A Perfect Union of Contrary Things

A Perfect Union of Contrary Things

Sarah Jensen

with

Maynard James Keenan

Backbeat
Books

AN IMPRINT OF HAL LEONARD LLC

Published in 2016 by Backbeat Books
An Imprint of Hal Leonard LLC
7777 West Bluemound Road
Milwaukee, WI 53213

Trade Book Division Editorial Offices
33 Plymouth St., Montclair, NJ 07042

Printed in the United States of America

Illustrations by Ramiro Rodriguez

Book design by Michael Kellner

The Jan Keenan photo is from the 1972 Mason County Central High School yearbook. All high school sports photos and the mock election photo are from the 1982 Mason County Central High School yearbook.

Lines from *Little, Big* by John Crowley, published in 1981 by Bantam Books. Used by permission of John Crowley.

Lines from "Burn About Out" © 1986 by Maynard James Keenan. Used by permission.

Lines from "Orestes" © 2000 by Billy Howerdel and Maynard James Keenan. Used by permission.

Lines from "Oceans" © 2011 by Maynard James Keenan. Used by permission.

Lines from "The Humbling River" © 2010 by Maynard James Keenan. Used by permission.

Library of Congress Cataloging-in-Publication Data is available upon request.

ISBN 978-1-4950-2442-9

www.backbeatbooks.com

For Kjiirt

Foreword

A Punk Psychopomp

Maynard James Keenan is a mysterious fountain of constant creation. From his soul-searing lyrics and extraordinary music in multiple bands to his astoundingly delicious wine, he has permeated our culture like no other artist. He straddles guises and genres and makes us wonder what could fuel such original superhuman output.

Behind every extraordinary person is a crisis overcome. Most fans of Maynard's work understand the significant impact of his mother's health and her faith. From the age of 11, Maynard was destined to be different, because his life at home set him apart from his peers. Both the creative artist and the shaman are classic outsiders to conventional society; their experiences of alienation, illness, and mortality give them a unique perspective, an altered state. This enables them to see what others cannot.

The native American Lakota people have a tradition of the *heyoka*, a contrarian, jester, or sacred clown. The *heyoka* speaks, moves, and reacts in an opposite fashion to the people around them. Maynard embodies both the trickster and medicine man archetype. It's not surprising that he lives in an area near Sedona where the kachina, the trickster god, and powerful natural forces are linked.

In my art for Tool's *Lateralus* album, the flaming central point is the throat. I saw the magic of the word empowering the music and giving it a unique poetic depth and height. Maynard swims in those depths, so his songs become the soundtrack of the soul, the confession of our united unconscious bubbling forward. I once visited his house in Hollywood Hills and saw his amazing collection of sculptures by outsider artist Stanislav Szukalski. Maynard's not only an artist, but he surrounds himself with eccentric and amazing artwork.

The rock star who writes songs sung by millions is a person of power. To ecstatically uplift packed stadiums around the world night after night is pure shaman magic. MJK is renowned for his uncompromising artistic integrity and a willingness to face frightening subjects. By luring listeners into the collective shadow, he guides us to face what is and what needs healing.

After all, why do we go to the rock concert or the shaman? The ecstatic leader is in contact with a higher level of creative spirit and becomes a channel of powerful transformative energies. We go to the show for a taste of that higher reality, the source of all things good, true, and beautiful. Without saying the word, we feel his love running through all he does. Maynard's message points us back to ourselves, and the lesson of his life is our artistic challenge: Be positively inebriated with life, be true to yourself, spiral out, keep going, keep growing.

Alex Grey
Cofounder, CoSM, Chapel of Sacred Mirrors
Wappinger, New York
February 2016

Prologue

The houselights dim and the crowd is on its feet, expectant. And when the man in the tailored Italian suit takes up his mic, they sway and nod in time to the drums and the bass and join him in every word.

He sings of the fire's spirit, of the taste of ashes on the tongue, of the truth on the other side of the mirror. He sings of the desert that is no desert place but a land breathing, flying, crawling, dying—alive with spirits of the ancestors and the untold tales of children to come.

Colored spotlights sweep over the house in a wash of color and the players move in a balanced triad of solemnity and chaos and easeful laughter. The duets and solos and skits tell the story of deception and pain repeated for millennia, and are reminders too of the eternal human capacity for selflessness and joy. And the dance is a celebration of ancient peoples not so different, the audience recognizes, from themselves.

The video against the stage wall is their own soaring flight among a shower of stars, triggering in them a pitched weightlessness as they look down upon canyons and mesas, the landscape created by flood and wind, a place hostile and somehow welcoming, too. And their heartbeats are one with the spiral of guitar and percussion and bass and keyboards and the strong, clear voice of the storyteller.

The tales the band tells are a prism of gone faces and lost hours, visions and tears and destruction, and the sonic river gathers speed and then cascades in arpeggios of love and of hope. Red glitter drifts in the spotlights. The players and the audience move as one, and together they dream the dream.

1

Spirito Marzo believed in alchemy. He understood how a hard day's work could transform weather and soil and fruit to a fine Barolo or Barbaresco. He'd spent his boyhood among the mountains and valleys of the Piemonte, where tending the vineyard was a matter of course.

Small, wiry, and jovial and as full of life as his name implied, he'd captured the heart of Clementina Durbiano, a no-nonsense woman who wore her dark hair parted in the middle and pulled back severely from her square forehead. By all accounts, theirs was a happy union, strengthened by a shared zest for adventure and rosy hopes for their children.

In America, they believed, lay their fortune. Anything might happen in a place where people were creating lightbulbs and phonographs and something they were calling motion pictures. And in the spring of 1902, the liner *La Bretagne* embarked from Havre, France, with Spirito, Clementina, and their two-year-old daughter, Luigia Ernestina, onboard.

Their timing was less than perfect. Spirito had imagined a future in lumbering, and they arrived in Leetonia, Pennsylvania, to find most of its forests gone to coal mine construction, railroad ties, and paper. For a few years, he took what work he could at the remaining mills and the logging sites, until, lured by the promise of a better life in West Virginia, he packed up the family and moved to Richwood to work in a tannery there. The company house was just big enough for the growing family, but in the yard was plenty of room for games of tag and pom-pom pullaway, for a vegetable garden and grapevines trained up over the wooden fence.

But by the 1920s, the hemlocks that had once covered the land in silvery green were all but depleted, and most of the West Virginia tanneries had closed. There was nothing for it but to pack their few belongings and sail—Spirito, Clementina, ten-year-old Peter, and baby Albert—for Italy. And there they made their home on a narrow street at the edge of the village where snowcapped mountains rose in the distance and vines grew green in the sunshine.

LUIGIA ERNESTINA HAD INDEED DISCOVERED HER FORTUNE in America. Not for her an alpine Italian village. She remained behind in West Virginia and took on the thoroughly modern name "Louise." And she set about capturing the heart of a dark-haired young man from Sparks.

Herbert Van Keenan had recently returned from machine gun duty in Saint-Mihiel and the battle of Meuse-Argonne, and his American roots ran deep. His father's ancestors had been among the first tide of Irish in the 1740s, and his mother was a descendent of Abraham LeMaistre, a French Huguenot who'd arrived in Maryland as an indentured carpenter in 1661. Abraham's great-great-grandson Benjamin had served in not only the War of 1812 but during the Revolution as General George Washington's courier at Valley Forge. And Benjamin's brother Joseph had been a part of the 13th Virginia Regiment at Brandywine and Germantown.

One couldn't be more American than that, Louise decided, and as proprietor of an Akron speakeasy and with a position with the post office in the offing, Van was assured of a fine future. In 1921, the two were married at the Methodist Episcopal church in Webster Springs, West Virginia, and, thrifty and hopeful, were by 1960 able to send their youngest son off to Kent State University in Ohio.

Mike, a star member of Kent's wrestling team, took his daily training run through nearby Hudson, past wide lawns and tidy lots and the house where the Dover, Ohio, chief of police lived. And one morning, he stopped running.

In the front yard, quite minding her own business, was Chief Gridley's daughter, Judith, and when Mike sprinted toward the front walk, she smiled. He stepped into the yard and they talked—about his classes, most likely, and her hopes of landing a job one day, perhaps of the fun she'd had in her high school drama club, her love of singing, and the tap lessons she'd splurged on.

After that, Mike called every morning at the white house with the black shutters. "She was the prettiest girl in the county," he would remember.

The baby with the big brown eyes and thick dark hair was born on the drizzly afternoon of April 17, 1964. They'd give him the middle name Herbert, they decided, after Mike's father and older brother. His first name would be James.

Mike took a job teaching science at Indian Lake High School a few towns west, and the family moved into a two-story house flanked by flower beds and vegetable plots with plenty of room for Mike's side business selling the pelts of animals he trapped and raised.

Laced with trout-splashed rivers and dotted with shadowy forests where Jim imagined deer and rabbits might live, Indian Lake was an idyllic place to be a little boy. He raised his baby eyes to see a bald eagle soaring to its aerie on Pony Island, listened to cicadas humming in the tall trees at the edge of the yard, patted his pet raccoon—tame as a housecat and all his. Scarcely tall enough to see over the sill, Jim would stand at his bedroom window and watch his father plant peas and lettuce in the garden below.

> I remember thinking, "OK, if I crawl up in the window and if I can get this screen open, I can get to that tree and climb down to help him." I could see that what he was doing was taking a while. He seemed to be struggling to get the shovel into the dirt.
>
> I tried to get up on the ledge of the window and realized, "Nah, there's no way I'm going to be able to get from the window ledge to that tree safely." I could tell the distance from the window to the tree was too far, so I got back out of the window and just watched my dad. But I wanted so much to help.

As idylls often do, the Indian Lake dream shifted to its dark shadow side. Judith eased her Volkswagen Beetle from the driveway and past the Italian cypress that lined the front walk. She held her arm across Jim's middle when she braked at the end of the driveway. Whether Mike's preoccupation with sports had distanced him from his family or Judith had had enough of opossums in the bathtub and a muskrat-skinning area in the basement, the rift had grown irreparable. Divorce papers filed, Judith packed into the VW a few belongings and Jim's green Gumby erasers and his crayons, and pointed the car toward Interstate 71 and Hudson.

Jim twisted in his seat and watched the house recede from view, hoping to catch one last glimpse of his father. Then he turned to his mother. "Doesn't he love us anymore?" he asked. He was three years old.

MOTHER AND SON MADE THEIR HOME with Grandma Gridley until Judith had set aside enough of her earnings from her job with Western Reserve Telephone to rent a place of their own—the rear portion of a farmhouse in Tallmadge. Judith did the best she could to mask the smell of the pigsty out back. "She painted every room and worked away at that house to make it a home," her half-sister Pam would remember. "She was like June Cleaver, always baking and cooking, doing whatever she could to be the perfect parent."

Nonetheless, Jim would recall the house as dark and strangely empty, and the swine farmers living in the front rooms as less than nurturing caregivers. Charged with watching over him while Judith was at work, they thought nothing of leaving him alone while they slipped out to the movies.

"She'll be back any minute," they reassured him, and left the four-year-old to wait the eternity before his mother came home again.

Jim slung a set of toy guns and holster around his hips the way he'd seen Marshall Matt Dillon do on TV or created swirling designs with his Spirograph, one after the other, and no two alike. And at bedtime, Judith sat at the edge of his bed and read from Andersen and Mother Goose and his collection of Little Golden Books about puppies and kittens and three little pigs. And she told him stories of her own, of her recurring dream that she stood on one leg, stretched her fingers toward the sun, rose with the wind, and flew over housetops and rivers and trees.

Judith recognized Jim's artistic inclinations and brought home one day a small organ so he might experiment with chords and tempo and simple melodies. And Aunt Pam, only a decade older than Jim, became more a sister than an aunt. "I had a cheap guitar and he was very interested in that," she would explain. "The first song he learned was 'Little Black Egg.'" On sunny afternoons, she'd climb with him into the shady cool of the oak tree in her parents' yard and read to him *Bartholomew and the Oobleck*. His pets were a cat and a canary—a combination that ended in tragedy and taught him early about competition and survival of the fittest.

He seldom saw his father, but Mike remembered him on birthdays and at Christmastime and faithfully sent Time-Life books about Native Americans or biographies of inventors and industrialists, stories of men who'd struggled against all odds and persevered just the same.

Jim looked forward most to holidays at Grandma Gridley's house, when aunts and uncles and cousins gathered to share stories of Christmases past and Grandma's sugar cookies. The real Christmas tree in the living room sparkled with tinsel and baubles, and on the top branches hung pipe-cleaner candy canes and paper stars. "We'd make handmade ornaments every Christmas," Pam would recall. "Each of us made one for everybody in the family. One year, Jim made macramé Santas for me and my mom, and when he was really young, he painted a pinecone to look like Santa."

On every street, one house becomes by unspoken agreement the place where children gravitate for hide-and-go-seek and tag and elaborate games of make-believe. The rambling ranch house on Hayes Road was the gathering spot of the neighborhood boys who became Jim's friends. Enclosed by a split rail fence, its deep front yard was big enough for ball games, and the white barn just beside was an open invitation to explore its shadowy mows. The backyard extended all the way to the woods, full of mystery and adventure.

When Judith remarried in 1968, they moved into the spacious house in Ravenna, a town of blue-collar workers lured from the Virginia hills by the steady paychecks and insurance plans offered by General Motors and the Goodyear Tire and Rubber Company in Akron. After a day on the assembly line, they'd drive the 20 miles home, smoke their way through the evening news and an episode of *The Sonny & Cher Show* or *Hee Haw* or *Laugh-In*, then rise in the morning to do it all over again.

For Jim and his friends, the house served as base camp for endless exploration and invention. Isolated in a pocket between highways and interchanges and three miles from the center of town, the neighborhood was far enough removed to feel to them like a world apart.

The small terrace surrounding the recessed flower bed in the side yard made a fine cockpit for a boy perched on the top step, the flagpole rising from the middle of the garden a perfect propeller post. From such a vantage point, the fields beyond were enemy territory concealing untold invaders or an arctic wilderness just waiting to be claimed.

The abandoned outbuildings behind the barn became bunkers and command centers where the boys reenacted movies like *Kelly's Heroes* and *The Bridge on the River Kwai*, or episodes of *Hogan's Heroes*, Jim taking on the Richard Dawson role. Trapdoors in the old chicken house were secret passageways where they could hide deserters and spies—and stay out of sight of enemy eyes.

Liberated from the classroom, Kirby and John and Teddy and Billy, who lived just next door, joined Jim in the barn on Friday afternoons and selected their allegiance—German or Ally or member of the French Resistance—and to formulate the weekend's battle plans. Strategies in place, they scattered home for dinner and reassembled after breakfast the next morning to resume where they'd left off.

They dispersed across the field and into the woods, enacting their carefully crafted drama. They crept through the tall meadow grass, darting behind trees and the van in the driveway if they sensed the enemy nearby. The opponents might not meet again until Sunday afternoon, when they came crawling on their bellies from the edge of the woods to take each other by surprise. In a flurry of toy rifle exchange and excited shouts—"You didn't get me! I got you!"—the battle was over in seconds, until it all began again the next weekend.

In winter, Jim moved the combat to his room, one place he might avoid his stepfather and sudden paddlings with bright orange Hot Wheels track. He created elaborate narratives of quests and battles, skirmishes and rescues carried out by his collection of Army figures and medieval knights and their steeds. Across the cellar floor, he constructed a vast landscape of castles and stockades, every miniature mountain range and bend in the river a setting for story.

Modeling clay was a block of nothing. Here was potential. You could create something from this nothing. When I was playing with the soldiers and knights,

> if there was some element of the story missing—a horse or a guy or a build-
> ing—I would create it. My imagination could transform this amorphous block
> into *something.*

RAVENNA OFFICIALS COULDN'T QUITE DECIDE to which school district the ranch
house belonged, and in the first six years he lived there, Jim was assigned to as
many different schools. No sooner did he make friends than he'd be shuttled
off by Betty, the bus driver, to a new school. First grade, third grade, fourth—a
continual adjustment to new teachers, new classmates, and confusion about
where to find the lunchroom.

> I was always introducing myself to new people. As an only child, I kind of lived
> in my head anyway, so I brought my friends with me, having many voices in my
> head. The glass-half-empty view of this is isolation.
>
> But the glass-half-full version is independence. I wasn't subjected to the
> hierarchy that had already been established with these kids who grew up to-
> gether and who knew each others' faults and flaws and what they could do
> well. I wasn't pigeonholed into the established social order.
>
> Every time I had to make an important decision, I could rely on my own in-
> stincts. I could rely on three voices: my head, my heart, and my gut. No outside
> noise can penetrate a solid sense of self-trust.

Jim didn't aspire to be the most popular boy in class or teacher's pet or the
one who got the best grades. His goal was to decipher the unspoken code the
other children seemed intuitively to understand. They raised their hands and
waited to be called on before they spoke. They formed orderly lines when they
walked outside for recess and knew the rules of the game when they stepped
onto the softball field—all apparently without being told. None of it quite
made sense to Jim, but he went through the motions as best he could, as if he
understood the plan. And sometimes, he defied the rules.

One afternoon, while his second-grade classmates sat hunched over their
penmanship assignment, he went to the pencil sharpener at the back of the
room. Curious, he removed it from the wall and discovered inside yellow curls
of wood shavings and bits of soft, black graphite. Impulsively, he smudged it
across his upper lip and cheerfully goose-stepped his way back to his desk.

His prank resulted in the first of many trips to the hall to endure a paddling from a paddling-prone teacher. After that, it seemed the slightest infraction—laughing too loudly, losing his place in his reading book, tasting paste—warranted the same punishment, and he soon gave up even trying to play by the rules. As soon as the morning bell had rung, he'd don another mustache or speak out of turn in order to get the anticipated spanking out of the way as soon as possible.

Judith surmised her son might benefit from an activity both structured and enjoyable, and suggested he join the local Cub Scout troop. Perhaps swimming and building balsa-wood airplanes and ascending the ranks with the other boys would help him develop not only social skills but a bit of much-needed self-esteem.

She drove Jim to his first meeting and he joined the pack around the Formica kitchen table. The den mother brought the meeting to order and set a fat white candle in the center of the table. She lit it and informed the boys that when it had burned all the way down, she'd bring out cake and cookies and Hawaiian Punch. If they misbehaved, she warned, she'd blow out the candle and they'd receive no treats that day. These were rules Jim could understand.

He returned the next week, eager to learn all about camping and hiking and pinewood derbies. The den mother lit the candle, and almost immediately, the other boys pursed their lips and began blowing gently toward the flame, delighting in its quivering dance. Jim watched them lean closer and puff harder until the flame went out. Young as he was, he was bewildered and appalled by their self-sabotage. Feeling more the outsider than ever, he vowed that his scouting days were over and worried whether he'd ever find the place he belonged—or recognize it when he did.

Jim's grades were solid in every subject, but not exceptional. His teachers noted on his report cards that he lacked focus, but the personality inventories he completed in those years suggested two areas in which he might excel: the military and art.

THREE TIMES A WEEK, Jim attended services with his mother and stepfather in a series of grim fundamentalist churches, each more devoutly self-righteous than the last. "It was horrifying to me when they started that," Pam would recall. "Once, they came over to my parents' after church. Jimmy was sitting on the sofa and doing nothing, not even talking. It was like he'd had a lobotomy. I'm like, 'Jimmy, what is the matter with you? What's happening? Let's go up in the acorn tree. Let's read.' Nothing."

Terrorized as he was by the threat of eternal damnation, Jim was uneasy with the pervasive hypocrisy he sensed among the pious. He watched ministers weep upon the altar, begging forgiveness as they skimmed from church coffers. He heard them preach of purity even as they imagined the next week's tryst with the deacon or enticing some small boy into the sacristy.

The congregations turned a blind eye to their pastors' crimes, believing absolution lay in accurately reciting Bible verses about the wages of sin. They cautioned Jim that his shortcomings—his less than stellar grades and classroom disruptions—marked him as a prime candidate for possession by Satan himself.

Life on the playground was no easier. He tried to emulate the other boys—boys who knew that athletic success was one of the few tickets out of a place like Ravenna. They'd mastered bats and balls and even strikes and spares long before, and Jim's was often the last name called when the two captains chose up sides for a game.

But with third grade came Jim's first distinguishing achievement. Clad in a tall red hat and black pack straps crossed smartly across his chest, he appeared as a tin soldier opposite classmate Kelly Callahan in the school play *Mr. Grumpy's Toy Shop.* When Jim turned the key on Kelly's back, her china-doll character was brought to life to dance on Christmas Eve with the Raggedy Anns and Andys and teddy bears that made up the rest of the ensemble. A small magic happened when he stepped center stage in full costume and character to play make-believe in someone else's story.

Not long after, Betty, the bus driver, phoned Judith with the astonishing news that Jim no longer disrupted her route by burning holes in his math book with a magnifying glass or singing too loudly along with the Fleetwood Mac tape in her eight-track player. Perhaps he'd changed merely because he'd turned nine. Or perhaps Jim's discovery that he could channel his gift of storytelling to productive ends left him little time for mischief.

The other sixth graders chose conventional topics for their end-of-year science projects, but Jim selected the Sasquatch. His presentation included a display assembled from pictures he'd found in magazines, and he retrieved the modeling clay from the back of his closet and created a detailed diorama of Bigfoot lumbering through the forest. More pseudoscience than fact, his elaborate project—his story—nonetheless impressed the judges and earned a blue ribbon.

And at home, he packed up his knights and soldiers and cleared the basement to make room for a makeshift stage delineated by cardboard cartons and stray lengths of lumber. At one end, he set a portable record player and folded out its built-in speakers. He flipped through the Alice Cooper, Joni Mitchell, and Kiss albums Aunt Pam had introduced him to, and at last slid his Jackson Five records over the spindle.

Improvised mic in hand, he stood alone on the little stage, accompanying the Jacksons on "ABC" and "I'll Be There." He gyrated his way through "Dancing Machine," and sometimes, when he managed to hit the notes just right, he imagined his cabaret was real, the bare bulb in the ceiling a colored spotlight, the music continuing long into the morning.

LIGHTS FLASHED in a pulsating strobe across the yard, and the wail of sirens echoed against the barn wall and over the field. Just inside the split rail fence, Jim stood alone, watching the team of EMTs as they bent over the blanketed figure that lay motionless upon a stretcher. He looked up when Billy's father from next door approached purposefully from the shadows and asked what the commotion was all about. "I don't know," Jim told him. "My mom's going to the hospital."

His curiosity satisfied, the man turned and walked back to his house, his own son safely asleep inside. He returned to his television and his recliner, leaving Jim on the other side of the fence in the sound and the light and the darkness.

Perhaps the aneurysm had been brought on by high blood pressure, and perhaps it had been a long time coming. Whatever the case, the vessel in Judith's brain had ballooned to the point of rupture. In the hospital, she suffered two more hemorrhagic strokes, leaving her half-paralyzed, half-blind, and unable to respond when Jim tried to talk with her. "You could see her struggling to make the word happen, but she couldn't say it," he'd recall years later.

Few support groups existed in 1976 to help families care for someone in

Judith's state. Her husband and son were on their own, and the counsel of their current church group was less than helpful. "She wasn't right with God," they told Jim. "That's why she got sick." They offered no assistance or listening ear, and took their good time deciding whether it was proper for Judith to come to church in the slacks she must wear over her incontinence pads.

"Judy had to wear some godawful ugly shoes because she was paralyzed, and they gave her a hard time about that, too," Pam would remember. "After the stroke, I took Jim to their church and the minister gave a sermon about how our blood was going to run four miles wide and four miles deep unless we came up and saved ourselves. So of course I took Jim and left. And I said that I would never, ever take him to church again."

> Though I did meet some wonderful people at those churches, people with a solid foundation of family and togetherness, they were caught up in dogma. It was my first brush with "Fuck your church." I knew in my heart that the universe is not that ugly and that nobody's sitting in judgment. There's just shit that happens, and if we all help each other, we can work through it.
>
> I knew these people were wrong. What they were saying had nothing to do with what I was forced to learn in Bible study. It was weird, crazy judgment and it made me not want to have any part of it.
>
> Even people in the family told my mother her affliction was God's punishment. Punishment by God for your behavior is not one of the things on the list of how the world works. What fucking God of love is that?

When one home health aide after another proved incompetent or unreliable, Aunt Pam stepped in to help with Judith's care. "I tried to make life as normal as I could," she would recall. "And Jim did everything he could for his mother. She was all he had."

Jim shadowed Judith in case she fell, helped her bake cookies or her favorite maraschino cherry nut cake, buttoned her into her clothes, and loaded her endless laundry into the washing machine. He accompanied her to the bathroom.

Often late for school because of his obligations, Jim suffered the taunting of classmates and scoldings from the principal when he ran down the hall to get to class on time. Yet school was a respite. He continued to earn good grades, and when the gym teacher introduced the 50-yard dash, he discovered a welcome release. He ran, and he learned he was good at it. His own speed rushing in his ears, he could focus on no one's performance but his own, forget for a little while the other boys and the teachers and the sadness waiting for him at home.

And all the while, he'd find himself watching, as if just over his shoulder someone might appear. Someone to catch his glance, understand an unspoken joke, ask to hear his story and stand beside him to help rewrite it.

2

The patchwork of fields and woods and highways tipped as the plane banked over the rainy Grand Rapids airport. Jim pressed close to the window and took in what he could of this Michigan, this flat, gray place he'd never seen before and would now call home.

Judith, in a moment of clarity, had realized caring for her and rushing sleepy off to school was no life for a 13-year-old. After a flurry of phone calls between Ohio and Michigan, Mike and his new wife, Jan, agreed the only sensible option was to bring Jim to Scottville to live with them.

Though they knew it was all for the best, they were ill-prepared for the sudden arrival of a nearly grown son. They enjoyed the students in their science and English classrooms, and Mike was a devoted mentor to the young athletes he coached on the high school wrestling team. But this would be a different matter altogether. "Even though I was around kids all day, I knew nothing about motherhood," Jan would recall. "Suddenly I'm inheriting a teenager."

And there was Jim, emerging from the burst of passengers at the arrival gate, already nearly as tall as his father, his dark, wavy hair framing his solemn face, his hand extended in polite greeting.

Covering their discomfort and doubt in smiles and small talk, Mike and Jan loaded Jim's carry-ons and oversized black footlocker into the back of their Toyota. Yes, the flight from Cleveland had been fine and he hadn't been nervous traveling alone. No, Judith's condition hadn't changed. His room on the second floor was ready for him; spring break was over and school would start again on Monday.

Once on the road, they fell into thoughtful silence, lulled by the rain and the unremitting sameness of the miles.

His son was plenty intelligent, Mike thought. He'd seen signs of that during his infrequent visits to Ohio, and Jim's graciousness at the airport had confirmed his belief. He imagined the perfect son he would become, a chip right off the old Mike block, a boy who'd make the honor roll and join the wrestling team next year when he was in high school.

A visit to J. C. Penney would be their first order of business, Jan decided. They could stop there when they reached town in about an hour. Jim's torn jeans—no matter how trendy—would never do for a teacher's son. She imagined the new friends he'd bring home—the quiet, well-behaved children of good families who'd cause no disruption in her well-ordered house. She wondered what was in the big black trunk. She sighed.

> I probably looked like some kind of derelict to them. This was something that had been tossed in Jan's lap, and if she had to deal with it, she was going to clean this thing up.
>
> When you settle into a pair of jeans, you love them, and new clothes are stiff and awkward. I didn't feel like they respected me, and I grumbled because they were trying to change me.
>
> But I took their lead because they knew these Scottville people better than I did. I had no idea if I'd fit in or not.

Jan and Mike didn't set out to transform Jim into someone he wasn't. With the best of intentions and limited experience as parents, they began innocently writing script and stage directions for a boy they barely knew.

While they planned his life, Jim sat quietly between them and looked out the rain-streaked windows. He wondered who lived in the towns they drove through, tiny towns with curious names like Rothbury and New Era. He read billboards advertising silver lakes and sandy dunes, took in a landscape different from the one he'd left behind, a landscape of rivers and forests and misty fields and a stand of pine trees arranged on a hillside in the shape of a star.

As they neared their house, Mike left the highway and took the county's back roads, muddy, uneven expanses rutted by snowplows only weeks before. Neatly kept barns and farmhouses stood well back from the roads, and massive maple trees clustered like sentinels at the ends of their driveways. Then the farms became less frequent, the ferny asparagus fields between them wider. At last, after a long stretch of uninterrupted road, Mike turned the car off Darr Road and parked before a compact house finished in rough-cut shingles and set amid tall second-growth pines. A redwood deck circled the front of the house, and the porch light was on.

On Monday morning, they piled back into the Toyota and made the four-mile drive to the new Mason County Central Middle School just north of town. It was Jim's first glimpse of Scottville: the block-long collection of hardware stores and coffee shops and drugstores bounded by railroad tracks to the south and the town's single traffic light to the north. The shops would be busy come Friday night when husbands received their paychecks and brought wives in for their weekly groceries. On Tuesday, farmers would truck their cattle to the livestock sale in the odiferous barn at the far end of the parking lot behind the bank. But this morning, the street was quiet, and Jim concentrated on his stiff oxford cloth shirt and new J. C. Penney slacks.

He'd spent the weekend adjusting to the routine of the Keenan household and suffering Jan's anger when she forbade him to tape his poster of Kiss bassist Gene Simmons and his unnaturally long tongue to the raw wood paneling in his room.

In comparison, getting used to a new school wouldn't be so hard, he knew. He'd learned a long time ago how to quickly assess the hierarchy of in-crowd and scholars and cutups and bullies and the invisible but impenetrable lines that separated them.

For their part, his new classmates had known one another since kindergarten and were just as practiced in dealing with newcomers. They knew from experience that in their eagerness to fit in, incoming students often overstepped boundaries, exaggerated their accomplishments, and disrupted classes in their bid for attention. They were generally given a wide berth until they learned the unspoken rules of the tribe and came to obey them. "As the new guy, you're under scrutiny on so many levels," he'd explain decades later. "You're being watched by the jocks, the middle of the pack, the farmers, the brainiacs. The rule breakers, the rule followers, everybody's watching to see what you're going to do."

They watched, and they saw that Jim was different from the typical new boy in town. He'd been shuttled off to new schools enough times that he wasn't particularly anxious about whether or not he made a good impression. He was comfortable in his own skin. His calm sincerity should have assured his classmates that he was exactly as he appeared, a boy they could accept into the fold immediately—were it not for the reputation of his parents as two of the most demanding and no-nonsense teachers at MCC.

They wouldn't experience the Keenans until they were in high school the next year, but they'd heard horror stories from older brothers and sisters about Jan's strictness in her Spanish and English classes and of Mike's humorless, hard-work approach as science teacher and wrestling coach. And this new boy was their son, someone best kept at arm's length until they were sure he was on their side.

Jim at first gravitated toward the unruly group that gathered with Camels and Salems around the trash barrel at the end of the sidewalk—the corner just past the high school known to generations as Burnout Corner. They liked Alice Cooper and tattered jeans and seemed likely companions, but their rebelliousness often led to trouble a son of Mike and Jan must avoid. The girls in his class seemed a safer choice. Their friendship was a haven from which he could observe and gauge his classmates' reactions when he hummed the songs he loved or gave in to the humorous streak that came so naturally to him.

He noticed which of them rolled their eyes and complained to the teacher when he inserted an *n* after the first letter of every word. "Wnhy dnoes thnis bnother ynou?" he asked evenly, and paid attention to which of them doubled over their desks in giggles. *They* were on *his* side and just might prove to be friends.

But despite his well-honed surveillance skills, there were some mysteries even Jim couldn't solve. No one batted an eye when the blond boy a few rows over unwrapped a sleeve of graham crackers in the middle of reading class. It seemed to Jim as if he were looking into a kind of fun-house mirror that distorted his every assumption about honesty and consequences. For as long as he could remember, he'd been punished and paddled for wrongs he'd never committed, and here was a boy breaking rules in plain sight and getting away with it.

"He's diabetic," one of his classmates whispered when he noticed Jim's stare. Jim didn't believe it for a second. He felt a twinge of envy—and a certain admiration for someone clever enough to manipulate teachers into letting him eat whenever he had the notion.

The boy kept his eye on Jim, too, noticed his quiet intensity, the confident way he spoke when he did speak, the often snide and humorous comments he made under his breath, as if he saw analogies and connections and twists of meaning the others missed.

And he admired the ceramic likeness Jim created as his final project in art class, a project he'd labored over all spring and that far surpassed the simple ashtrays and lopsided teacups the other students produced. The clay face captured perfectly the features of Gene Simmons, tipped up at an angle to reveal a flawless Simmons tongue and meticulously painted in full Kiss makeup.

As Jim grew more comfortable with his classmates, he teased them for their uncool wardrobes or inane jokes—but only those who should have known better. The privileged, popular, all-A students were fair game. But the timid ones, the weak and powerless whose talents and confidence were regularly snuffed at home with beatings and ridicule—and worse—were off-limits. "I looked at those guys and felt like that was me back in Ohio," he would explain. "You don't have a clique, so you get singled out. You're like a wounded antelope."

MAKING SENSE OF THE TACIT LAWS OF THE CLASSROOM was one thing, but adapting to the habits of the Keenan household was another matter. The room at the top of the open stairway would be all his, to decorate as he pleased, so long as its paneling remained pristine. He spent his first drizzly weekend there unpacking pens and sketch pads and modeling clay from the black trunk while Mike sat at the edge of his bed and asked about things he thought a dad should ask about: friends and how he was doing in math and whether he'd considered joining the wrestling team next year. Jim answered in monosyllables, unsure of what was expected of him.

He tentatively brought out his folder of drawings and fanned them out across his bedspread. Mike gasped. Here were pen-and-ink portraits of Kiss band members Gene Simmons and Paul Stanley and Peter Criss, the likenesses sure, the perspective and shading controlled. "His drawings were way beyond what I could even imagine," Mike would remember. "You could just see the talent." Maybe his son's creativity could be put to use in the gardens come summer, the extensive perennial plots in which Mike took such pride. Before Jim had arrived, he'd already begun to clear away last year's fallen leaves, and maybe in a month or two, they could work together tending the lemon balm and echinacea and flowering shrubs that lined the meandering pathways. They could dig and plant and prune and talk, creating the bond he fancied his students had with their dads.

Jan imagined such things, too, and plotted the household regime that would create order from the chaos. Jim would receive an allowance, yes, but he must work for it. He'd make sure the woodpile was stocked and he'd bring logs inside to feed the woodstoves. And every Saturday, he'd vacuum, dust, and scour the bathrooms in exchange for his $10—or $8 if the job wasn't done to her satisfaction. She was of the everything-in-its-proper-place school of housekeeping, and she'd impress upon Jim the importance of the house remaining as tidy as it had been before he'd arrived.

And if they repeated the routine enough times, they'd come together as a real family over Sunday drives and visits with neighbors and meals together every evening as she suspected all happy moms and dads and sons did.

> At breakfast and dinner, we usually sat at the bar in the kitchen, just like we sat in the truck with me straddling the gearshift. We were three people sitting elbow-to-elbow in a line and not facing each other. The mission at hand was finishing the meal or getting to town.
>
> That arrangement doesn't help much with intimacy.

And once the dinner dishes were cleared, they went their separate ways, Jim behind his closed door with his stereo and clay and pen and paper, Mike and Jan to the living room to grade homework. They'd never replaced the television set destroyed in a lightning storm some years before, and in the long evenings, when those other families tuned in to *M*A*S*H* and *Fantasy Island* and *The Incredible Hulk*, the Keenan house was quiet, the silence a chasm none of them knew quite how to bridge.

Rainy April made way for sunny May, and anxiously determined to be the relaxed, involved stepparent she'd read about in women's magazines, Jan invited Jim to join her in the kitchen one Saturday after he'd completed his chores. She brought out flour and vanilla and eggs and chocolate chips and showed him how to chop and measure a cupful of walnuts. She asked him how he was getting along in school, if he missed his friends back in Ohio, what music he was listening to these days.

"This isn't the way my mom makes cookies," he said.

The Sugar Ridge Church of the Brethren stood surrounded by bean fields and cornfields, its windows looking out over gently rolling hills and the narrow dirt road. Its steeple had over time fallen into disrepair, and the carpenters among its members had mounted the bell in a triangular frame set on the front lawn where the congregation would pass it when they came to church on Sunday mornings.

Soon after arriving in Scottville, Jim joined a handful of classmates who attended services there, diligent, industrious students who would become class presidents, graduate with honors, and continue their good-natured competition for high achievement even after they reached college and the corporate world. These were peers Jim might emulate—and who were, in the eyes of Mike and Jan, unlikely candidates for pilfering from the corner store, raiding their parents' liquor cabinets, or frequenting Burnout Corner.

Presided over by the Reverend Paul Grout, an antiwar activist and former art teacher, the congregants were among the most intellectual of the county's citizenry, parishioners focused on social justice and the peace movement.

> Paul showed me that there's a difference between following the road and following the map. He taught me that when you focus on the teller of the tale or the hand pointing to an idea, you miss the whole point.
>
> I really didn't want to go to church, because it seemed like it was all about maps, and flawed maps, instead of being about the road. But the Church of the Brethren was different. They weren't idol worshippers.

The church welcomed Jim as its newest choir member. His strong young voice added refreshing harmonies to "There's a Wideness in God's Mercy" and "I'll Count My Blessings" as he stood at the little altar holding his worn copy of the Brethren hymnal.

At home, he turned to the music he more closely identified with: the hard-rock theatricality of Kiss. The band's studded black leather costumes, teetering platform shoes, and white face paint intrigued him, and the driving dark rhythms drew him into the mystery of what the group might be all about.

He turned his stereo up loud. Jan passed his open door and watched him mime Simmons's guitar licks, lost in fantasy and frenzy. She held her tongue, but her disapproving silence was audible above the music. If Jim noticed her before she turned away, he answered with a silence deeper still.

His seeming obsession left Jan and Mike concerned about the influence of a band whose name they'd heard was an acronym for Knights in Satan's Service. "We thought he was some kind of degenerate," Jan would recall. "From a teacher's perspective, he was going down the tubes."

No one quite remembers whether they suggested Pastor Grout talk with the boy or whether Jim approached him in search of a listening ear. What is certain is the meeting that took place following the service one Sunday.

Pastor Grout led Jim up the narrow staircase, motioned him toward a comfortable chair in his office, and closed the door. "So tell me about these guys," he invited. Over the next hour, Jim explained Kiss as best he could. He told of their fire-breathing, blood-spitting performances, the smoking guitars, and the makeup that concealed their offstage identities. He told of their comic book character personas and their lyrics of love stolen and dreamed of, hard luck women, and rocking all day and rolling all night.

Far from worried, Grout became fascinated. Decades later, he would recall his reaction to the things Jim had told him. "I was more interested in what he was finding in the music than alarmed by his interest in Kiss," he explained in a 2013 interview. "I wasn't concerned about him, just the opposite. Jim was interesting and funny and comfortable to be with. And he had such a creative edge."

When Jim had finished his narrative, Grout reassured him, pointing out aspects of Kiss beyond their music. "They sound like interesting characters telling an interesting story," he said. "Don't worry about anyone judging you about this. Focus on what you like about it and what resonates with you."

As SUMMER APPROACHED, Jim found himself looking forward to the annual campout of Brethren youth from across the district. The highlight of his last Ohio summers had been the respite of 4-H camp, a week of canoeing, singing, and sharing s'mores. Every evening, the older children had stood in formation, holding aloft blazing torches to light the path to the campfire. Though one of the youngest, Jim had been named Camper of the Year after his second summer and given the ceremonial duty of carrying the flame—a lighted roll of toilet paper skewered to one end of a long stick.

Camp Brethren Heights was only an hour's drive from Scottville, but to Jim and his fellow campers, it seemed a universe all its own. The week at camp was a vacation from family and day-to-day cares and a chance to test their self-reliance and interdependence, to live in heightened awareness of birdsong and weather, the taste of breakfast cooked over an open fire, chilly lake water against their sun-splashed skin.

They turned up their noses when gas bubbles rose from the marshy muck, skimmed the curious duckweed from the lake's surface, examined the delicate purple flowers of the loosestrife. They watched the leaves of the maples on the hill above the campground turn against the approaching rainstorm and kept watch for the skunk and bobcat rumored to live nearby. In the morning, they identified fresh deer tracks along the shore, sharp and distinct as their own attentiveness. Together, they discovered talents they'd never known they had: an ability to harmonize, skip stones across the lake's surface, comfort the lonesome bunkmate who'd never been away from home before.

In the evening, they brought branches from the woods to feed the fire, a chorus of bullfrogs calling from the gathering dusk. They talked then, celebrating one another's triumphs and gently exploring their worries. They took turns telling their own stories and stories from the Bible, stories that seemed to Jim less about the wages of sin than dilemmas of real people just like him.

The fire cast the profiles of his friends to bright crescents against the night. He watched the flames spew crimson sparks into the darkening sky, up, up into the starry night where the orange moon floated fat and full.

PASTOR GROUT UNDERSTOOD the double-edged sword of their experience. The Sunday after camp week, Jim and his friends took their places in the pews beside the adults, smiling furtively at each other across the aisle as if sharing some great secret.

"Moses cannot truly express what he saw on the mountain," Grout told his congregation. "He goes up, he sees a miracle, he's given his instructions, and when he comes back down, there's no way he can describe to anyone what happened. The people are just going on about their business, worshipping and celebrating in the same way they always have. Of course they are, because they didn't see what Moses saw. He came down from that mountaintop experience glowing."

Jim and the other young people exchanged quick, astonished glances, scarcely daring to believe Grout's sermon was directed at them and not at the adults who listened from the stiff wooden benches.

"Your mountaintop experience is also a lonely experience," Grout continued, looking from one to another. "You come back with mixed feelings because you'd love to share this wondrous thing, but you realize no one can quite understand what you saw. It resonated with you, and on some level, it changed you. You must embrace that. Resolve to go on, to use this experience in a positive way. Carry this with you and express it in a way that others may have their own experience."

As he listened, Jim began to suspect that there might be more to the stories he heard in Bible study than just accounts of make-believe people who lived a long time ago. It just could be that the magic of stories lay in making them his own, he thought, until he felt this pitched weightlessness Pastor Grout's words seemed to trigger. Maybe the stories of Moses and Abraham and his cabinmates at the lake weren't so different from the stories Kiss sang as he stood alone in his room with his stereo.

Maybe—just maybe—there was only one story, an endless story with infinite variations, but one story all the same, populated with characters in a boundless array of costume and mask whose job it was to recognize and celebrate the mysterious tale they carried deep inside.

3

When school started again in the fall, Mike, in his hope that Jim begin high school on a positive note, urged him to choose some sport he might excel in.

Eager to please his father, Jim geared up in chin strap and shoulder pads and joined the junior varsity football players on the practice field behind the high school. At only 105 pounds, he quickly realized he was no match for his teammates, the solid, muscular boys who'd grown up hauling bushels of string beans and stacking bales of hay on their fathers' farms.

"I went to two practices and decided I need to run the fuck away from that," he would recall. "I just sat on my ass in these shoulder pads that I couldn't even see over." He needn't have worried about his father's reaction. Before he said a word, Mike suggested that cross country might be worth a try. Jim agreed, and what seemed at the time a small decision proved to be a deliverance.

STEVE BISHOP WAS THE RARE TEACHER who delighted in watching students' eyes light up when a lesson in American history or social studies sparked their interest. His passion for learning was contagious, and his students ignored the echoes from the overhead air duct in their classroom. They were captivated by Bishop's seemingly boundless knowledge and his enthusiasm when he led them in discussions of war and economics and the voting process. Almost without realizing it, they learned what no textbook could teach: the confidence to move from adolescent insecurity to a belief that their ideas mattered.

Bishop applied the same methods as coach of MCC's cross country and track teams. He made it a point to understand his athletes' strengths and weaknesses, the potential they'd never before considered. The cross country team that fall included some of the best senior runners in the school's history, but he devoted as much praise and attention to the novices as to the champions.

Early each morning before school started, he accompanied them on distance workouts and training runs along the roads just outside town. Every afternoon, he sprinted with them up hills and jogged along the piney trails of the state park and the dunes above Lake Michigan. He stepped aside only when timekeeping or observing the team was necessary, allowing them the freedom to discover on their own just what their limits might be. And from the first, he recognized Jim as a runner.

Bishop and his wife often joined Mike and Jan for dinner and conversation and swing dance classes in nearby Ludington. But in their five years of friendship, Mike hadn't once mentioned a son.

"All of a sudden, there was Jim," Bishop would later recall. "I couldn't imagine what it was like for Mike and Jim to be together after such a long estrangement." When Bishop looked at Jim, he saw a sensitive young man uprooted from the familiar and forced to adjust to not only high school but a home life more regimented than the one he'd known.

And he saw something else. Decades later, he would remember the quiet boy in social studies class and his insightful comments about the branches of government and the articles of the Constitution. He remembered the determined runner eager to see what might be beyond the next bend of the road or the next stand of red maples blazing against the October sky.

The state cross country finals were held in nearby Clare, and Bishop, believing that all the boys, no matter how skilled or unprepared, should have the chance to participate in every event, arranged both a JV and a varsity race on the same course. Jim came in at speeds faster than anyone else's—outpacing not only his fellow freshmen but the stellar members of the varsity team as well.

His performance did not go unrewarded. At the cross country banquet that fall, Bishop presented Jim with his first varsity letter.

He'd run as he had in the long-ago war games in the Ravenna field, understanding now that work and discipline spelled success—his own and that of the team. "Even though Bishop and my dad hung out, he didn't cut me any slack. He expected a lot from everybody," he would recall. "He was like, 'We're going to get things done, and we're going to do them right.'"

Jim sensed that his growing collection of awards was only a beginning. He recited his coach's oft-repeated mantra: Never give up, and you'll be victorious. He wondered if the letters weren't the first small step toward some even larger goal he couldn't yet imagine.

CROSS COUNTRY IN THE FALL, wrestling in winter, track in the spring: Jim's sports triad brought structure and the satisfaction of knowing his talents contributed to a larger effort. The starting gun sounded and the race became a race against himself. The whistle blew and he was alone on the mat, his contest as much about besting himself as his opponent.

By the end of his freshman year, Jim had excelled in mile and half-mile track events and earned another varsity letter. He looked forward to working with his mentor in the seasons to come, but his dream was short-lived. That spring, Bishop announced his resignation and transfer to a school downstate. Losing a coach was one thing; saying goodbye to the man who'd believed in him during those first uncertain Scottville days was quite another. Jim grieved.

It wasn't long before the effect of Bishop's absence was obvious. His replacement lacked the skill and passion to coach the runners to anything near victory, and their morale and performance plummeted. By junior year, Jim's frustration had reached the breaking point and he took it upon himself to reverse the situation. "The teams weren't motivated and the coach wasn't pushing them," he recalled in a 2012 interview. "If we were going to succeed, I would have to step into Steve Bishop's shoes."

Jim took charge of the underclassmen, who soon looked to him as their unofficial captain. He led them in training runs that looped from Gordon Road to the east all the way to Crystal Lake northwest of town. And he ran with them, just as Bishop had, through fallow fields and autumn woods, pushing them no harder than he pushed himself. They pulled on their blue and gold team T-shirts and tackled the marshy lowlands of Amber Road and the long, hilly stretch of Stiles, every practice a test of their endurance, a challenge to always run faster and longer than they had the day before.

> You can be a warrior on the field, on the mat, on the track, but at the end of the day, it really isn't about pummeling your opponent. It's about understanding how much better you can do.
>
> The other teams—the guys from Shelby and Benzie Central and Hart—they're all snow shovelers just like you. I always thought you should go at the end of the event and thank those people for giving you the opportunity for another step toward finding your strengths or limitations. You should recognize that the hurdle is you, and then acknowledge the person's role in your learning about yourself.

Sometimes, weary of shin splints, blisters, and aching calf muscles, they complained about Jim's punishing workouts, and their less-demanding coach would take over for a little while. But before too long, they missed Jim—his arduous regime tempered with his teasing humor. They missed the exhilarating sprints down unforgiving gravel roads and the intense camaraderie they felt when the team became a single being, each member a crucial part of the whole.

"Jim was a great leader," recalled Ed Sanders, a freshman runner under Jim's captaincy. "He made us work hard, because you didn't want him coming after you. We'd heard stories about how tough he was, how if someone wasn't working hard enough, he'd rip their shorts off and make them run back to the school in their underwear."

There was no truth to the stories, of course. They were tales shared in the locker room, myths repeated by boys in awe of the upperclassman's drive and his ability to transform his visions into action.

"We all wanted to emulate Jim. I wasn't worried about disappointing the coach. I didn't want to disappoint Jim," said Sanders, who later would become Scottville's phys ed instructor and cross country coach. "Jim showed us what leadership was all about. I use what I learned from him to this day: the respect he showed for others, the things he did to motivate us to work harder."

Another freshman on the cross country and track teams was Tim Genson, now Scottville's high school athletic director. "Other than Jim, we were extremely young and not a very good team," Genson would recall. "Jim's prodding and pushing certainly allowed me to be better than I would have been."

On blue fall afternoons, Jim led Genson and his teammates along Darr Hill, the quarter-mile upgrade past his house and the bane of MCC runners, shouting encouragement every step of the way. Taking a page from Bishop's coaching manual, he created a team of comrades who knew their success depended as much upon their shared empathy as upon their speed and stamina. He taught them to be always aware of the discouraged teammate in need of an extra boost of confidence or a heartening word and that celebrating triumph was as important as learning from defeat.

"We were novice, wet-behind-the-ears runners," Genson said. "But with Jim's leadership, we got as much out of ourselves as we could. He made us care about what we were doing and helped me understand that teams are at their best when players, not coaches, hold each other accountable.

"I remember the first time that switch clicked on for me," he would recall. "We were coming back from Darr Hill and I was keeping up with the lead group, which was always Jim. Watching him, I thought, 'I can do this!'"

> Once, we were at a conference meet, and we were all running strong. These guys aren't even my team. They're from Muskegon Oakridge. Those are some of the best times I ever ran, when we connected and pushed each other even though we were on opposite teams.
>
> Before the race, we'd all decided that we were going to let the younger brother of one of the runners win. Me coming in first or second or third wasn't going to make any difference in the big picture. But we pushed that kid harder than he'd ever been pushed so he'd get his first first-place conference medal.
>
> He'd kept up the whole time and we were within milliseconds of each other, but this kid couldn't get to the finish line without hanging with us. In the last 100 yards, he had to run faster than he'd ever run.
>
> The rest of us just slightly hesitated at the finish line to put him in, and we all went over the line together. He earned that medal.

Drawing pen always at the ready, Jim whiled away a few spare moments during the invitational meet at Ferris State College that autumn. He laced up his running shoes, did a few stretches at the edge of the field, and before the race began, doodled an elaborate 12-pointed figure on his palm. And then he ran, his footfalls a counterpoint to the wind rushing in his ears.

At the finish line, he held open his hand to accept his medal. The coach pressed the award against Jim's outstretched palm, where it fit almost exactly within the ink outline he'd drawn. He looked at it in wonder, this award for doing what he most loved to do, this award in the shape of a star.

"MIKE SCARED THE HELL OUT OF ME," recalled Jim Allen, who joined Scottville's wrestling team as a freshman in 1977. "As small in stature as he is, he was so intimidating. He always demanded respect." Since coming to coach at MCC, Mike had led his wrestlers to dozens of league, district, and regional championships, and two of his men had won individual state titles. Allen had good reason to feel anxious.

Choosing wrestling had been a most fortuitous move for Jim. He observed his father as the professional he was and learned the skills of the sport in their purest form. The hours they spent together in training and competition were the safe framework where they could explore their new relationship. Even Jan accompanied them to out-of-town matches, and, inching along the snowy Michigan roads in the Toyota, they imagined themselves—for a little while anyway—a real family.

Mike wasn't one to play favorites. He expected his son to complete the same rigorous training exercises as others on the team—and then some. On the way home from school, Jim listened as his father repeated theories about fitness and dedication and the importance of sensitivity to an opponent's every nuance. And on practice nights, he joined his teammates in the gym for round-robin matches, pull-ups, and what Mike called "killers." The boys would drop from standing to a push-up position, then pop back to their feet in one sharp motion—again and again and again. "Then we'd run laps in the halls until we about bled," Allen would recall.

Up and down the halls they ran, past darkened classrooms and tall windows overlooking the courtyard where snow swirled and drifted against the foundation, their steps echoing from the metal lockers lining the empty corridors. The halls smelled of chalk dust and sweat, of tomorrow's bread baking in the cafeteria oven, and of the strong detergent in the custodian's wheeled scrub bucket. The boys' flat shoes played havoc with their arches and shins, but at Mike's command, they ran. He was free with praise for a job well done, but the boys knew if they slackened their pace or lost focus for even a moment, they'd hear Mike's shout—"Get over here!"—and be subjected to a punishing bout on the mat with him.

Jim completed his wrestling career at a respectable .600, consistently winning more matches than not. Early in his freshman season, he proved himself a key member of a winning team—a team that placed first in the annual Scottville Optimist Wrestling Invitational in January. Every Scottville wrestler placed, Jim Allen third and Jim fourth in the consolation finals in what the *Ludington Daily News* called an "awesome display of team power."[1]

"Mr. Keenan expected so much of everybody," said Allen, Scottville's wrestling coach since 2009. "I coach the way he did to this minute. If you expect a lot, you get a lot."

JAN WATCHED FROM THE BLEACHERS, and Mike stood nearby, arms akimbo, as his son approached the mat. Jim, his body and his instinct tuned to the job at hand, faced his opponent, aware of his every movement and intention. It was as if some inner voice directed him in the grappling dance, created the image of the next step he must take. He heard Mike's voice, too, the words he'd repeated in the hallway, in the Toyota, in the one-on-one practice matches: "Make it a challenge and not a chore." The task was up to him, and he stepped into his vision's reality.

Wrestling and running wouldn't guarantee Jim a place in MCC's inner social circle. That honor was reserved for the quarterbacks and point guards destined to date homecoming queens and be named Most Popular in the mock election come senior year. Always under the watchful eyes of Mike and Jan, he wasn't included when classmates ventured down remote two-tracks to experiment with strawberry Boone's Farm and a pack of Marlboros.

He hung images of Devo and the Pretenders and the Plasmatics inside his locker where others taped the homecoming week schedule and pictures of the Bee Gees and Olivia Newton-John. His awareness of the latest hits only distanced him further from peers whose only music exposure was the local Top 40 radio station.

Jim's grades had convinced him he was at best an average student. Scottville's

---

[1] George Wilson, "Central Captures Own Mat Invite," *Ludington Daily News* (Michigan), January 8, 1979, 6.

administrators were convinced, too, and placed him in introductory courses separate from his college-bound classmates. While his Sugar Ridge friends tackled Algebra I, he was relegated to the remedial course and spent the entire year studying concepts they covered in two weeks.

> They stuck me in pre-algebra because based on my junior high grades, I supposedly couldn't count or add. I just wasn't challenged enough during my time in Ohio's so-called educational system.
>
> Pre-algebra was all repetition and open-book tests. I was pretty bored. It didn't exactly inspire me to learn, so my grades hovered just above who-gives-a-shit.

And then there was Boots Newkirk. Beloved and feared by generations of students as the teacher who provoked them sometimes to tears, Boots was known as much for his unexpected outbursts as for his love of knowledge. He wasn't past crashing his history textbook to the floor if a student dozed in class, and he was vocally intolerant of the teen angst that led to dramatic locker slamming after a romantic breakup. He called out students he'd seen the weekend before tossing Budweiser cans from their cars into what he sneeringly called the "puke weeds" alongside the road, and challenged their naïve political views, often switching sides mid-debate in an attempt to force them to examine their preconceptions.

Boots's students graduated able to defend and articulate their beliefs. Fearing his wrath if they came to class unprepared, they learned to list every U.S. Cabinet department and its purpose. They spent hours before the hanging maps in the school library and learned forever to identify a Mercator projection and the rivers of Africa.

> I did not see eye to eye with Boots politically or religiously, but I found a connection with him because he was adamant about the best parts of those things. He saw through bullshit. He didn't expect you to adopt his views, but he did expect you to behave like an adult.
>
> Every day, he would ask, "What's the price of gold this morning?" and no one would know. The next morning, same thing, and no one would know. Then the next day, you'd have the kiss-asses who would know the answer, and Boots would go, "So what?"

> He got you to pay attention, but just because you can answer the question
> doesn't mean you know the why. So you know the price of gold today. What
> does that mean?

Despite his often self-imposed isolation, Jim wasn't lonely, and in truth was never altogether alone. He had only to turn and notice the blond boy from eighth-grade reading class, the one classmate willing to admit disdain for the superficial, ready to trade snide remarks about the contest for popularity, eager to share the unspoken dream of discovering just what might lie beyond their little town.

JIM LEARNED TO CHART THE SEASONS' CYCLE in the first trilliums emerging white in the April woods, the trout returning to the Pere Marquette River. In May, he awaited blossoms in the apple and peach orchards surrounding the Darr Road house and climbed the tall wooden ladders come harvesttime in July, earning for his efforts pocket money for new records, pens, and sketch pads.

In the summer, he rose with the sun and knelt beside Mike in the gardens. Side by side, they removed weeds from the bleeding heart and iris and marigold beds. They trimmed Mike's sculpted shrubbery and cleared debris from the winding paths between bee balm and day lilies and clematis while chickadees and nuthatches swooped to snatch birdseed from the hollow Mike had formed in the top of his cap.

Clipper and trowel in hand, Jim watched chipmunks and squirrels approach from beneath bushes and brush, wary at first, then bravely scampering toward Mike, their tiny black eyes intent on his face as he crouched and extended his hand. They ate the seed he offered, then darted back to their hidey-holes beneath the peonies. "It was my first exposure to the consciousness of nature," he would later recall. "It wasn't like the animals were hanging out and talking to us. It was all based on survival, on forgoing fear in order to eat, the natural process of the earth."

Jim called Judith when he could, eager to share with his mother news of his improving grades and mentions on the sports pages. Each conversation was more frustrating than the last as she struggled to find the words and Jim tried to be patient.

The students in Anne Meeks's junior English class responded with wide-eyed panic when she announced their English assignment. "Some of them said they didn't like the ending of *Lord of the Flies*," she would recall. "I asked them to rewrite the last chapter as they'd like it to end." Jim faced the task with aplomb. Writing was almost second nature to him now, and the idea that it was permissible to alter someone else's story was a revelation. Instead of passively accepting an outcome, he discovered it was within his power—was, in fact, his duty—to create it.

The assignment changed more than the book's ending. Reworking William Golding's ideas forced Jim to place himself at the heart of the story, to understand character and plot more deeply and recognize his own importance in the creative process. The exercise was the catalyst to view his own art in a new way, to admit that it was no longer a solitary pastime to fill his empty hours. It was, in fact, his strength.

Suddenly, it seemed imperative to take advantage of every moment that could be spent writing and drawing and discovering a new song. He decorated his binders and book covers with his sketches and carried them about the school for all to see. He made no secret of his adoration for Kiss and Devo, and poured his passion into his classwork. And this time, instead of marking him as introverted and aloof, his talents were recognized and supported.

"It was interesting to watch the transformation," recalled Ted Winkel, whose psychology class met in the classroom adjacent to Meeks's. "Around junior year, we started to see another side of Jim. All of a sudden, a very creative side emerged with the artwork and sketches and poetry. Obviously, there was a part of him that was yearning to be free."

As Winkel lectured on Pavlov's dogs, Jim filled his notebooks with drawings and verses, and he generally ignored the work Meeks assigned in journalism class. Instead of concentrating on ledes and the inverted pyramid, he turned in poems and drawings, prompting her to incorporate into the course a unit on poetry. "I encouraged his poetry because he was good at it," Meeks admitted. "He had a good sense of irony, and his drawings contained wonderfully subtle humor."

Classmates relied on his poems to help them cope with sibling rivalries, parents who just didn't understand, and crushing romantic breakups—a more productive catharsis than locker slamming. Unpolished juvenilia to be sure, Jim's limericks and simple verses urged them to ignore the judgments of others, to think for themselves, to fearlessly face both joy and sorrow. Between classes, he surreptitiously slipped the poems among their books and binders, poems he signed Count Malcolm Gridley.

Count Malcolm Gridley was the larger-than-life myth who allowed no sentimental self-pity, a man behind a mask who offered challenge and comfort. Jim named his alias for Malcolm Young, the AC/DC guitarist who, from the shadows just outside the spotlight, created the rhythms that unified the band's words and music. He chose as his wizard's last name Gridley, Judith's family name.

> I started to put words together and people actually responded in a positive way. I felt like I was onto something. If people were going through some fucked-up situation, I'd get in my head and write about it. To see the look on their face when I somehow touched on what they were going through—well, you get a little praise for something, you follow up on it.
>
> And being from a family that didn't communicate very well, it felt good to express myself.

Of course, everyone knew the poet was really the quiet boy in the next row, the boy in pristine T-shirt and freshly pressed Curlee trousers, the boy with the growing collection of cross country and wrestling medals. "He wrote about deep emotions and used dark images, but there was nothing frightening or sinister about his poetry," Meeks would recall. "Some people might have had that impression, but I don't think he was ever serious about that. Jim didn't take himself seriously, but he took life very seriously."

By now, Jim knew what to expect of a Michigan winter. The incessant blizzards and lake-effect squalls off Lake Michigan might bring days of seclusion along roads impassable with drifts. After stoking the stoves, he listened with Mike in the dark mornings to the radio reports of school closings and blocked secondary roads that even the plowing crews dared not venture down.

On those snow days, he'd curl on his bed, the tangy scent of woodsmoke filling the house, the wind rattling the windows in their frames. Before Meeks's English class, Jim hadn't been an avid reader, but now he took from his bookshelf a neglected copy of *Cry Geronimo!*. He learned of the Apaches' struggle to defend their land and their tradition, and as he merged their story with his own, the book became weightless and forgotten in his hands.

He ran with them through the Sierra Madres, past the oddly familiar pin oak and prickly pear and saguaro, one step ahead of the cavalry and Mexican army intent upon their women and their scalps. He listened with Geronimo for the voices of earth spirits and mountain spirits, and he understood what it was to call upon them for protection and strength. He felt the cool of nighttime desert beneath bare feet, saw at the horizon boulders red with sunrise. Across canyon and creek bed, he ran through the night to the Cochise stronghold, juniper heavy on the air, the Dragoon Mountains rising dark against the spangle of stars in the Arizona sky.

Jim looked forward to the short-lived January thaws, the crystal-bright days that allowed a drive between towering snowbanks and rivulets of melt to Ludington, the county seat seven miles away. Most of his classmates had by now completed driver's ed under the severe instruction of Boots Newkirk, and in their fathers' sturdy Fords or well-tested farm trucks, they chauffeured Jim to town, where he'd rendezvous with one or another girl from his class for burgers at McDonald's or a showing of *Private Benjamin* at the Lyric.

When icy winds and whiteouts kept his friends at home, Jim trudged through the drifts to spend an afternoon with his friend Andy Green two houses distant. An evening at the Greens' meant catching up on *The Dukes of Hazzard* and *Saturday Night Live*, and between episodes, a chat with Andy's father.

> Butch Green was an amazing man with great stories. I would pick his brain about how he got his sled dogs to eat from his hand and the time he hitched them up to the sled and went into town for food when everybody was snowed in.
>
> And he introduced me to T. Rex. He would talk about how music, if it really resonates, will beat somewhere right near your heartbeat. That music will make sense to you, he told me, because it's in rhythm with your soul.

FAMILIES AND FRIENDS FILLED THE BLEACHERS and the folding chairs set in the space usually reserved for basketball and PE class. The members of the high school choir stood in formation on the stage at one end of the gym, their voices blending in *Muppet Movie* medleys and ballads of Dan Fogelberg or Joni Mitchell.

Jim had joined the choir early in sophomore year, and performing in recitals proved to be more than a pleasant diversion from sports. Director Ann Johnson began at the beginning, teaching her charges to properly breathe from the diaphragm to avoid straining their young vocal cords. She introduced them to the behind-the-scenes tasks required to mount a performance, from placing announcements in the *Daily News* to the ins and outs of acquiring performance rights, and her choir members collaborated in selecting the popular songs they performed. Jim took his place at the bake sale table and the chocolate bar concession, raising funds for the construction of an acoustic shell and the purchase of sheet music for *Oliver*, the musical they chose to stage that year.

Cast as the cocky charity boy Noah Claypole, Jim called upon his wrestling skills to add realism to his fight scene with the title character. His vocals were limited to group numbers, but even so, his powerful tenor rose clear among the voices of the ensemble.

"Jim could pick out a harmonizing line and improvise," Johnson recalled in a 2013 interview. "His intonation was always spot-on. I remember wishing I could hear those internal harmonies the way he did."

IN MAY, ANNE MEEKS OPENED THE WINDOWS of her classroom to the school courtyard, admitting soft breezes and the muted voices of honor students allowed to spend study hall on the lawn. They sprawled among dandelions and abandoned textbooks, comparing notes on the gowns they'd wear to the upcoming junior prom and speculating on how well the Detroit Tigers would do that season.

Restless with spring, her students were hard-pressed to pay attention to their lessons, but distracted as they were by the just-reopened Dairy Queen down the street, they snapped from their reveries when she distributed their end-of-year gift. She'd collected their work throughout the semester and compiled it in *Aurora*, the class literary journal. They turned the pages of the little magazine, pungent with fresh ink and still warm from the press in the art studio down the hall, and for the first time, saw in print their verses and stories and bylines. Illustrating Jim's poems were his pen-and-ink drawings of a small, wiry character he called Maynard.

Every morning, Jim set his cup of tea at the edge of his drafting table, taped paper to the drawing board, and arranged in a line his pencils and Staedtler erasers. He'd discovered in drafting class a way to blend the artistic and the practical and apply the geometry he'd struggled with sophomore year. He still ignored Meeks's journalism syllabus, but when challenged to draw a 3-D view of the threads and mechanisms hidden inside a machine assembly, he gave his full attention.

"I'd have a hard time finding anything wrong with his work," student teacher Kjiirt Jensen would recall. "I'd have to get on his case because he couldn't do the proper lettering too well. He always tried to do it his own way."

The most advanced student in the class, Kjiirt had completed every drafting course the school offered, and at a loss over what to assign him next, Mr. Ingraham had enlisted him to assist with grading and keeping his class on track.

Instead of creating a competitive distance, Kjiirt's critiques only drew him and Jim closer. Ever since eighth-grade reading class, each had always found in the other an empathetic outsider. At the periphery of a party or during a pep rally in the gym, they'd whispered snarky comments and recognized a safe if tenuous kinship. But working together in Ingraham's class, they discovered their mutual passion for art and a shared drive for perfection, and before long, the two were inseparable.

"They always walked around the school with these little impish grins," choir director Ann Johnson would recall. "It was as if they were in on something that nobody else knew about. You saw them and thought, 'What are those two up to?'"

Here at last was Jim's counterpart, a tall, blond opposite to catch his glance and see with him past hypocrisy and blind conformity, a bright equal with a perverse sense of humor that rivaled his own.

> Kjiirt and I saw things differently. We'd read the newspaper or hear something on the news, and go, "That doesn't sound right. That seems like a very ma-

nipulated statement that's not reflective of the truth. I'm calling bullshit on that one."

If somebody was all excited and asked us if we were going to the football game, we just didn't get it. That was the kind of thing we just didn't line up for.

On prom night, Kjiirt went way formal, like he was James Bond or somebody. I bought a plastic top hat and spray-painted it green and rented a green tuxedo and a frilly white shirt with green highlights. I looked like a leprechaun. I took one of our best friends instead of an actual date. We hung out for an hour and then went to a drive-in movie.

They spent weekends on Darr Road, where Jim took album after album from the big black trunk—the Jacksons and the Bee Gees, Adam and the Ants and Patti Smith, Devo and Kiss. Kjiirt's LP collection was limited to the lyrical James Taylor and Jimmy Buffett available at Sounds Good, Ludington's provincial record shop, and he listened, rapt. Jim's music was a revelation, a portal to a place of sound and color and emotion alien to anything he'd ever experienced in Mason County.

And on Saturday nights, Kjiirt drove them in his dad's immense Buick to nearby Custer and teen night at Johnny's. Roller rink by day, dance emporium by night, Johnny's had been for generations the destination of young people from all corners of the county. Romances bloomed and ended here, jealousies ignited, and hardly a week went by without an altercation in the parking lot between aggressive boys just off the farm.

Inside, Johnny's was all cavernous shadow, tables set about the wooden dance floor, and clusters of friends daring one another to ask an upperclassman to dance. Presiding over it all was Johnny himself in pompadour and dinner jacket. Little at Johnny's ever changed, least of all the music. When Jim and Kjiirt stepped inside, they invariably heard the same Village People and Donna Summer that had been popular years before.

But they danced—sometimes with classmates, sometimes with girls from Ludington or even Manistee, girls they found fascinating and sophisticated, if only because they didn't live next door. The strobes flickered, the DJ replaced "My Sharona" with "Sultans of Swing," and they moved across the floor, forgetting for a little while the shabby décor, the smell of stale beer and cigarettes, the long, straight roads and acres of string beans outside.

An evening was never complete without the drive afterward to Ludington, the radio tuned to a station Kjiirt's dad, with a bewildered shake of his head, would have to change in the morning. A ritual visit to the town's western edge and Lake Michigan was almost mandatory for Mason Countyites. Every departure, every return was marked by a drive along the shore, a glance at the vast inland sea that meant home.

Their visits might include only a spin past the beach and a possessive look at the lake raging with whitecaps or placid in moonlight, the sky awash with stars. More often, though, they'd park the Buick and walk barefoot across the cold sand and along the breakwall to the lighthouse.

The silence and the darkness invited confidences, and Jim and Kjiirt talked— in the somewhat guarded way of teenage boys, to be sure—of synchronicity and mystery, of the wheelsmen who maneuvered the carferries through storm and fog across the lake, of what might lie on its opposite shore.

"One night, he told me a story," Kjiirt would recall. "He told me about a girl he'd known in Ohio. I don't remember if he told me her name or if she was still there or even what their connection was." Kjiirt may not have remembered the details, but he remembered the sadness in Jim's voice and the depth—uncharacteristic in someone so young, he thought even then—of his words. "He looked up," he recalled. "And he said, 'She's looking up and seeing the same moon.'"

Before long, their walks to the lighthouse came to include another ritual, a ritual of their own making. When the time came to abandon a childhood dream, if a certain girl decided she no longer wished to accompany them to the Lyric, when a friend moved away or proved to be not such a good friend after all, they tossed talismans of ending and beginning into the dark water. Moon and stars their only witnesses, they sacrificed a photo or a letter, a coin, a ring, a stone—silently closing one chapter and opening the way for the next.

SPIRIT WEEK WAS THE LONG-ANTICIPATED AND OVER-THE-TOP EVENT of the sports-centered school, the annual celebration of star players and winning teams. All week long, every Scottville Spartan dressed in the school colors of blue and gold, and alumni returned from colleges and careers to attend the homecoming football game at MacPhail Field. In the crisp fall evenings in advance of the game, students gathered in some classmate's barn to decorate flatbeds with tissue rosettes and papier-mâché goalposts to create the floats that would make up the halftime parade.

They constructed in the school's corridors elaborate tableaux honoring their team, each class sure their effort would be voted the most creative. The Class of '82 commandeered B Hall, the long corridor outside Meeks's and Winkel's and Boots Newkirk's classrooms, and erected larger-than-life images of the graduating football players. The mannequins stood shoulder to shoulder on either side of the hallway, identifiable as the real boys by their numbered jerseys. Imposing yet minimalist, the images evoked a walk through the Pro Football Hall of Fame, a tribute to victory and achievement, the embodiment of possibility. They were the handiwork of seniors adept with paintbrush and glue, but the idea was all Jim's.

Cross country runner Ed Sanders, by then a sophomore, would later recall the display. "Jim had a different vision from what everybody else had," he said, remembering the crepe paper streamers and foil stars that made up the other class exhibits. "We'd walk down the senior hall and think, 'Well, our display is going to lose.'"

Students auditioning for the spring musical had much the same reaction to the sudden public appearance of Jim's talents. Eager to explore yet another artistic avenue, he—rather on a whim—responded to the casting call and arrived for tryouts. He'd enjoyed the movie version of *The Sound of Music* and imagined performing as he had in *Oliver* the year before, perhaps as one of the von Trapp children. The pianist made her way through the intro to "Edelweiss" and then nodded toward Jim to begin. His strong tenor echoed across the empty stage with the intensity and heartbreak the song demanded.

The director looked from Jim to the pianist to his classmates, who sat in stunned silence. "They were all looking at each other," he would remember. "And I'm thinking, 'Am I fucking this up? What the fuck's going on?'" No one in the church choir had ever commented on the quality of Jim's voice. His work with the school chorus had been limited to ensemble singing, and his solo abilities had never been singled out. But now, the drama director admitted he'd never heard a high schooler's voice so pure, so clear, so confident.

As much to Jim's surprise as everyone else's, the role of Baron von Trapp was his.

The spotlight and the chance to sing were as tempting as they'd been since he was small, but the rehearsal and performance schedule would conflict with regional track meets and the final conference race of the year. He took his time contemplating his decision—too much time—and when he finally phoned the director, the part had been given to someone else.

Perhaps one day, he'd have another chance to take the stage, Jim rationalized. Another lead role might someday be his. In the meantime, it was probably best to stay the course and complete his final season of track. Abandoning his teammates this late in the game would be tantamount to walking away in the last mile of the race. He'd set his course long ago, and there was nothing now but to see it through to the end, earn one more varsity letter, reach the goal he'd envisioned freshman year—even if it meant delaying another.

The song that would represent the Class of '82 seemed a foregone decision. Only one song appeared on the ballot circulated by the class council, "Believe It or Not," the sprightly theme of the television comedy *The Greatest American Hero*. But Jim believed his class deserved a song of more depth and complexity, and he spent the weeks before graduation petitioning for the more appropriate "Dream On." He approached student after student, explaining the inspiring lyrics and calling their attention to the innovative musical riffs, until even classmates who'd never before heard of Aerosmith joined his camp. In the end, "Dream On" won by a landslide.

> When they decided that the *Greatest American Hero* theme would be our class song, I hit the roof. I was never so active in student government as I was that month getting signatures for "Dream On." I wasn't going to go down as having my class theme song be a bouncy TV show bullshit song.
>
> Whatever mascot they wanted to attach to us, whatever they chose for our class colors and our class flower, OK. But that song? Absolutely not. Our fuckin' graduation song should be one you can look back on in 20 years and reflect on where you came from and where you're going. This is our song, not the convince-yourself-everything's-OK song.

When mock elections were held that spring, his classmates voted him Most Pessimistic—not because he took a hopeless view of the future, but quite the opposite. He'd become known for his outspoken intolerance of complacency and the status quo, and instead of ostracizing him for his outlook, they'd honored him. They'd seen, too, his talents, and, in a rare mock-election hat-trick, also named him Class Artist and Most Talented.

And his four years in cross country, wrestling, and track meant an even more prestigious honor. In the spring, Jim became the first in the history of the school to earn 12 varsity letters. At the varsity dinner that spring, his achievement somehow went unmentioned.

THE GRADUATES STOOD ABOUT THE SUNNY COURTYARD, toying with their betassled mortarboards and accepting the congratulations of relatives and friends. In keeping with Midwestern tradition, the afternoon would be an endless series of sliced-ham-and-potato-salad luncheons, gatherings of aunts and uncles who unfailingly traveled across the state to honor such triumphs.

> All my relatives were in Ohio, so I planned my own open house and invited a bunch of people. Not a single fucking person came. A lot of them went out drinking instead, because you couldn't drink at my dad's house. Nope. Not a single person came.

Kjiirt escaped as quickly as he could from his family obligations, and he and Jim drove to the lake to hold a ceremony of their own. They walked to the lighthouse where Jim took from his pocket a tiny balsa-wood cross he'd carved with names of musicians recently gone, musicians who'd left voids no one would soon fill—AC/DC vocalist Bon Scott, Quiet Riot and Ozzy Osbourne guitarist Randy Rhoads, Led Zeppelin drummer John Bonham. Kjiirt stood beside him, and Jim tossed the cross into the dark, silent water, marking their passage.

Jim's classmates graduated with their plans intact, with engagement rings from their high school sweethearts, offers to manage the family farm, scholarships and internships and pictures in the yearbook proclaiming them Most Likely to Succeed.

Even Kjiirt planned to leave his job as stock clerk at Farmer John's supermarket to study architecture come fall, but Jim had never seriously thought about a career. He loved to draw and to write, to imagine what might be and to set about creating it. There wasn't much economic value in such things, he realized, and Mike and Jan told him in no uncertain terms that if he expected to stay at home, he must earn his keep.

Jobs in the county had never been plentiful or especially lucrative, and in truth, Jim couldn't imagine spending his days pumping gas or flipping burgers simply to turn his paycheck over to Mike for his room and board. Conforming to the corporate world felt equally distasteful.

He wanted to study art.

"I was worried about his future," Jan would recall. "I remember thinking that he wasn't grounded enough to have a career." She and Mike were hesitant to finance four years of college in light of his dubious prospects, and they particularly balked at the idea of art school. They'd envisioned a stable career track for their son, perhaps a management curriculum, as so many of Jim's Sugar Ridge friends had entered. Perhaps, they thought, he should become a teacher.

But Jim wanted to discover the practical application of his passion, to follow the inner voice telling him that sketching and writing and maybe even music were the things he was made to do.

The year before, he'd seen the movie *Stripes*—the tale of two friends weary of meaningless jobs and vapid love lives who join the Army in search of direction. He'd admired the snappy military uniforms and Bill Murray's comedic timing. And since active combat was remote in the peaceful summer of 1982, three years of stateside service would be a tolerable enough existence. The real lure, of course, was the Army College Fund, which in those years provided tuition monies to those who satisfied a six-year military commitment—three years of active duty followed by three inactive—and just might be his ticket to art school.

In June, Jim completed the Armed Services Vocational Aptitude Battery, the survey that determined enlistees' suitability for service. The delayed entry program would mean two months of freedom before he must report for duty.

He and Kjiirt would live that summer by their rules and their rules alone before the inevitable constraints of college and the military. Jim moved his Izod shirts and Members Only jacket to the back of his closet and replaced them with jeans skintight at the ankle and trimmed with a scatter of Sid Vicious–inspired safety pins. With a box cutter Kjiirt had borrowed from the market, he slashed to fashionable threads his T-shirts bearing the logos of the Smiths and Adam Ant.

Many of their classmates still indulged in Saturday night house parties, blowouts that had never held much appeal for Jim, who had no interest in alcohol or insipid small talk. But now, he and Kjiirt avoided them altogether, knowing they'd end as they always had—in chugging contests and slurred arguments and much retching in the bathroom—until the Blatz ran out and everyone dispersed until the next weekend.

On Kjiirt's days off, they'd stake out a spot on the white sand beach, a supply of Mountain Dew and Snickers bars and strawberry Twizzlers in tow in case Kjiirt's blood sugar levels fell. Theirs was a summer of drives along the dunes at the edge of the lake, matinees at the Lyric, music and dancing and late-night pizzas.

AND THERE WAS JOHNNY'S, ALWAYS JOHNNY'S, where no matter how much Jim and Kjiirt longed to escape the county, they always returned. Johnny's, where at last the DJ spun the Plasmatics and the Romantics and Devo. The summer brought new dancers, a whole table of them—Kathy and Tracy and Kim—young Ludington girls who dared appear in public in the big hair and bright New Wave colors and strategically tied bandanas that typified the era. "They looked like they just fell out of MTV," Kjiirt would later recall.

The girls arrived at Johnny's ready to dance—and ready to accept Jim and Kjiirt into their cutting-edge circle. "We did our own thing, had our own style," Kathy Larsen would later recall. "We purposely tried to be different. We were rockin' the '80s big-time."

And the girls became a part of the beach-day afternoons. Jim and Kjiirt considered them more than companions, beyond girlfriends. They were trusted sisters who shared their laughter and their fears and their dreams.

> I got to hang out with the hot, edgy girls from the big town, but we really weren't on their radar.
>
> They were probably thinking, "There's no way this guy's going to get a job at Dow Chemical and hang around here and help me raise my babies." I wrote poems and wore a green fuckin' top hat. If I wanted a girlfriend, I was probably going about it all wrong.

A Perfect Union of Contrary Things

The Ludington girls were among the few in the county who believed the vow Jim made before he left for basic training, his pledge that when his stint was over, he'd return in a Mohawk and full punk regalia, a uniform of freedom following the restrictions of military life, a fitting costume for an art student.

THE DRIVER ADJUSTED HIS MIRRORS and pulled the Greyhound slowly from the curb outside the bowling alley. Jim pressed his face against the streaked window, straining in vain to catch a final glimpse of the lake and the lighthouse. Then he settled back in his seat for the long ride to Detroit, wondering at the wisdom of the path he'd chosen.

4

Detroit's Military Entrance Processing Station was a windowless barn of a building set 20 miles from the city in a no-man's-land of wide boulevards and acres of parking lot. Inside, Jim joined the crowd of young people from throughout the state, the latest group of enlistees arrived for a day of endless paperwork, interviews, and physical exams, their voices echoing from cinder-block walls and the high ceiling.

Lines formed and re-formed as recruits were directed from desk to cubicle to private office. Jim thought of the mazes he'd worked in the *Highlights* magazine in the dentist's waiting room back home, the puzzles he'd never quite solved before the hygienist would call his name.

He moved from station to station, completed a questionnaire here, spoke with a uniformed counselor there, tallied childhood mumps and measles and chicken pox at the medical technician's table, all the while imagining some logic to the chaos. Failing to discover a method to the bureaucratic madness, he resigned himself to following barked orders: Move to the background screening interview, report for the eye and ear exam, stand in this line until it is divided and rearranged, wait here.

The results of his ASVAB test indicated that Jim was highly intelligent and would adapt easily to military life. His impressive scores had qualified him to select the Military Occupational Specialty he wished to choose—that of infantryman or electrician or military policeman—and he'd set his heart on MOS 82 Bravo. As a mapmaker, he'd merge his interests and his abilities and create surveys and charts, channeling his talents with pen and ink as he so loved to do. An understanding of spatial concepts had always come easily, and his grades in Mr. Ingraham's drafting class were all the résumé he'd need.

The MOS coordinator glanced at Jim's transcript, then at his spreadsheet of available positions. He frowned, then brightened. Plenty of enlistees had already been assigned as 82Bs, he informed Jim. But a related MOS—82 Charlie—was wide open. He turned then to Jim's paperwork, clicked his ballpoint once or twice, and entered Jim's assignment on the blank line: artillery surveyor.

Jim gleaned from the coordinator's brief explanation that surveying had something to do with using the sun and stars and nearby trees to determine positions on the battlefield. He wouldn't sit at a lamplit desk in the company office drawing maps after all. He'd plot diagrams and escape routes for his battery—in the midst of simulated warfare.

The noisy room, the stale air, the shifting groups of young people converged into one sinking realization: that this was only the first of many military moments when expectation would dissolve in the face of baffling reality.

> The processing station was like the bargain basement in a department store. All this activity going on, and the same disappointment. Oh, look at that wonderful thing! Ah, they don't have it in my size. Or if it is in my size, somebody grabs it right out of my hand. You want to be a mapmaker? Don't we all! Here's the artillery.

By the time Jim stepped from the final cubicle, the last box on the last form checked, he'd been reduced to the most vital of statistics. Differentiated from all the others, he was distilled to the essential Private James Herbert Keenan that would be his identity for the next three years.

It was easy enough to find one's way through a maze, he reassured himself. Hadn't he heard the secret once, the secret of always keeping the left hand against the labyrinth wall? No matter how many times one had to retrace one's steps, no matter how much backtracking was involved, the method would always eventually lead to the way out. He wondered if the theory was true, and he wondered at the map he could devise that would include such touchpoints all the way to the exit.

That night, he had only to venture as far as the hotel across the street from the MEPS building. He lay awake and thought of the countless boys who'd spent sleepless nights on this thin mattress, wondered where they'd gone when they'd left Detroit, what their lives might be like now. Morning light filled the drab room, and he rose to dress for his flight to Oklahoma and Fort Sill.

Jim stepped into his barracks, his shirt collar already damp though it was barely noon. The room provided little relief from the heat and humidity that had plagued the area for days. The parched fields surrounding Fort Sill were broken by scattered groves of trees, their leaves drooping, and the gentle hills far in the distance shimmered in the heat.

Sixty-four identical beds lined the concrete bay, beds separated by back-to-back metal lockers at their heads offering only the slightest degree of privacy. Jim fit his black trunk into the bottom of his locker, changed into a fresh shirt, and made his way to the reception hall to report for his first Fort Sill assignment.

Fort Sill had been built during the Indian Wars as a stronghold to subvert tribal raids into neighboring states. Now it was the training ground for Army field artillery soldiers and Marines, the preparedness center that Jim would call home for nearly five months.

He didn't know it yet, but the fort had also been for a time home to his literary hero, Geronimo. In 1894, the Indian leader had been captured along with 341 other Chiricahua Apache prisoners of war and had lived in a village on the post until his death in 1909.

One end of Jim's bay opened into the dayroom, a sunny space furnished with tables and chairs and plastic M16s lined along one wall, one for each of the soldiers. In one corner of the dayroom stood a television for the enjoyment of the sergeants venturing from their offices on the floor below. A pleasant room, inviting, and a room the trainees must not enter without permission.

Jim understood the reason for such rules. The television was off-limits for the same reason his Adam Ant–logo T-shirt and his long hair were forbidden. He understood and appreciated that when he'd entered the military, he'd put on a uniform, and with it, a persona that, until the day of discharge, he would never entirely put off. He understood the need for the soldier to relinquish his individuality, to sacrifice personal desires, not through mindless conformity but a dedication to the one overriding goal: to be ready at a second's notice to move and act with his battalion as one cohesive being.

He understood, but he bristled.

His days began at 0400 hours with a regimen of push-ups and sit-ups and pull-ups and runs. Under the demanding Staff Sergeant Lawrence Brew, he learned of triage and CPR and the use of tourniquets on the battlefield. Brew stood over him while he took apart his M16 and tried his best to maintain his focus while he reassembled it. "Just as you're getting good at this," he would explain, "they come up and start yelling at you. It's not about speed. It's about putting it together under stress."

Brew shouted his orders, and Jim and his battalion marched and turned, marched and turned again at his command, until they learned to move as one across the training field, not a footstep out of place, not an arm out of sync.

In the afternoon, they loaded their backpacks and set out on ten-mile marches to the edges of the compound. Exhausted and thirsty, they pitched their tents, longing for rest under the canvas shade. Invariably, a smoke grenade lobbed from some unseen position would interrupt their work, and they'd drop their ropes and bedrolls to defend their position—having received little training in exactly how such a thing was to be done.

By 2000 hours, after eating dinner at record speed in the mess hall, they were back in their bunks, only to wake in the morning to repeat the grueling routine.

More than two weeks after arriving at Fort Sill, Jim at last had a short respite, a few hours he was allowed to call his own. He lay on his bunk and tried to ignore the 100-degree heat, the cicadas buzzing incessantly in the trees outside, and wrote a letter to Kjiirt.

He was honest with his friend about his unhappiness and vague sense of depression, but in true Jim fashion, he sprinkled the letter with his signature humor. Along one side of the page, he drew a stick-figure character who demonstrated the two swift motions required in digging a hole and tossing the soil over one's shoulder, a job Jim had done every morning that week. Then his character morphed into a two-step diagram of the choreography involved in performing Devo's "Jerkin' Back and Forth"—a dance he and Kjiirt had not so long ago perfected at Johnny's.

Aug. 19, 1982

Hello Kurtis Jensensis.

Things have been jerkin' right along here. I don't really like it, but what can I do about it? I'm goin crazy with no music and I haven't had a Dew* + Snickers* for ages, or so it seems. I miss Johnny's a whole bunch.

The beds suck as do the uniforms. Basically I don't like it but I'm not really sure yet. I must give it a chance. I miss the beach with all my heart and tan. Only 3 more years and I'll be home for good but until then I'm counting the days.

Be good.

James H.K.

*Mountain Dew + Snickers are®

The summer of chocolate bars on the beach and late-night dance marathons at Johnny's had left Jim in less than prime physical condition. Nevertheless, he approached the two-mile footrace with the same confidence he'd brought to every cross country and track event, determined to give it his all.

Held during the first weeks of basic training, the race was yet another test of enlistees' abilities, one more way to ascertain the individual training they might require. They changed into running shoes, the commotion and voices and Sergeant Brew's orders echoing from tile and metal, amplified across the indoor course.

Jim ran, the sound of footsteps hard at his heels. No matter how great the surge of energy he summoned, no matter how intently he concentrated, he could not outdistance the sound. His own speed whistling in his ears, he evoked every pointer Coach Bishop had suggested freshman year, determined to stay ahead of whatever it was that pursued him.

At the finish, he looked back. Far behind him, the nearest runner sprinted breathlessly. The steps he'd heard had been his own.

GERONIMO, JIM HAD LEARNED, had at least once tried to escape Fort Sill and run through the night toward his home in Arizona, only to be captured the next morning and brought back to the prison. As much as Jim dreamed of freedom, he'd meant what he'd written to Kjiirt. He'd give Army life an honest chance, knowing the discipline and the skills he'd learn there would only serve him well, knowing a full term of service would mean tuition and art school.

"I was surprised that he joined the military. I always thought of him as a free spirit," choir director Ann Johnson would reflect years later. "I didn't know if he would tolerate the imposed discipline, but his choice was a reflection of his incredible focus. Jim had a plan."

So long as he held fast to that plan, the rigors of Fort Sill would be tolerable. He took advantage of the moments—however brief—that sustained his sense of self. The men he befriended were the gifted but underestimated boys of working-class backgrounds similar to his own, the few who shared his taste in music and a refusal to completely abandon their more unorthodox qualities.

On the nights when he wasn't assigned fire duty and could sleep undisturbed, Jim pulled his pillow over his head, lowered the volume of his Walkman, and listened until he fell asleep to the Sex Pistols, the Plasmatics, the Pretenders, and Judas Priest's latest release he'd found at the PX.

His exemplary performance in basic training qualified him for yet another test, a lengthy evaluation that seemed to him unfocused and pointless. He handed the completed exam to his superior and watched it disappear into the mysterious ether that he'd learned by then was the military.

And on commencement day, he discovered that his performance and test scores had also qualified him to be named the battery's distinguished basic training graduate. His cumulative scores and rankings were the highest in the group, and his speed in the footrace had broken every record in platoon history.

The countdown he'd begun in August had, if not reached an end, grown noticeably shorter. Private E-2 Keenan packed his cassettes and his Walkman, eager for a brief holiday leave in Scottville, more than ready to depart Fort Sill, its battered fields, its groves of oak and hickory, the cramped bay, the stone pyramid in the Apache Indian Cemetery that marked Geronimo's grave.

Snow fell upon the flat Kansas plains and the rows of buildings, their uninspired architecture repeating itself endlessly across the Fort Riley complex. It was home to more than ten thousand soldiers and their families, its barracks and schools and medical facilities extending across the fields. The fields, Jim knew, would be the setting of maneuvers and marches and mock battles.

He crossed the yard and climbed the stairs to the second floor and his room, a stately space compared with the bay at Fort Sill. Three bunks stood against one wall, separated from the sitting area by a divider down the room's center. One of the bunks, Jim discovered, was assigned to Jeff Parks, a Fort Sill buddy and an avid Michael Jackson fan, his presence a welcome continuity. The three roommates pooled their pay for a small television and placed it beside a portable stereo on the table beneath the window. Their battered metal lockers were subject to inspection at a moment's notice, but their private bathroom was a luxury after the pandemonium of a communal latrine.

Frequently, Jim was assigned fire guard duty or to keep watch over tractors and heavy equipment parked in the lot across the street from the barracks. More often, he and his battalion were dispatched to field exercise, bivouacking on the grounds and engaging in protracted and realistic battle. He packed the essentials he'd need during the long day and night: his compass and levels and coils of measuring rope. And more important, the Sterno kit to make more palatable the cans of beans and franks, the mysterious corn hash, and the paste-like chicken concoction that no amount of heat or salt and pepper could improve. He packed, too, the envelopes of laxative preparation necessary to counteract the fiber-free and binding C rations. At night, he lay in his bedroll on the hard Kansas ground, dreaming of the ice cream parlor back home and of the butter pecan and black cherry he'd enjoyed as if it would last forever.

Advanced Individual Training was no game in a sunny Ravenna meadow where the game was interrupted when the sun went down. It was a monthlong combat enactment, a day-and-night simulation of war.

> No one was pushing the idea that actual war was a possibility. But it became immediately apparent to me that we were doing desert training. We weren't that far out of Vietnam, and it seemed to me we'd pretty much screwed the pooch over there. So what were we doing? Didn't we have our asses handed to us in the marshlands? Shouldn't we be doing wetlands training so that didn't happen again?
>
> We were being prepared for desert warfare. Something was already up in 1983, but nobody tells you things like that.

Ahead of the tank batteries, the 82 Charlie team crossed the rutted field in their weathered jeep, stopping to set up sextants and tripods and to install hubs alerting the batteries of their location and targets. The artillery squad fired, fired a second round into a barrage of rifle shots, then retreated into the turmoil of smoke and shouts and black boots trampling the brown grass. Dummy rounds and smoke grenades bursting on all sides, Jim and the other surveyors darted laterally among the troops, determining their coordinates and the likely locations of the enemy, the classroom geometry and algebra at last beginning to make sense.

Dusty and weary, Jim envisioned another two and a half years of charting stars and treetops, 30 more months of unquestioning obedience, of every trimmed hair in place and boots polished to an acceptable shine, of donning the costume of good soldier and perfecting his performance in the tragedy of imitation warfare. Two and a half years—an eternity before he'd spread across his desk a sheet of clean white drafting paper, his collection of pencils and drawing pens in a squat jar just within reach.

DESPITE ITS RIGORS, Fort Riley offered a freedom unimagined in Oklahoma. On Saturdays, Parks took his car from the adjoining lot and drove Jim to the Colonial in nearby Junction City, where they saw *National Lampoon's Vacation* and *Trading Places*. The more lax barracks rules allowed Jim to add personal touches to his room: a hot air popcorn maker and an electric kettle in which he boiled water for soup and Earl Grey to enjoy from his own mug.

On the days they didn't go to the field, the battalion gathered for lunch in the mess hall and then were allowed a few minutes in their rooms before beginning their afternoon duties. Jim and his roommates tuned their television to *The Young and the Restless*, propped the door open with a boot, and kept an ear cocked for the sergeant's call to formation.

When they were summoned, they fell in and received their orders for later in the day. As soon as they were dismissed, they darted upstairs to continue their escape into the world of ill-timed pregnancies, returns of long-lost relatives, sudden amnesia, and the appearance of evil twins. The drama and emotion-torn relationships reminded Jim—however unrealistically—of the civilian world he'd left behind. "I didn't give a fuck about that show," he would later recall. "I couldn't tell you what it was about. All I know is that it was all we had."

And at bedtime, he triple-stacked Pink Floyd or REM on the stereo and fell asleep to A-side songs one night and B the next.

LATE THAT SPRING, A LETTER ARRIVED with the results of the test Jim had taken months before. Of the thousands of enlistees who'd completed the exam, Jim was among the few whose scores qualified them to attend West Point's preparatory school, the first step toward admittance to the military academy.

He didn't weigh his options or seek advice. Before he reached the end of the letter, he'd made his decision. Prep school would be the end of muddy fields, of tins of pale roast beef, of the isolation of Fort Riley life. He imagined classrooms and libraries, discussions over coffee with students as bright as and brighter than he, music and art and knowledge beyond firearm assembly and transit lines—and the leisure to discover them.

Nearly a month of accumulated leave meant PFC Keenan could pay an extended visit home before he must report to New Jersey as a cadet candidate. It meant a July amid acres of sweet corn and string beans and the flowers in Mike's elaborate gardens, refreshing displays after the brown, parched expanse of Oklahoma and Kansas.

On Kjiirt's days off from the grocery store, the pair returned to their spot at the lake, the cooling breezes a reprieve from the 90-degree heat, the tubs of Blue Moon and Rocky Road at the ice cream parlor indeed inexhaustible. The two found they'd outgrown the adolescent dramas of Johnny's and spent afternoons walking the trails at the state park and splashing in the shallow end of the lake there, speculating about what the future might hold. And in the evenings, Jim discovered the local girls a year older too, a year more mature, and ready to explore with him new levels of intimacy.

Jim downplayed his prep school offer and shared his plan with only Mike and Jan. Remote and provincial as the county seemed to him now, he believed few there would appreciate the magnitude of his achievement. He felt he owed them no explanation, and instead quietly focused his sights on the design he'd put in place the year before.

Jim soon discovered that prep school, though it meant the end of C rations and night patrols, wasn't without its difficulties. Shortly after arriving at Fort Monmouth, he reported in to Kjiirt. "Am I sore all over er what?" he wrote. "I am totally tired from intense push-ups and pull-ups. Our hours are 5:30 to 10 p.m. The food is OK if you get the time to taste it—they rush us so fast through the mess hall. There are girls everywhere, but the 'Look But Don't Touch' rule is *not* in effect. You can't even *look*. What would Devo do in a situation like this?"

The U.S. Military Academy Preparatory School was a complex of austere concrete buildings and parking areas, a stark, treeless tract belying New Jersey's designation as the Garden State. Jim was heartened to learn that his relative freedom there would allow visits to nearby Eatontown and the ocean only five miles distant. And more tempting, a rail line at the western edge of the post offered connections that would take him all the way to Manhattan.

His room was an improvement over the quarters at Fort Sill and Fort Riley, carpeted and furnished with stylish wooden lockers and bed frames. He shared the double room with a country music lover given to chewing tobacco and spitting the dregs into a coffee cup. It was all Jim could do to put up with his albums, and his roommate felt the same about Jim's Mötley Crüe and Sex Pistols. But in spite of their differences, the two found common ground in their mission to compete on the prep school wrestling team and their drive to succeed at the academy.

Half the 360 men and women in Jim's class had entered USMAPS directly from high school. They were the exceptional athletes and team captains who required a taste of military life and an academic refresher before entering West Point as members of its lacrosse and cross country and football teams. The others were basic training graduates like Jim who would spend the next months in class preparing for the rigors of military school. And after working their way through algebra and trigonometry, after memorizing endless vocabulary lists, after more push-ups and pull-ups and track meets and wrestling matches, after learning the fundamentals of military science, only half would receive a West Point appointment.

For most of the cadet candidates, West Point was their one channeled aspiration, and they lived and breathed the USMAPS motto: Desire—Faith— Effort. They'd been winnowed from thousands of hopefuls and now jockeyed for one of the coveted 180 appointments. In their zeal, they exercised sometimes underhanded tactics to protect their own place in the hierarchy of contenders. They kept an ear trained on idle conversation, the innocent speculations about the wisdom of attending West Point, and might report to their higher-ups as little as an innocuous remark spoken over coffee.

> Even in idle conversations, you had to be careful what you said, because anything you said might be construed as a lie and make it easier for others to get in. As a creative person, I had to be very careful of how I talked.
>
> It wasn't so much the administration watching you. Your best friend was your worst enemy. The Cadet Honor Code said we wouldn't lie, cheat, steal, or tolerate those who do. "Tolerate" is the part that gives everybody license to kick out their roommate.

Jim was careful to keep his true plans to himself, but his frustration with the blind loyalty and the snitching was clear in his letters to Kjiirt. "If I'm not discovered soon by EMI records and get taken away from this stuff to become a rock star," he wrote, "I think I'm going to have to become a famous war hero."

JIM DEDICATED HIMSELF to USMAPS cross country, track, and wrestling with the same focus he had in high school. His contribution, he knew, would bring the Black Knights to victory in meets with other East Coast institutions and their archrival, the Naval Academy Prep School.

He sprinted with the cross country team in distance training runs along Asbury Park's beach and boardwalk, Coach Beal running alongside them. Jim and his teammates grew to expect Beal's shout that opened each practice: "Gentlemen, double knots," a reminder to discourage them from pausing to retie their shoelaces mid-run.

Beal possessed the self-assurance and natural grace of his East Coast heritage. Both USMAPS dean and cross country coach, Beal required every action in the classroom and on the course be completed with alacrity and dispatch. Beloved despite his gruff manner and exacting expectations, the practical and unbiased Beal was ever willing to support the lonely, the discouraged, the CC in need of an ally.

Often, he invited Jim and a few fortunate others to join him in conversation and challenging Socratic dialogue. He prefaced each session with the same request: "Allow me to pontificate just for a moment, if you will, gentlemen." His rhetorical exchanges challenged the CCs to think beyond the obvious, and when they failed to uphold their end of an argument, he sternly accused them of suffering from diarrhea of the mouth or constipation of the brain.

> He would go into a conversation, and you would soon realize that he was ex-
> plaining to everybody that they had their heads up their asses and they needed
> to figure out how to pull them out. He didn't care about your political or social
> background as long as you were focused on how you could be better.
>
> He said he'd help people to a point, but if they weren't helping themselves,
> it meant nothing. He'd go, "I have 10 percent for everybody. You need to do
> the other 90."

JIM STOOD AT INSPECTION, his slim, athletic figure showing off the cut of his dress greens to perfection. Every seam was knife-blade sharp, his cuffs fell just so over his insteps, and the brass buttons down the front of his jacket shone. He looked the methodical military man living exactly the life he wished to live.

Even as he presented the outward image of a compliant and proper CC, he managed to maintain a degree of personal integrity. On his shirtfront, hidden beneath his black necktie, he attached three safety pins and an earring made from a razor blade.

> The one time anybody found out about anything like that, they just laughed.
> They didn't want to bring it up because they didn't want to champion it.
>
> We'd gone to West Point to watch Army play Notre Dame, and when we
> got there, I realized I'd forgotten my tie and my white shirt. The plebes I was
> rooming with didn't have anything I could borrow. They have a whole different
> set of uniforms. I went, "Does anybody have safety pins?"
>
> Somebody had a pair of scissors, so I cut the elastic waistband out of my
> sweatpants and safety-pinned my black socks to it so it went around my neck.
> Under my dress greens, I'm wearing my Why Be Normal shirt, and if anybody
> made me open up my jacket, there would be this foot going to the right across
> my tit.

Jim worked as hard as the others to become the model soldier, but he already considered himself an artist. And with the artist's instinctive need to rearrange life's tidy boundaries, he grew impatient with the cosseted life of comfortable bus rides to cross country invitationals and the warm, carpeted room at the end of the day. The others unquestioningly accepted their protected existence, an existence uncomplicated by the messy disorder of half-learned guitar riffs, in-progress poems, and paint-splattered studio floors.

He chose extracurricular activities that allowed him to create and to sing, attending at least one editorial meeting of a student newspaper, the *Knight Crier*, and caroling in Eatontown with the Glee Club at Christmastime.

Jim took his turn at all-night charge of quarters duty, fielding phone calls and announcing the next day's shifts, taking advantage of the quiet and the office typewriter to work on poems and letters to Kjiirt. He'd been away long enough to regard Scottville as isolated and behind the times, a place where an evening's entertainment might at best include creeping about a moonlit field engaging in the time-honored rural fun of cow tipping. "As you know, cows sleep standing up," he wrote. "What you can do is push the fucker over and run, cuz when he hits he's gonna wake up and chase; more fun."

Life, he reminded his friend, was meant to be experienced firsthand rather than observed from within the boundaries of a quiet Midwestern town.

THE ESCALATOR CLIMBED FROM THE PENN STATION CONCOURSE and delivered Jim and his Fort Monmouth buddies into the bustle and chill of Midtown. They wandered the crowded avenues among purposeful secretaries and street sweepers and dancers hurrying off to auditions. They dodged bold bicycle couriers and black-clad punksters in spiky leather wristbands and carts high-piled with nude mannequins. They started at the shrill whistles of doormen beneath awnings of fine hotels and stepped into clouds of cologne escaping the revolving doors of Macy's and paused to examine new cassettes in record shops. They roamed Times Square, its theater lobbies bright behind tall glass doors.

At last, they turned onto Sixth Avenue where the deco and neon of Radio City Music Hall rose against the darkening sky, the block-long marquee announcing the evening's performance.

Kiss fans eager to experience the band's New York stop on its *Lick It Up* tour snaked around the corner and partway down 50th Street. Jim and his friends took their places at the end of the line, tickets firmly in hand, their toes tingling. They stamped their black boots against the cold, watched the impatient crowd, watched yellow cabs pull up at the curb, watched as Gene Simmons, Paul Stanley, and the rest of the Kiss entourage pushed past them toward the entrance, close enough to recognize, close enough almost to touch.

Jim returned to Fort Monmouth eager to share his adventure with Sarah. She would appreciate the thrill of standing among thousands swaying to "Young and Wasted" and "Detroit Rock City," his own heartbeat in time with the rhythms. As best he could, he'd tell her of his sudden sense of pitched weightlessness, as if his every choice—however small—had led inexorably to this swirl of colored spotlight and costume and story, this warm theater and the snow falling gently over the city.

Sarah Llaguno was the sole woman on the USMAPS postseason cross country team. Jim was one of the ten men who'd qualified for the team, and they'd discovered in the sport their common bond. They ran side by side during training runs at Asbury Park, each understanding with a glance the other's unspoken jokes and straining to glimpse the ocean behind the rows of garish hot dog stands and clamorous pinball arcades that lined the boardwalk.

Before long, Sarah and Jim were constant companions, discussing over tea the movies they saw together in Eatontown and the music they loved. On Saturday afternoons, they walked to nearby Monmouth Mall to flip through the bins of Psychedelic Furs and the Pretenders, albums brand-new to Sarah. "Jim had such a sense for music," she would recall. "If he thought a new release was good, you could almost assume that band was going to make it."

The two looked as if they belonged together, Sarah slim and petite and Jim toned and fit and more and more resembling his high school illustrations of the small, wiry character he'd called Maynard.

They spoke of marriage, albeit knowing neither was ready for such a commitment. Jim referred to Sarah in a letter to Kjiirt as his "one and only," while Sarah struggled with the realization that she most probably was gay. Their intimacy, though, was deeper than sexual. Theirs was the nonthreatening, respectful relationship Sarah required and the foundation of a lifelong friendship. "Jim is the only man I've ever allowed to hold my hand," she would admit decades later. He would change who he was for no one, she recalled, and he instinctively extended to her the same expectation of integrity.

EARLY THAT SPRING, in another of the military's unexplained reorganizational maneuvers, the CCs were allowed to select new roommates, and Jim requested of his section captain that he room with John. Six feet tall, sensitive, and a skilled concert pianist, John struggled through his days at the prep school, his attendance there a fulfillment of his parents' wish that he become a soldier.

Jim had heard his flawless performance at the piano and seen the lengths to which John went to be accepted among the more aggressive CCs. He'd watched him return from evenings with his tormentors, seen him subject his previous roommate to inebriated stupors and their messy aftermaths. "I was like, Jesus, dude!" he would recall. "This must be breaking your heart!"

> John was clearly unhappy, in prep school only to please his parents and going along with what the others forced him to do. They'd pour all this shit in a glass and spit in it and dare him to drink it. And then he'd completely puke all over his blanket and bed. It makes me retch thinking about the shit they did to him.
>
> He would come in drunk and I would fucking drill sergeant all over his ass, lay into him and go, "You don't need to fucking listen to these assholes," just trying to push and push and push him to what he really wanted to do, which was play piano. It burned me up to see that he could do something better than most people, and yet he wasn't doing it. I couldn't sit back and watch this happen. I told him, "You're your own person. You don't need to behave this way. You're loved. You're talented. You don't need to do these things to impress these knuckleheads."
>
> But he was smart and did all the testing properly and he ended up getting his appointment to West Point and came out as a private. Of course, there's a punch line: John couldn't take the pressure and later committed suicide.
>
> Who knows. He may have gone down that path anyway, even if he'd become a pianist. But at the time, I knew something was wrong, that he wasn't supposed to be there.

"When Jim saw someone who wasn't following their heart and was choosing the wrong path, he tried to bring out what they should be focusing on," Sarah recalled. "He was always impatient with people who just followed the crowd. He had a name for people like that. He called them tools."

"Good News + Bad News! I need a good tan and I've got the ultimate solution to get one," Jim wrote Kjiirt in early May. "I received my appointment to West Point last week and turned in my declination of appointment card. I've been re-stationed at Fort 'Microwave of Armpits' Hood, Texas, hence the awesome tan."

The decision had not been an easy one. Jim had enjoyed his success at prep school and had forged comfortable relationships with the like-minded Sarah and Dean Beal. Accepting the appointment was tempting, yet he felt he'd come too far to relinquish the dream of art school.

As his grades continued to improve and his skills on the mat and track brought him recognition, Jim had begun to suspect that his achievements might just qualify him for the appointment. And if he accepted, his fate would be sealed: He'd be groomed for a military career as an officer, and he knew that if he were to make such a commitment, he'd take it seriously and see it through to the end without a backward glance at the tuition fund he must forfeit.

He could think of no one to ask for unbiased advice. Even Sarah, her own direction clear, hadn't known him long enough to truly understand the doubts and certainties he held in equal measure. Mike, convinced of Jim's eventual acceptance, had proudly announced it to his fellow teachers months before. The people of Scottville equated West Point with achievement and prestige, and Jim knew that if he turned down the appointment, he must suffer the dismay they'd feel as deeply as if his decision represented some failure of their own.

> At that moment, all these voices are ringing in your head, telling you what you're supposed to do. I knew I'd hear the wind go out of my father if I turned this thing down.
>
> And I heard Newkirk pounding his shoes on the desk going, "Don't let anybody influence your decision. It's your life. It's your choice. Don't just jump on the cheerleader bandwagon."

And Jim knew, as he'd known for a long time, which was the right path. He moved his belongings across the courtyard to the washout section, the barracks where those dismissed for misconduct or failing grades were sequestered while they awaited their orders.

His West Point slot was returned to the pool of willing candidates, and only weeks before the USMAPS Class of '84 graduation, Jim said goodbye to Sarah and departed for Texas to serve the final 15 months of his military commitment.

Two days in 90-degree heat had burned his skin to a redness no Solarcaine could relieve—had any been available in the field miles from the post. He scooped water from his steel helmet and splashed it across his face in a vain attempt to remove the thick film of dust. He could feel the grit caked deep in his nostrils and his ears, and he ran his fingers through his hair, an immobile mat of grime and sweat. "My hair feels like one of those horsehair doormats after Uncle Bob and the kids have wiped their muddy boots on it," he wrote Kjiirt.

Field training at Fort Hood had begun only days after his arrival with cavalry and fire brigades stationed about the massive installation, the all-too-familiar western landscape otherwise barren but for sparse stands of mountain laurel and red oak.

His bay was a mirror image of his Kansas room, austere but comfortable enough. His roommate, Wayne, bright and personable, welcomed him, and he in turn extended his hand and introduced himself as Maynard.

Early on his first morning at Fort Hood, Maynard came downstairs and crossed the lawn for formation in the parking lot at the front of the barracks. He stopped short, overcome by an unexpected vertigo. The asphalt, the vehicles along its periphery, the tall lampposts undulated in black waves, shiny in the sunshine. He blinked, regained his balance, and looked again. Crickets, black crickets, thousands of them hatched in the relentless Texas heat and humidity, had settled across the lot, where they would remain all summer long. The wriggling landscape seemed the plague and pestilence Maynard had been warned about from the pulpits in Ohio. As he stood at attention amid the heaving blanket of chirping insects, he performed a quick calculation. In 440 days, his only concerns would be turning in a drawing assignment on time and sweeping spilled Cheerios from the floor of his own apartment.

Many of those days he'd spend at the shack behind the barracks inventorying the battalion's survey equipment, or in the motor pool servicing its fleet of jeeps and Gama Goats, six-wheeled semi-amphibious vehicles last driven through the jungles of Vietnam. He'd check oil levels in vehicles never moved from the lot and order replacement parts long obsolete, just as he'd ordered them the day before and the day before that, just as sweaty, dusty men before him had ordered them each day for the past ten years.

Every few weeks, the battalion marched with tents and equipment and a limited water supply to bivouac in the dry fields and take part in combat simulations at Fort Irwin. They sat upon the ground at mealtime and opened the foil and plastic MRE pouches, the ready-to-eat pork patties and stew and diced turkey with gravy no more appetizing than the C rations they'd recently replaced.

Maynard knew next to nothing about cars. He'd never found the need to complete driver's ed or earn his driver's license, able always to ride with friends into Ludington and run to and from school each day as part of his cross country training. Even so, he was assigned the duty of taking the wheel of the Bronco and transporting the battalion's command sergeant major throughout the encampment. If he didn't quite understand gears and power train suspension, Jim consoled himself with the fact that he was upholding a family tradition by acting as chauffeur, just as Grandpa Gridley, a member of the 20th Armored Division, had when he'd driven his colonel behind German front lines during World War II. It passed the days.

WALLED BY STEEP CLIFFS of the Tehachapi, San Gabriel, and San Bernardino mountains, the Fort Irwin National Training Center was an ideal location for desert training, situated as it was at the southern edge of Death Valley. Only the occasional Joshua tree interrupted the flat, arid canyon, a canyon continually swept by hot, dry winds that kept the valley in the 80s even through the night. The Fort Hood group fought a losing battle on their opponent's home turf. The resident battalion was accustomed to the climate and the terrain, and Maynard watched buddies drop in the heat, overcome by endless darting among smoke bombs and dummy rounds in the 120-degree afternoons.

Once they were back in Texas, he and Wayne tried to forget the punishing days in the desert. Maynard exhausted his pay at the record store at Killeen Mall, where he discovered Bauhaus and the Ramones and Romeo Void. He discovered, too, the nearby Irish pub and its happy hour club, a program he eagerly joined to help offset the doldrums of the otherwise temperate Bell County.

One lonely Saturday, Wayne off on adventures of his own, Maynard sat at the bar and quickly downed his two tequila shots in a race against arriving late for the showing of *Ghostbusters* at the cinema next door. He entered the already darkened theater and slid into a seat in the front row. Craning backward, he found it almost impossible to focus, and in his distraction, the laughter behind him sounded oddly out of sync with the action taking place on the screen.

He thought of crickets and of dust, of the music and shouts and taxi horns of Manhattan, of Lake Michigan, of the seat beside him where Sarah should be. Perspiration trickled from his armpits and down his sides, cold beneath his sweater. His salty fingers gleaming with butter and shards of popcorn kernels, he wiped sweat from his face, and his calculations muddled in his head: Three hundred days? Two hundred fifty?

And before the autumn was over, he'd completed his art school application and walked it confidently to the Fort Hood mailroom.

"From deep within the plum I pull the pie," he wrote. He'd begun to approach his writing with a seriousness befitting an art student. Still unpolished to be sure, the poems he wrote in his Fort Hood room reveal a maturing sensibility, an adept use of metaphor and inverted language, a lyricist's talent for conflating the visual and the aural to create a provocative synesthesia. No doubt as much to convince himself as his readers, he took as his theme his bold belief that dire straits might be transformed to triumph with only a shift in perspective.

Eye of the Needle

Waking from a bed of nails
I slowly lift my tattered sails
Against the cruel and cutting winds.
I march the world in seconds flat
And use the ball to hit the bat.
I'm free of rights, moralities, and sins.

Drawing pictures you can hear,
I squeeze a river from a tear
And move a mountain breathlessly at will.

A Perfect Union of Contrary Things

I stroll atop the estuary
In a world so sanguinary,
Loving not the death but just the kill.

Holding whispers in my palm,
I bring the troubled waters calm.
From deep within the plum, I pull the pie.
I make the fox run from the rabbit,
Impossibility my habit,
Passing in and through the needle's eye.

By January, he was traveling often to Austin, 60 miles distant, attending Black Flag's *Loose Nut* tour concert there and dancing at the city's New Wave mecca Club Iguana with Cheryl Carney, a nurse in Fort Hood's medical division. He found in Cheryl a perfect companion, she with her spiked, bleached hair and he in neck chains crafted from razor blades and padlocks, both of them in dark eyeliner that matched their black spandex and fingerless gloves.

"Cheryl taught me how to be yourself while you're also being somebody else," Maynard recalled in a 2012 interview. Living off-post with her husband and concealing her lesbianism from the military community, Cheryl had discovered ways to wear the mask within her mask and yet never sacrifice the integrity of either role. "She was able to put on her Clark Kent at work and then turn into Superman when the music started," Maynard said.

He grew his hair as long as he dared, keeping its sides neatly trimmed and tucking the wavy top beneath his cap. But on club nights, he tousled his curls and pulled them down across his forehead, one bleached strand extended over one eyebrow. He bleached tiger stripes down one leg of his tight jeans, tied a colorful scarf around each ankle, wrapped his waist in studded belts. A package of strawberry Twizzlers open on the bar beside his 7 and 7, he practiced the aloof attitude required of the serious punk, secretly pleased that this could be his way of life in 200 days and counting.

AND ON AUGUST 4, the countdown reached its end.

Sunshine flickered through Maynard's window as the plane banked gently in its descent over Grand Rapids. Below were green fields and forests, lakes and winding rivers, and somewhere in the distance, the campus of the Kendall School of Design.

Just inside the arrival gate, he spotted Kjiirt standing near the newspaper kiosk and raced to tell him what their first stop must be. They loaded the oversized black footlocker into the trunk of Kjiirt's father's Buick and made their way out along Patterson Avenue and 28th Street to Woodland Mall and the J. C. Penney hair salon. Still in his dress greens, SP4 Keenan placed his Penney's credit card on the receptionist's desk and politely asked a stylist to shave his hair into a Mohawk.

5

The strip malls and office parks of Grand Rapids gave way to fields and maple groves already here and there bright red and orange. Maynard was as eager for school to begin as Kjiirt was about his upcoming move to Boston, and during the drive to Scottville, the two plotted how they'd spend their brief time together before embarking on their new ventures. They'd reestablish connections with old friends certainly, classmates and fellow cross country runners and girlfriends Maynard hadn't seen since entering the service three years before.

A few miles past Muskegon, Kjiirt replaced the cassette in the boom box. They looked at each other and grinned. REM's eerily appropriate lyrics urged them never to return to the wasted years of dead-end factory jobs in some faraway, xenophobic small town.

"I heard you are a punk now," Maynard's grandmother had written from Ohio soon after he'd turned down the West Point invitation. "I thought being in the Army would make you grow up." Hers was a typical reaction.

Mike and Jan hid their shock when they saw his haircut, and Jan eventually admitted that the Mohawk was a fine example of creative expression. And once he reminded them that attending art school had always been his goal, they let go their disappointment over West Point and admitted their pride in his Kendall acceptance.

But his former classmates quickly found excuses to cut their visits short. He watched them go, most likely to down a McDonald's vanilla shake spiked with peppermint schnapps in preparation for another night at Johnny's.

> I came back to Scottville and was completely ostracized and crucified by these
> guys and ignored by the girl who I took to the prom. I came back after the
> Army with my hair shaved into a Mohawk and they went, "Get thee behind
> me, Satan!" Come on, dude. I told you I was gonna do this.

As always, Maynard and Kjiirt found in each other all the company they really needed. Maynard shared with his friend the EP club mixes he'd brought from Texas: Gary Numan, Alien Sex Fiends, dark ballads of Lords of the New Church, the experimental structures and atmospheric harmonies that satisfied their search for the new, the different, the daring.

They talked through the night, imagining Boston and the clubs and music and friends Kjiirt would find there. His plan was to follow no plan, travel with no map, experience to the fullest whatever the city might hold. He'd worry about a job when he got there. After all, he and Maynard agreed, the key to success was to first prepare the scene, like a stagehand dressing the set, and then to step confidently into it.

MAYNARD SETTLED INTO THE APARTMENT he'd share with fellow student and White Room guitarist Chris Ewald. The house stood at the edge of Heritage Hill, the neighborhood of stately Greek Revival and Queen Anne homes built for the city's lumber barons a century before. Only a few blocks from campus and downtown Grand Rapids, Cherry Street seemed the ideal location for a student eager to explore the city.

Grand Rapids offered the diversity and cultural attractions of a major metropolis—fine restaurants, museums, and resident symphony, opera, and ballet companies. Even so, the city retained the closed-minded aura of an isolated small town, numbingly conservative and proud to be home to the central offices of the Christian Reformed Church.

By the fall of 1985, gentrification was already in full swing, forcing black families far from the neighborhoods they'd called home. Angry minorities and a religious Right nonetheless joined against a common enemy: art students in chains and spiked hair. Warnings to stay on one's side of the tracks were meaningless in a town like Grand Rapids, where invisible boundaries separated the districts. Downtown was uptown was crosstown was collegetown, and Maynard soon learned that his best defense was a thick skin and a lead pipe tucked in one sleeve of his leather jacket.

> Whatever that particular religion was, they'd apparently found a clause in their
> good book that justified oppression. People in the black neighborhoods were
> being treated horribly, so the pushback was that any time they had a chance to
> beat the shit out of a student with a baseball bat, they would. That put me at
> risk whenever I wanted to go to Subway for a sandwich.

Most of the time, the attacks were only derogatory shouts from the safety of the opposite side of the street. Indifferent to the taunts, Maynard focused on his part-time job assisting with demolition and painting and hanging drywall at another of his landlord Bill's properties—and felt the safest when he lost himself in a frenzy of crayon and paper and pen and clay.

He discovered the fine arts program to be Kendall's redheaded stepchild, second fiddle to the school's more conventional design department. Not surprising in a town nicknamed "Furniture City," Kendall focused on preparing students for careers at nearby American Seating and Steelcase, lifelong careers designing desks and file cabinets and laying out four-color magazine ads. The curriculum provided a solid foundation, but left little room for exploration and innovation.

Maynard sought out the department's renegade subculture, the small cadre of nonconformists keen to invent their own personae and their own art, the fringe group that embraced their individuality and outsider status. He found in them comrades in music, prepared to discuss with him Nick Cave's chord progressions and the poetry of Joni Mitchell's lyrics.

Yet even among the avant-garde punks and armchair anarchists, Maynard—in his tight leather pants and jacket trimmed with bleached chicken bones and a coiled bass string—stood out and to everyone's surprise, was named student council president in the fall.

> The art students used spray fixatives to preserve our charcoal drawings, but
> there was no ventilation system in the studios. I went to the foundation to get
> them interested in our health, but they didn't do anything.
>
> So I tried to get the students to come to a meeting and demand action. I
> posted notices in the break room and circulated a petition, but they didn't pay
> any attention.
>
> Finally, I drew a really aggressive Sid Vicious on bright red paper and made

a poster saying that we'd talk about it at the next student council meeting. A lot of people said the flyer was offensive and too punk, but people showed up who never came to a student council meeting before.

They came because they were pissed off about what I'd drawn. That's the difference between illustration and design. You put something controversial out there, and people notice and actually do something.

My marketing prowess ended up with my getting elected student council president.

"Maynard was an advocate for justice at all levels," Kendall drawing instructor Deb Rockman would later recall. "He was all about creating the best possible experience for students."

AN ICY DECEMBER SQUALL rattled the windows of Kendall's break room, where students sat with books and Walkmans, their late dinners a hodgepodge of the few selections still available in the cafeteria. One glanced nervously outside, where snow fell faster. He must brave the 45-minute trip to his parents' house, he told his friends, the drive he made to and from school each day. Maynard recognized him as Ramiro Rodriguez, the diligent student whose sure lines and warm palette he'd admired all semester, whose intriguing images skillfully combined the mythological and the familiar.

Ramiro had noticed Maynard, too, his combat boots and white anarchy symbol painted across the back of his jacket. He looked up from his plate, unsure for a moment just how to respond to Maynard's announcement of a vacant room at Cherry Street. "Coming from a small town, I was amazed that there was anybody like that around," Ramiro would recall. "Maynard was one of a kind, even in art school. But I was desperate to move closer to campus, and my car was dying."

The next day, Ramiro arrived to find the apartment strewn with canvases and brushes, a four-track recorder, two guitars propped against chairs as if they'd been set there mid-song, and a crowbar against the wall near the front door.

"I'm not sure what convinced me that living there was going to be all right," Ramiro would confess. "I was totally out of my element, but I thought, 'Well, he seems like a decent enough guy. He dresses weird and all, but living here might be kind of exciting.'"

Friends gathered at the Cherry Street apartment at all hours to exchange cassettes and their latest drawings and poems. When Maynard's part-time job didn't require him to head across town to paint or hang drywall at another of his landlord's properties, he and Ramiro prepared quiches and casseroles for their guests with fresh vegetables and lentils from the nearby food co-op.

"Planting acorns. I'm planting acorns," he'd answer when asked about his activities, as if he realized that given enough time, the most esoteric of skills, the most dubious of investments might one day provide a return.

AT THE END OF THE SCHOOL YEAR, Maynard was one of only ten students—and the sole freshman—whose work was selected to travel the Midwest as part of Kendall's recruitment effort. His charcoal life drawing would be displayed at college fairs and career days representing the exceptional quality of Kendall students' work.

He proudly told Kjiirt of the honor when Kjiirt visited Grand Rapids that spring. On high alert, the pair walked about the Cherry Street neighborhood beneath greening ash and Norway maples, Maynard's lead pipe hidden inside one sleeve. Kjiirt described the wonders of New England: the endless selection of beer at the Wursthaus in Harvard Square, the ornate Symphony Hall, and the gritty Rathskeller, the center of Boston's rock scene. He told him of his job as wine buyer for Martignetti Liquors and his study of aldehydes and maceration and *vins* both *ordinaire* and premium in order to master his craft.

Back at the apartment, Maynard cleared cassettes, crimped tubes of oils, and hog hair brushes from his kitchen chairs. He brought from the dish drainer two tumblers while Kjiirt lined across the table the half-dozen bottles he'd brought from Martignetti's high-end lockup.

Maynard sipped the 1961 Krug rosé, mystified by his friend's talk of tannins and complexity and balance and varietals. He marveled at Kjiirt's ability to detect base notes of oak or citrus or vanilla in what he called the wines' finish.

Baffled, Maynard set his glass on the Formica tabletop and turned to the subject of his drawings, his excitement over his growing understanding of line, shading, and perspective, of his sometimes girlfriend Laurie Rousseau, and of the plan for the next evening. They'd visit the Ice Pick, he told Kjiirt, the punk music venue in the Muskegon countryside, the raucous club where not long ago he'd performed with the area's newest group, Children of the Anachronistic Dynasty.

For all its straitlaced conservatism, Grand Rapids was the vortex of a lively music scene, one of the many such areas that had emerged in the mid-'80s to cater to unconventional young people living far from the cities. Their guide was Steve Aldrich, host of WLAV radio's weekly *Clambake*, the alternative music program featuring punk and New Wave and local indie bands. With a keen ear for quality and an unerring sense for the next big thing, Aldrich gave Western Michigan youth their first taste of the latest sound.

Primed for the real thing, they bought fresh packs of clove cigarettes and attached a few more safety pins to their shirtfronts. They made their way to shows at the Ice Pick and in function halls and condemned storefronts on Division Street where the only stage lighting might be fixtures fashioned from bulbs and coffee cans.

"All the top hardcore bands were coming through Grand Rapids," Aldrich would recall. "People could see the very best, and I think that influenced a lot of them to put together their own bands."

The shredding guitar riffs and anti-establishment lyrics were a call to break free of the disco years and the narcissism of the Me generation, just as the music ignored conventional structures and traditional rhyme schemes. Musicians took up their drums and guitars whether they understood chord changes and rhythmic patterns or not, these hipsters intent upon bringing music to the masses in new, non-elitist forms. "The early punks didn't want to turn into Michael Jackson or be on the cover of *Tiger Beat*," Maynard would explain. "They felt privileged to be hearing stuff no one else had discovered."

Maynard and Laurie drove along Alpine Avenue to Top of the Rock, an isolated warehouse of a building deep in the woods. Punks and goths and sensitive art school students paid the $3 cover to experience live bands and Thursday's Alterative Night, a celebration of anarchy in the middle of farm country. "Maynard showed me there was another way of looking at the world," Laurie would recall. "There were people making music and art who saw things differently than the mainstream and acted on those views. I'd been on the outside for so long growing up that it was a relief to find them."

The DJ spun Fear and the Cure, Erasure and New Order, and in Doc

Martens and dog collars and multicolored mullets, the crowd came forward to dance. Partway through the evening, the more timid among them retreated to the shadows as the dance floor became a slam pit where skinheads and the most radical of the punks hurled themselves against one another in a frenzy of head-banging and unchoreographed flailing, until inevitably, one fell—and in the spirit of solidarity, the others scrambled to help him to his feet.

Maynard had the inkling that visual art wasn't after all the medium for him. He preferred the collaborative atmosphere of the punk clubs, the almost palpable sensation of energy that flowed between musician and spectator. Band members turned to one another and their audience, attuned to their every nuance, drawing from the energy in order to cocreate an experience that excluded no one.

> Art exhibitions seemed self-indulgent, and all these sycophants showed up claiming to understand the paintings. It had been so long since I stood in front of something original and said, "Wow! That changed my life!"
>
> It felt like advertising and design had no soul, no pulse. Then I'd look at what they were doing in the visual arts and think, "Just go get therapy."
>
> When I saw a roomful of people literally and figuratively tuning into each other to create rhythms and images, it just made sense.

IN THE FALL, MAYNARD AND CHRIS TOOK AN APARTMENT in another of Bill's buildings, a semi-refurbished house at 649 Evans Street. Ramiro, concerned that the hammering and drilling and drywall dust would disrupt his studies, opted for a less chaotic space a few blocks away. But for Maynard, whose only requirement was room for music gear, the apartment was ideal.

The canvases in his living room and his half-empty tubes of oils would last until another odd job turned up, he calculated, and he withdrew what he dared from his college fund. With it, he purchased a Peavey Black Widow amp, a Korg drum machine, and a Tascam four-track recorder and turned to his writing with a new seriousness.

He took as his influences the bands whose styles most intrigued him: Depeche Mode, Ministry, Black Flag, Kiss, of course, Nick Cave and the Bad Seeds, and local punk-meets-metal fusion group Born Without a Face. He created linear soundscapes embellished with mantra-like drones and crafted minimalist lyrics that left room for listeners to inhabit the songs and fill the silence with stories of their own. Yet the complex constructions were all his.

"I was trying to abandon the easy intro-verse-chorus-bridge-chorus-chorus format," he would explain. "You can take almost any popular song, whether it's rock or pop or R&B or country, and lay them right over the top of each other and they all match up. There's nothing different about them."

And with a little help from his rhythm guitarist friend Kevin Horning, C.A.D. became a reality, if not a live band. Recorded in his living room and duplicated at a recording studio north of campus, its two cassettes, the 1986 *Fingernails* and *Dog House* in 1987, sold for $5 each and realized enough sales to cover Maynard's modest rent.

The quality of the cassettes was remarkable given the simple equipment Maynard worked with in his living room. He'd learned to program the Korg to create delays and overdubs of sound and echo, producing tracks like the haunting "25 Hours," a strident sermon sampled beneath the repetitive melody and segueing into a chant evocative of the sound of an army marching in lockstep into battle.

He included with each cassette a copy of the C.A.D. manifesto, a rambling screed addressing materialism, AIDS, and global warming, issuing a call for the union of opposites in a polarized world, and ending in a message of hope.

CHILDREN OF THE ANACHRONISTIC DYNASTY 1987

Based on our being merely average in the field of "Corporate Middle-Class, T.V. watching, American-Consumerism" . . . We . . . the CHILDREN, have reached the following conclusions/predictions…out of need. What need? Well, we needed to know why things don't work . . . why we cure cancer with cancer and pursue peace by building bombs. We needed to know why we know the ozone is the problem by manufacturing and producing #28 X-tra strength sun screen by Tropical Blend. We needed to know why we, in our advanced state of space travel and genetic research, haven't discovered a cure for AIDS as of yet . . . and why we attempt to end racial prejudices by acknowledging the separation. We needed to know why we think that he who dies with the most toys is the winner and why all that we consider success can be physically taken away from us.

A Perfect Union of Contrary Things

Why? Because we are victims of a dualistic, cause-effect paradigm that merely lacks empathy. 1+1+1=1 unless you are a slave of this dualistic, western, Rambo-culture, and then 1+1=2. No longer do we experience the harmonious interaction between each other and our environment.

All that we see experienced here is in twos, like opposites . . . black + white, good + bad, us + them . . .

Therefore, We, the CHILDREN, have reached the fear of the following.

In five years we will discover a cure for AIDS merely because it began to seriously effect heterosexuals one year previous.

In ten years there will be no more cold winters.

In ten years heat from unfiltered ultraviolet sun rays will result in drought and frenzy. Drought and frenzy will result in mass starvation and race riots.

In ten years those without toys will take from those with toys, and soon all those toys will break, become meaningless, and be forgotten.

In ten years the Mercedes, the job securities, the stocks, the bank accounts, and the masters degrees will no longer be considered elements of success.

In twelve years . . . safe shelter, food, extra ammo for the rifle, surviving a raid or making a profitable raid, and just plain surviving will be considered true success.

In 15 years fewer and fewer will be successful because of lesser and lesser food for which to be successful.

In 15 years those who established isolate strongholds because they felt they were a superior breed or race will find that the person in the bunk next to them is more of a derelict and an imbecile than the person or persons they burned or murdered 5 years earlier merely because of their color.

In 15 years this tape will not matter. The instruments used to play and produce it will not matter . . . and whether you have the few dollars it takes to purchase it will not matter.

But what is said on it is timeless. It cannot be erased or taken away from us. It is forever.

And in 20 years when the ice caps have melted, Mother Nature will have another go at it. . .and hopefully as time progresses in this new world there will be no need for another bloodline of misplaced youth. amen. thank you, we are **C.A.D.**

MAYNARD'S SENSE OF HUMOR INTACT, he became a devotee of another local group, the acerbically humorous TexA.N.S.

TexA.N.S. was Tex and the Anti Nazi Squad, their music a comedic offshoot of alt rock. Led by Grand Rapids punk rocker Clint "Tex" Porker, TexA.N.S. was a talented lineup including Horning and keyboardist Mike Meengs but, as Maynard learned after attending only a few of their performances, sorely lacked a bass player. With his dwindling funds, he brought home a Hohner knockoff Steinberger bass.

"I didn't know how to play bass, but I knew I could figure it out," he would recall. "I thought, 'It can't be that hard. It has only four strings, so I'll even have an extra finger to use.'"

Maynard's short time with the band was a period of concentrated creativity, a time to explore his potential as a musician and to hone his performance and recording skills. Soon he was appearing with TexA.N.S. at the local venues he'd visited only weeks before, this time center stage, bass in hand.

TexA.N.S. recorded its February 1986 performance for its first release, *Live at Sons + Daughters Hall*, a collection of 16 songs including the tongue-in-cheek "Big Dead Things," a warning to step carefully across the kitchen and the front lawn.

Maynard collaborated on the band's second release, *Never Again*, an independently produced 17-track cassette of garage punk. He did the best he could on bass—and unwilling to completely abandon the visual, created album art for both *Never Again* and local band Reel Bodeans's single "I Won't Take It."

Porker's unexpected move that spring left the band without a vocalist, and Maynard stepped up to fill the role. With a bass player and rhythm guitarist, a drummer, and Kevin on lead guitar, the band was complete. But it wasn't long before Maynard realized it wasn't merely TexA.N.S. reconfigured. The band was C.A.D.

Maynard's '76 Plymouth Arrow with its Batman logo and tiger stripes soon became a familiar sight on the Grand Rapids streets. Between classes, he dashed to the copy shop to run off fliers announcing upcoming C.A.D. performances and crisscrossed the city to attach them to message boards and lampposts, creating a grassroots buzz that reached the WLAV studios.

"The station did special programming for that kind of music," Aldrich would recall. "Some of C.A.D. was almost novelty, some of it was noise. But then there was a sound like early Tangerine Dream. There were things in C.A.D. that if Maynard had had a producer, they would have gone, 'Oh my God!'"

C.A.D. saw its media debut in April as part of public access station GRTV's 1987 Peace Day programming. The 26-minute performance featured seven songs, Maynard, his eyes rimmed in black eyeliner, glaring intermittently at the camera as he sang. In his black tank top and tight black pants rolled midcalf just above the laces of his Grecian sandals, he tossed his head in time to the music to better call attention to his Mohawk and the bleached strands in his long curls. He strutted back and forth across the stage, his single metallic earring glittering.

In an interview following the performance, Maynard explained the meaning of the acronym C.A.D. "It's not really a band name," he said. "It's more a concept behind what we're all about. It stands for Children of the Anachronistic Dynasty, which is kind of like a bloodline of youth born out of sync with time, out of sync enough to where they sit back and observe rather than just take things for granted."

Maynard wasn't content to limit his work to one band and branched out with Meengs to form the short-lived Malicious Sissies, a hybrid punk-digital duo locally known for a time for its songs "Hallucination" and "Who Leads You?"

> Mike was a computer dude who loved drum machines and programming and sequencing. He and I would go to Gaia, this coffee shop and organic restaurant on Diamond Avenue. They had an open mic night that was mostly acoustic, and "Last Train to Clarksville" was always the closing number.
>
> Mike and I get there with a drum machine and I'm singing with a delay pedal through the mic. We were doing a very digital thing in a very crunchy granola setting, and people actually paid attention.

But C.A.D. was the band that true punk aficionados followed from gig to gig, from the Intersection bar downtown to the City Centre Mall, where shoppers paused in their quest for golf shirts and pillowcases and oversized chocolate chip cookies to stand and listen.

C.A.D. STOOD BENEATH THE FLASHING LIGHTS of Top of the Rock, the audience clustered at the stage, eager to be among the first to hear "Burn About Out." They swayed in the spiral of staccato percussion echo, Maynard's insistent lyrics rising above the surge of sound. Count the bodies, he urged them, take note of the specter lurking just behind

Waiting like a stalking butler
Who upon the finger rests.
Murder now the path of "must we"
Just because the son has come.

"Keep going with that," Chris Ewald told Maynard after the show. "That's the song. Whatever that is, keep pursuing it."

With C.A.D.'s popularity came the attention of Grand Rapids girls keen to date someone just like Maynard. It was the rare evening that no one waited for him after a C.A.D. performance or accompanied him to one of the clubs downtown.

> A guy in a leather coat and a Mohawk is absolutely the polar opposite of what their fathers would choose for them. I'm the outsider, the guy not allowed to pollute the gene pool in any way. And I had the keys to the chastity belt. There was a lot of making up for lost time in those years, and I definitely made some mistakes, but I wouldn't change any of it.

The highlight of the summer would be Black Flag's Grand Rapids stop as part of its 1986 Michigan tour, Maynard's opportunity to once again experience the band he'd seen in Austin, this time in the more intimate setting of Burton Hall. Drugstore turned punk venue, the hall had been gutted of all but a dysfunctional sink in one corner, and the space promised plenty of room for a packed house and a slam pit.

He arrived early, surprised to find no line at the door. He'd been certain a crowd would turn out to see Henry Rollins, if not the opening band, Das Damen. But with the first notes of the second opener, he forgot his surroundings. Gone, the instrumental side project of Black Flag guitarist Greg Ginn, exploded in a fusion of sound and fury. Ginn's crashing guitar, the percussive power of longtime Black Flag drummer Sim Cain, and Andrew Weiss's ferocious bass transformed the drab hall to a swirling eddy of energy. Weiss's was bass as Maynard had never imagined it, true playing, not merely a striking of strings in time to a kick drum, an artistic level far beyond his own anemic attempts.

Gone was followed by the equally commanding Painted Willie, the L.A. punk group formed by drummer and filmmaker Dave Markey, and by the time Black Flag took the stage, Maynard was aware only of the intensity, the professionalism, the purity and energy of a reality he could only hope to inhabit.

Then Ginn picked up his guitar again. His intense attack underscored Rollins's vocals and his message of rebellious individualism and defiance of authority, the fierce lyrics of fear and isolation. Black Flag's 90-minute set was a controlled bedlam of sheer sound, a crashing riot of syncopated metal, astonishing jazz fusion, and inventive percussion that brazenly defied traditional rhythmic structures.

But Burton Hall remained virtually empty, the sadly underpromoted show having attracted only a fraction of its capacity. "It was amazing to see these bands playing to the sparse crowd," Maynard recalled in a 2012 interview. "The energy they put into their performance was breathtaking."

HIS MUSIC MIGHT TURN COMPLETELY FROM THE EXPECTED, Maynard thought, and envisioned an instrumental trio of his chordal base, Ewald's guitar rhythms, and inventive percussion. And when Chris brought Steve Aldrich into the discussion, he agreed to come onboard. "I was way up for that," he recalled, confident the sonic spaces he created with his Yamaha drum kit would complement the sound Maynard had in mind. "The music was going to be very, very dark," Aldrich would explain. "It wasn't going to be hardcore, but somewhere not too far from Killing Joke."

Brainstorming sessions were sporadic and rehearsals few, but the three believed in their collaboration. This band would be so unique, so unconventional, so postmodern, that its very title must be unspoken. Maynard designed the symbol that would serve as its name, a black and white UPC bar code.

After their meetings, Ewald and Aldrich urged Maynard to join them at a nearby pub. "We tried to get him out of the house and have a beer with us," Aldrich would recall. "He always said no, he had music to work on. He was so very, very dedicated."

Focused as he was on his art, Maynard nonetheless made room for the comedic.

> A friend and I would make mixtapes for a woman he knew. One day, we started fucking around in the studio making really dumb songs to send her as a joke.
>
> Then we dressed all up and rented a VHS recorder and did one of those songs on camera. We wandered around Grand Rapids in stupid outfits filming each other being silly. Our film ended with me walking in our door with cigarette butts stuck up in my lip and a baseball cap on sideways. On camera, my friend punches me in the face and I spit my teeth across the room. We called that character Billy Bob.

Maynard sat back on a bench in the downtown amphitheater. The early-July sunshine reflected from windows of banks and department stores surrounding the park was warm on his face, and he remembered the recent festival of disillusioned rebels on nearby Punker Hill, the chaos of leather and goth and spiked hair. But he couldn't waste the afternoon in reminiscence. He must stop at the pet store for seed for the latest addition to the Evans Street apartment, the newly hatched zebra finch, the little bird with bright orange beak and shiny black eyes he'd named Harpo.

He watched a giddy group of neo–flower children in tattered jeans and bright flounced skirts weave hand in hand under the brick arch and up and down the tiered risers. They paused in their dance and breathlessly approached Maynard, eager to share their excitement. The Rainbow Gathering, they announced. The Rainbow Gathering in the Smoky Mountains, and they were going there now, and he must join them.

Maynard had considered visiting Scottville during his summer break, but four days in the mountains and valleys of North Carolina was tempting. He loaded his Chevy Sprint with a few essentials, left Harpo in the care of his roommates, picked up his friend punk musician Jonathan Haner, and set out for Franklin, North Carolina.

He wasn't alone. From all across the country, New Agers and retro hippies and spiritual seekers descended upon the Nantahala National Forest to join the event billed as a week of peace, love, harmony, and freedom. They arrived by the busload, by car and by van and by thumb, and an assemblage of saffron-robed Hare Krishnas rode in on the back of an elephant. Whatever their reasons for coming, whatever their beliefs, they entered along the same gravel drive, each of them passing beneath a sign that read WELCOME HOME.

They pitched tents and teepees on the mossy forest floor beneath old-growth sycamore and basswood, and washed in the waterfall nearby. They wove for each other beaded bracelets and braided their hair with purple asters, and despite run-ins with state troopers and wildlife officers, dedicated the week to their mission of achieving universal consciousness. Swept in the infectious communion, Maynard and Jonathan surrendered to the experience and all it might offer.

In the afternoons, they joined the others in the meadow and listened to the words of Medicine Story, the graying Indian who'd been a Gathering fixture since the first was held in 1972. The eagle feather he held was passed next to a shaman or a neo-pagan, a Buddhist or an orthodox Jewess. Their stories of journeys and myths and mystical awakenings seemed to Maynard stories of people no different from himself.

In the gathering dusk, he helped bring branches from the woods to feed the campfire and sat in the circle of drumming and singing and more storytelling. Crimson sparks drifted into the darkening sky and the first-quarter moon gleamed white above the oaks and tulip poplars.

And in the early morning of July 4, the stories came to an end. The 7,000 walked quietly from their camps to the Main Meadow. In tie-dye and saris, faded jeans and black leather, they formed circles within circles and joined hands. Their silent meditation continued until noon, their breathing one breath. The sun rose high in the sky and a collective "Om" rose above the grasses and field flowers, echoed through the valley, and culminated in joyous shouts as children paraded from the Kiddie Village to the center of the circle, where they leapt and danced in the sunshine.

> When thousands of people gather in a circle in a three-hour silent prayer, that shit's powerful. Think about all we could do if we were just quiet and agreed on something. Imagine marching on Washington with 30,000 people not saying a word and then one person coming forward and saying, "This is what we want done."

> When we open our mouths, we screw it all up and assert our agendas.
> But if you're quiet, you feel the energy you visualize. You don't feel it until you
> shut up.
>
> All these people holding hands were dead silent for hours. And even in that
> wonderful moment, I become aware that I'm stoned, wearing only a loincloth
> and sandals.

Maynard came home to find Grand Rapids going about its usual business. Housewives drove in from the suburbs to look at the new summer dresses at Herpolsheimer's, kids practiced skateboard heelflips in the amphitheater, and office workers paraded to their cubicles in the morning. The Rainbow Gathering hadn't transformed the world after all. But Maynard returned buoyed by four days of heightened awareness amid birdsong and sunshine, meals from the Hare Krishna kitchen, the hundreds of hopeful gathered for the express purpose of celebrating their collective tale. He'd never find words to explain it to Laurie or his bandmates, he knew, but it somehow didn't matter. The experience had been his, one he would remember and draw upon later, and that too, he realized, was a part of the tale.

Neither did it matter much in his pitched state that while he'd been away, Bill had begun major renovations on the house, requiring his tenants to live elsewhere. Maynard's roommates, accustomed by then to his impetuosity, had assumed his North Carolina jaunt was no jaunt at all but a permanent departure. He returned to find them gone along with most of his possessions—sold or discarded or taken as their own.

In one corner of his bedroom were his belongings: a few items of clothing, sketch pads and a clutch of Sheaffer pens, a black footlocker, and Harpo's cage. Maynard unhooked the latch, and Harpo, a bit thinner perhaps after four days of neglect, fluttered out, perched on Maynard's shoulder, and took the seed he offered from his hand.

MAYNARD AND RAMIRO SET UP THEIR STEREO in the living room of the apartment they rented in the fall. They filled the bookshelves with albums, Ramiro's Led Zeppelin and Foghat and Maynard's Cocteau Twins, Depeche Mode, and Ministry.

In the corners of the living room hung cages for Harpo and his offspring and the collection of finches that completed Maynard's aviary. They flitted from potted ficus trees and back to their nests, where hungry chicks demanded to be fed. The birds trusted only Maynard and settled in his palm for their dinner of millet and grass seed.

On most evenings, Laurie joined them in spirited discussions of punk trends and anarchist ideals, the theories of Joseph Campbell and Carl Jung that Maynard and Ramiro studied in their history class. They'd found most fascinating the concept of synchronicity, a theory they thought just might have something to do with the odd coincidences and misfortune that seemed to be associated with Led Zeppelin's "Kashmir." "We'd notice whenever it was played," Ramiro would remember. "It was always when something important was happening. I think it was just making us aware of things we might not otherwise have noticed. But we also liked the idea that it was some kind of mystical connection."

And they talked too about the merits of sobriety. "'Nothing to excess' was a popular subject with all of us," Laurie would recall. "We saw others around us doing too much anger, alcohol, or drugs, and we resolved to be careful not to do the same."

The group looked forward most to movie night. After they'd finished their homework, Maynard and Ramiro would bring home *Blue Velvet* or *Repo Man* from the market nearby, often inviting Bill the landlord to add a generational dimension to their cinematic conversations.

They envied his ability to set his own hours, to sit back at the end of the day and enjoy the fruits of his labor and another viewing of *Female Trouble*.

MAYNARD RAN THE HOOVER over the floor, and Harpo, terrified of the noisy vacuum, perched on the relative safety of his shoulder. While he swept, he imagined lyrics and melody and the wild idea that even humor could be incorporated into his act.

The lack of rehearsal space in the new apartment—and lack of motivation among his bandmates—had meant the end of C.A.D. and his duties as manager, accountant, advertising rep, and cheerleader. Unrestricted by the group's wishes and abilities, he allowed his imagination free rein. He incorporated in his music Eastern mantras, the African rhythms of Dead Can Dance, and spare industrial elements borrowed from Swans.

He emptied his footlocker and pulled it to the middle of the living room, creating from it a makeshift acoustic box. He held above it a length of heavy fencing chain, dropped it at regular intervals, and recorded the sound with his Tascam. Afterward, using sound delays and looping techniques, he cut into the recording his minimalist chant: "Anahata, not hit. Anahata, not struck."

He and Ramiro had learned the word in Professor McCaffrey's history class, the mysterious Sanskrit word meaning "unstruck," the word associated in the yogic tradition with the heart chakra. Anahata, the only sound not made by one thing striking another, Anahata, the creative hum of the universe, the silence containing the antecedent of all things, Anahata, an echoing stillness rising over a meadow in North Carolina.

Ramiro provided a steadying counterbalance to Maynard's growing attraction to the mystical. He included Maynard in family holiday gatherings and invited him on Sundays to share his mother's tortillas around a dinner table lively with conversation and laughter.

And one afternoon, they returned from their errands to find the back door torn from its hinges, their television, their boom box and cameras, the four-track recorder and the stereo gone—and with it, Led Zeppelin's *Physical Graffiti* album, the album that included "Kashmir."

"We were left without media," Ramiro would recall. "In hindsight, that was probably the best thing that could have happened to us. We started reading."

With no television or stereo to occupy their free time, they took down their few books: cookbooks, a volume of da Vinci colorplates, *The Portable Jung*, and the volumes they'd read in their history course, Joseph Campbell's *Myths to Live By* and *Hero with a Thousand Faces*, the only texts they hadn't resold to the student bookstore at semester's end.

Ramiro had begun to struggle with the tenets of his Catholic upbringing, and Maynard's memories of the Ohio churches had led him to abandon organized religion altogether. But mysteries remained, and they visited tarot readers and studied cults ancient and new age, doubting there was such a thing as a spiritual path in the first place. And they found in Campbell a gentle guide.

They spent long hours discussing—and arguing—Campbell's views on various belief systems, but found common ground in his more practical theories. The ultimate goal, Campbell insisted, was not to discover the meaning of life, but the experience of life, to listen to one's heart and to fearlessly follow one's passion.

A Perfect Union of Contrary Things

> I came at Joseph Campbell from a "fuck Christianity" perspective. I was really
> into what he had to say because I loved the idea of undermining the funda-
> mentalists. It was an interesting jumping-off point after being in the middle
> of all that shit as a kid and watching people make decisions based on what
> seemed illogical.
>
> But Campbell turned out to be somebody who could actually give me the
> facts about mythology and archetypes and break apart the dogmatic views of
> religion in a way I could understand and appreciate. Professor McCaffrey really
> pushed us to see beyond the obvious and see the things that connect cultures
> and different peoples rather than set us apart.

ONLY AFTER PROVING COMPETENCE IN THE BASICS were Kendall students allowed
to experiment and bring personal expression to their work.

Maynard generally ignored his instructors' preoccupation with classical
elements. Rather than concentrate on vanishing points and shadowing and
negative space, he preferred to embellish assignments with creative twists and
to work beyond the exacting boundaries to discover approaches and interpretations all his own.

Ramiro would later recall spending an entire week on the self-portrait assigned by instructor Sandra Stark, a project she'd explained must contain specific elements: a horizontal orientation and the presence of a mirror within
the frame, the entire piece done in graphite. The night before the assignment
was due, Maynard assembled his drawing tablet and charcoal. He managed to
incorporate most of the required elements but departed from the assignment
just enough to produce a portrait that unmistakably reflected his unique style.

During the class critique, Stark pointed out the areas he hadn't drawn according to her guidelines, but even she admitted to the quality of his piece.
"There was always that rebel side to Maynard," Ramiro would recall. "It was
part procrastination because he was busy with music, but also part 'I'm not going to do it exactly your way.'"

Drawing instructor Deb Rockman understood Maynard's dilemma. "The
portrait studies Maynard did for my class were excellent, but he was very, very
conflicted about what he wanted to pursue," she would recall. "I could see his
talent and could see that he was struggling to decide whether to focus on art or
music. I certainly didn't try to sway him one way or the other. I just listened."

He transferred that spring to Grand Valley State University, a few miles west of Grand Rapids. GVSU offered a course in printmaking, a less traditional program that would allow him the freedom to push conventional boundaries. "I liked the process of taking blank pieces of copper and getting an image on paper," he would recall. "Including all the things I could do wrong."

His enthusiasm was short-lived. Art, he thought as he drove home late one night from Top of the Rock, must unite the practical and the purely artistic, a combination his new school stressed no more than his old.

> If I was going to do art, I was going to do some kind of functional art. If I'd stayed in the military, I would have probably been the guy going, "No, no, this backpack is all wrong. Let me design this more ergonomically so that when you reach your arm back, your hand lands on whatever you need without your having to think about it."
>
> I would have designed vehicles or gear to be utilitarian.

He thought of how his landlord managed to balance work and leisure and his awareness of manual labor as an investment in after-hours enjoyment. Perhaps an evening with him was just what he needed to help put his priorities in order.

He replaced the cassette in his tape deck as he neared Bill's house. Crickets chirped from the grasses along the roadside, their song a chant-like chorus filling the silence between Kraftwerk's rhythms.

STAYING IN SCHOOL WOULDN'T BE THE END OF THE WORLD, Maynard told himself. He could, if he must, conform to the status quo, stay in the safe cocoon of Grand Rapids and live out his career designing ergonomic office chairs and easy-to-open filing cabinets. Or he could take time out to regroup, step from the downward spiral of academic disappointment and financial insecurity.

His time in the Army certainly hadn't prepared him for the economic juggling act required to live on his own. The military had provided his wardrobe, a bed to sleep in at night, and a wakeup call every morning. If he'd spent his stipend on the latest releases of Violent Femmes and REM, his meal card had still guaranteed him dinner until payday. Since returning to civilian life and with only a rudimentary understanding of budgets and interest and

Clementina and
Spirito Marzo
sailed from Italy
in 1902 to begin
a new life in
America.
Back row: Marzo
sons Peter and
Albert. *(MJK
collection)*

Judith Marie Gridley, "the prettiest girl in the
county." *(MJK collection)*

James Herbert Keenan, the baby with the big
brown eyes. *(MJK collection)*

Mike introduced his son early to the gardens and trees surrounding their Indian Lake, Ohio, house. *(MJK collection)*

Jim took an immediate interest in his aunt Pam's guitar, and his friends joined him in learning simple chords and rhythms. *(MJK collection)*

Jim made his stage debut as a tin soldier in the third-grade class play, *Mr. Grumpy's Toy Shop.* *(MJK collection)*

Judith allowed Jim to choose the outfit he wore for his fifth-grade class picture. *(MJK collection)*

"Suddenly, I'm inheriting a teenager." Mike's new wife, Jan, was unprepared when Jim came to live with them in Michigan.

Returning Lettermen

Front row left to right: Jim Keenan, Jeff Hansen, Lawrence Golay, and Andy Green. Back row left to right: Pat Gilbert, Sam Hodges, Scott Dittmer, and Rob Schrink.

Jim, always the sartorial rebel, returned to the wrestling team for his fourth season in 1981. Coach Keenan held his son to the same standards he did the other members of the team.

Under coach Steve Bishop, Jim excelled in high school track and cross country, winning his first varsity letter when he was a freshman.

MOST TALENTED: Jim Keenan and Julie Edel

His classmates named Jim Most Talented in the mock election senior year—as well as Most Artistic and Most Pessimistic.

In 1982, Private E-2 Keenan graduated from Fort Sill the distinguished basic training graduate in his battery.

PFC E-3 Keenan in a moment of levity while bivouacked with the 82C survey team in Fort Hood, Texas, 1984. *(MJK collection)*

During their time at USMAPS, Sarah Llaguno and Jim ran on the cross country team and shared a passion for cutting-edge music. *(MJK collection)*

Jim returned from the military with a new name and a Mohawk. Among the few friends who accepted his outré persona were Kjiirt Jensen and Kjiirt's cousin Julie Vanderwest. *(Photo by Sue Ellen Jensen)*

Maynard vamped with fellow Kendall School of Design students at a 1985 Halloween party. *(MJK collection)*

C.A.D. performs at Maynard's Evans Street apartment in Grand Rapids in 1986. Left to right: Maynard, Tom Geluso, Kevin Horning. *(MJK collection)*

C.A.D.'s 1986 CD featured album art
by Maynard. *(MJK collection)*

Maynard took a break between TexA.N.S. and C.A.D. rehearsals to tag the wall behind his Cherry Street apartment. *(MJK collection)*

In the late '80s, Maynard was introduced to fine wines that Kjiirt brought to holiday dinners in Boston's North End. Right: Fellow Midwesterner Tracy Nedderman, their Ludington friend who'd joined the community of Midwestern expatriates in Massachusetts. *(Photo by Sarah Jensen)*

late fees, he'd used his credit cards to finance C.A.D.'s nonpaying gigs and to purchase recording equipment and the Chevy Sprint, running up balances he was in no position to pay.

He relied on the car to travel to and from the Grand Valley campus, but the bank didn't take that into consideration. One afternoon, he returned to the apartment to find the Sprint gone.

Maynard had been uprooted often enough. He knew the essentials he must pack and the things he could leave behind. And Boston wasn't so far away; he could be there in no time, and the fold-out foam chair in Kjiirt's living room would be comfortable enough until he found an apartment of his own.

> In theory, the energy of the universe wants to go in some direction. You have a goal, and the push and the pull of opposites is what gets you there. Grand Rapids is a Garden of Eden where rents are cheap and family is nearby and most people aren't motivated to leave because it's so easy to stick around.
>
> Here in the Garden, everything's cozy. One school of thought says we've reached our goal when we have everything we need and there are no distractions pulling us toward anything more. Keep all the conflict and the darkness away and life is perfect. Then you have the other school of thought, which is, No, get out of the Garden. Go into absolute chaos and struggle, and force yourself to accomplish something. In essence, Lucifer, or the serpent, is actually a necessary disruption, a motivation to get us moving toward our goal.

"I didn't really think he would actually leave," Ramiro would recall. "And then suddenly one day, he was gone."

6

Boston's distinct neighborhoods were still intact in that summer of 1988. The homogenization and gentrification that would come with the end of rent control was still far in the future, and the most struggling of artists could easily afford a walkup in the North End or a spacious room in a Somerville triple-decker.

Maynard arrived in early August at the peak of a crippling heat wave. Brownstones and cobblestones remained unbearably hot long into the night, train tracks warped into hazardous heat kinks, and children splashed in the welcome coolness of the Frog Pond on the Commons.

Mike and Jan were perplexed by his move. At last, they'd believed, he'd found his calling at Kendall. They'd driven to Grand Rapids to attend a C.A.D. show and to admire his drawings, and they interpreted his sudden departure as an abandonment of his art, a denial of his talents.

"Art school seemed disconnected from reality," Maynard would recall. "I didn't see how I could ever create art and be compensated for it." He most wanted to make music and paintings and sculpture, but he realized it made little logical sense to dash madly from class to rehearsal to performance in a spiral of diminishing returns. "I went to Boston looking for structure," he explained.

The move was a chance to set aside for a while his plan and to discover a way he might alter his story. It was time, he knew, to step from the predetermined path, to establish a routine that would allow space for the synchronistic accidents that might determine his course. And with Kjiirt to share his exploration, the search might prove easier.

A Perfect Union of Contrary Things

The blue fold-out chair in Kjiirt's living room was comfortable enough, but certainly unsuitable for the long term. After only a few restless nights, Maynard was ready for a room of his own, and when a Somerville apartment became available, they packed their bags. It took only an afternoon to transport their few belongings to the house on the back side of Winter Hill, a neighborhood of young families and Tufts University students, towering shade trees, and sprawling nineteenth-century homes. Maynard lugged his black trunk up the front steps and to his room and then stepped out to decipher the transit system and explore the city.

DAMIEL AND CASSIEL LOOKED DOWN upon a black and white Berlin. Maynard sat back in the air-conditioned chill of the Nickelodeon and watched them go about the silent business of guardian angels: comforting the fretful subway rider, encouraging the frustrated poet, consoling the dying man sprawled at the curb. From the first soft-focus aerial pans of the city, Maynard was lost in the rhythmic narration, the agonized longing of the angels, the visual poem that is *Wings of Desire*.

Breathless, he watched as the angels, creatures out of time and of all time, observed and witnessed and took nothing for granted. He watched as they took out notebooks and documented for eternity the smallest raindrop on the most obscure raised umbrella, recorded humanity's story even as it endlessly unfolded. Maynard yearned with Damiel as he drew from the rock the spirit of the rock, ached with him to feel its coolness, its sharp edges. And when Damiel discovered the portal to the human world of taste and color and raucous punk clubs, of love and at last of loneliness, Maynard rejoiced.

> Being an only child, I'd listened to my inner dialogue all my life. Suddenly, I was watching characters on the screen doing essentially the same thing. They were immediately comfortable sharing their thoughts with this angel, not realizing they'd been speaking to him forever. No matter what they were going through, someone—whether they could see him or not—had always been there to offer nonjudgmental support, to listen to their story. It all seemed so familiar.
>
> And I understood the commitment of that eternal being when he took the plunge into the polarity of existence. For the first time, he was living within the

A Perfect Union of Contrary Things

|| ticktock of time, something precious and expendable. Every choice he'd make
|| in this world of time would have its benefits—and its consequences.

The lights came up and the theater doors opened to admit the humid rush of Boston afternoon. Maynard looked across the street toward Boston University, its rooftops in sharp relief against the cloudless sky. The sidewalks shimmered hot beneath his shoes, and the smell of car exhaust reached him from the curb. The taste of salt and butter still sharp on his tongue, he started at the taxi's blare, heard a Led Zeppelin riff drifting from an open window not far away.

In the distance, he knew, were the punk clubs along Lansdowne Street. Further still, whole lambs hung in the windows of North End butcher shops, and beyond lay the salt spray beaches of Rockport and Manchester-by-the-Sea. He was anonymous here, free to walk about in receptive uncertainty, to be anyone he chose—or no one at all.

An aura of expectation and hope permeated the city. For a long time, headlines of global unrest, hostage taking, and armed combat had lulled too many into apathetic indifference, and the time was ripe for a backlash, a collective quest for heightened consciousness and a more authentic life. The PBS series aired that summer had brought into the most no-nonsense of living rooms Joseph Campbell's theories of universal archetypes and the power of myth. Artists and poets and New Agers had embarked on heroes' journeys of their own, convinced that embracing Eastern thought and whole grains and natural fibers would encourage a pendulum swing toward peace, love, and understanding.

Boston hummed with the contagious energy. Maynard found the streets confusing at first, their meanderings so different from the Midwest grid pattern that had determined his direction for years. But there, all squares and rotaries and diagonal paths converged at lively cafés or opened to sudden surprise: a mural in the narrow passageway beneath the overhead expressway, the lone sax player in the moonlit concrete canyon of City Hall Plaza.

He walked among the purposeful crowds on their way from yoga lessons to the herbal supplement aisle in the organic market, to adult ed courses that promised to teach them psychic skills. He passed contemporary gypsies, their bright, gauzy skirts billowing as they stepped over steam grates, healing amethyst and carnelian strung on silver chains about their necks. He paused at the window of Seven Stars bookstore and its display of incense and tarot decks and brass likenesses of Hindu goddesses, their many arms battling the many forces of evil.

As skeptical as he was of the ability of the hierophant and the hanged man to foretell his future, he entered into a sort of Pascal's wager with the gnostic: Even if magic were humbug, he'd lose nothing by believing. And if a nugget of alexandrite in his pocket really could increase his creativity, he'd choose to trust its powers. "I know on some level, most likely all that is bullshit," he'd later admit. "But I'll buy into it because it puts me in a headspace that anything's possible. If you're an artist and don't believe in some kind of magic, your art probably sucks."

COLLECTORS RELIED ON THE SHOP IN UNION SQUARE for the handcrafted frames and acid-free mats that would protect their fine paintings and photographs. A short bus ride through the Somerville morning took Maynard to Stanhope Framers and his first full-time job. A sweet-smelling haze of oak and cherry dust hung over the woodshop where Maynard's coworkers cut and finished the custom frames and then delivered them to his worktable.

He determined their proper alignment and hinged a lightweight scaffolding to their backs. He fitted the glass and cleaned from it every streak and speck before wrapping the finished Monets and Sargents and György Kepes prints for shipment to homes and galleries throughout Boston.

> You see the artistic and the utilitarian colliding right there in Stanhope Framers. I had to put the right angles together and follow a structure and package it. We were containing and bringing structure to whatever happened in the minds of these crazy artists.

The work was more difficult than he'd expected, but the steady pay was a chance to eliminate some of his debt. Besides, he realized, an honest week's work was a small investment if it meant free hours to keep to the plan he and Kjiirt followed, their plan of no plan at all. They would live for experience only, their radar ever trained on possibility, their senses tuned to the invisible energy crackling in the summer air.

At 5 o'clock, Maynard replaced his brad puller and stapler in the cubicles above his table and spread across it a fresh sheet of white paper. In the morning, it would begin again: the focused concentration, the precise fitting and polishing, the battle against the most imperceptible fingerprint and the tiniest mote between print and glass. Try as he might, smudges and dust remained. Maynard was good at his work, but an upscale shop like Stanhope required an attention to detail that he knew he lacked.

And then he saw the flyer advertising a position at a pet shop. He'd watched baby opossums in the bathtub thrive under Mike's care and had recognized the bond between his father and the wild birds that had fed from his cap. He'd raised Harpo from a helpless chick to a healthy, happy bird, and he gathered his internal advisory board to weigh the pros and cons of a career change.

"My bliss was not cleaning glass with ammonia and alcohol," he would recall. "My bliss was with birds and animals. I was drawn to working in a pet store, where everything around me was breathing, flying, crawling, living, and dying."

Boston Pet Center, a privately owned shop in the Lechmere section of East Cambridge, specialized in saltwater fish—bright angelfish and clownfish and dottybacks. Beyond a glass door in one corner was the aviary where finches and cockatiels fluttered from perch to nest, and parrots followed with their beady eyes the customers who came to admire their plumage.

It was Maynard's task to take up broom and mop to keep the place tidy, and he soon came to recognize the birds' individual personalities. He reassured the boldest, whose loud squawks, he knew, were merely compensation for their fear, and interacted with the timid until they became brave enough to light on his shoulder when he entered the room. He befriended Bobo, the shop's hyacinth macaw, who in no time bonded with him and never refused to perform for customers, falling trustingly from his perch into Maynard's outstretched hands.

"Maynard would call me late at night and tell me about his job," Deb Rockman would recall. "We'd talk about music and what he was doing in Boston, but the main thing I remember about that period was how he was really grooving on the birds."

He'd indeed found his passion in the bird room, but at Boston Pet, Maynard discovered skills he'd never known he had. One afternoon, he watched as a coworker knelt in an aisle assembling a display of puppy toys. He placed box after package on the shelves, duplicating the same uninspired pattern arranged by countless stock boys before him. Maynard had never set up a retail display, but it seemed to him that the squeaky balls and plush monkeys could be more attractively positioned. "You know, if you arrange this differently," he suggested, "maybe by shape and by putting similar products together, it could be more logical." His coworker glared, resentful of the newcomer's intrusion, and responded with his own suggestion, that Maynard be off with his mop to sweep up the bird droppings as he'd been hired to do.

Maynard hadn't noticed store manager Debra Alton, who stood just out of sight behind a nearby endcap. But she'd overheard the exchange. "She came up to me and said, 'Seriously, how would you do that?'" he would recall.

Alton invited him to try his hand with a display of parakeet seed and cuttlebones. Intuitively, he rearranged the products according to size and shape and color, leaving just enough room between each to allow customers to easily remove them from their rows of hooks. Alton smiled.

"I'd been in retail management my entire career," she would explain. "There's nothing creative or clever about pet supplies, but Maynard could take a pile of stuff and turn it into a beautiful display."

Maynard remembered the lessons on perspective in Mr. Ingraham's drafting class, the castles and fortresses he'd built in the Ravenna basement, the C.A.D. album art and the Kendall assignments—random successes that seemed now but preparation for one moment on one afternoon in a pet store in Lechmere Square. "This was more fun than it was a job," he would recall. "It was like a living, moving sculpture in the form of a pet store."

It wasn't long before Alton appointed him merchandise manager in charge of the display crew. When the store took on new lines of cat treats and aquarium accessories, it was his job to reset the aisles, and when the rawhide candy canes and pet-sized Christmas stockings arrived in November, he created cheery displays to highlight the seasonal goods. "They actually recognized that I might have valuable input," he explained. "They gave me a shot and I didn't blow it. I took the opportunity and made the best of it and I thought, 'Here we go.'"

Maynard took a critical look at the shop's layout and suggested the bags of dog and cat food be moved from just inside the entrance to the rear of the store. His proposal met with not a little resistance. The bags were heavy, his coworkers reminded him, and relocating them would mean customers must lug an unwieldy 30 pounds the length of the store to reach the exit.

But the shoppers didn't mind. En route to the one product they'd intended to buy, they passed plastic aquarium plants and name tags and hairball treatments and impulsively filled their carts with the pricey extras in their belief that their Tippy truly wanted a bright pink collar and Puff deserved a brand-new catnip mouse. "I invented the chew-bone pickup," Maynard would explain.

For all the rhetoric of universal harmony and brotherhood of mankind, Boston remained a provincial small town where invisible boundaries kept outsiders at some remove. The stereotypes Maynard had been told of before he'd come east had proven true: The fabled Yankee attitudes of steadfast self-reliance and guarded privacy prevailed in this place where newcomers were suspect until they'd established themselves—a mysterious process that might take generations.

> Being in Boston was like moving to Scottville all over again, back in a town where everybody knows you don't belong here and you have to prove yourself. Kjiirt and I would go to Shays in Harvard Square for a beer. It was a nice little bar and I wanted to make it my home, but it just didn't happen. Half my experience in Boston was like that. Nobody really wanted to open up.

Ever up for the newest of new music, Maynard and Kjiirt joined in the head-thrashing and moshing at Axis and Avalon on Lansdowne Street and when hardcore acts appeared at the Channel in Fort Point.

They watched the spotlights play over the Ramones or Devo and slammed with the metalheads and goths in the sunken pit, replicating the "Jerkin' Back and Forth" dance steps they'd perfected at Johnny's. The wooden floor bounced beneath their jumping and colliding, and the overhead speakers swayed precariously. The crowd moved as one with the driving beat, and when it became unruly, he and Kjiirt moved to the far edge of the dance floor just in time to avoid being led away by bouncers fearful for patrons' safety.

Maynard approached band members during set breaks and asked about their innovative riffs and chord progressions. Unaccustomed to serious questioning from their fans, they turned a deaf ear to his natural Midwestern gregariousness. "He tried to talk to the bands, but they never seemed to be able to put two words together," Kjiirt would remember. "We were the only ones talking to these guys in the entire Channel."

The silent treatment didn't diminish Maynard's elation after a night of clubbing. At closing time, he and Kjiirt stepped around overindulgent revelers passed out in the parking lot and began the four-mile walk back to Somerville. The T had shut down for the night hours before, but, wide-awake in the evening's aftermath, they made their way across the Mass Ave bridge, imagining what it would feel like to play music under the colored spots at Axis.

"Neither one of us had any idea what we actually wanted to do," Kjiirt would admit. "We just felt like Boston was a transition point, and we knew we weren't going to live in this uptight New England town forever."

IT WOULD BE IMPOSSIBLE, Maynard realized, to win over the icy Bostonians. He was drawn to the few he could count on, the few who, like himself, had migrated from elsewhere: Ian and Elias, recently arrived from Brazil; Somerville neighbors Tina and Liz, whose warmth and sincerity marked them as not-quite-true Bostonians; the homeless man who could have been from anywhere but always offered a kind word when Maynard passed through the little park in Harvard Square. And, as he'd foreseen, Kjiirt and his sister.

Maynard and Kjiirt climbed the narrow staircase to Sarah's fifth-floor apartment and stepped into a kitchen warm with roasting turkey or leg of lamb from DiPaolo and Rossi around the corner. Small as it was, the North End apartment always had room for one more, one more Midwest transplant whose pocketbook or family dynamics prevented their going home for the holidays. Their common roots made of them immediate family gathered to share in celebrations to which Maynard was not so much invited as expected.

They wedged mismatched chairs around the folding table in the living room, the table set with goblets for the Gewürztraminers and Malbecs selected by Kjiirt to accompany each course. Maynard might contribute an hors d'oeuvre tray, ripe olives and deviled ham and string cheese he'd braided for the occasion. He might bring, too, a guest of his own—someone he was dating, and never the same someone from Thanksgiving to Christmas to Easter.

Maynard and Kjiirt and the others stayed as long as politely possible. Their laughter echoed far into the morning in this unheated apartment in the heart of this impersonal city, this home where a candle burned and no one was alone.

MAYNARD'S HAVEN WAS THE NEIGHBORHOOD, the cozy Union Square restaurant operated by the convivial Borgeses—Mario, master of Portuguese cuisine, and his sister Sheila, the feisty waitress in big hair and halter top.

He and Kjiirt took their usual table at the rear of the restaurant, eyeing the heaping plates of eggs and linguica and home fries, waffles and pastries and bowls of special-recipe Cream of Wheat.

> There are places that have resonance. The Neighborhood is one of those places. I'd get there, and Mario would say, "Sheila, your friend Myron's here. Gaylord? What's his name? The guy." He couldn't remember my name, but he knew I'd order the seafood omelet.
>
> You gravitate to places like that. Mario and Sheila were my Boston family. I could rely on them just being there for me.

And Sheila was there for him immediately, snuffing out her cigarette and answering his call: "Judy Patootie, get your ass over here and bring me some coffee right away!"

"This is not an easy town," Sheila admitted in a 2013 interview. "It's cold as hell. No one talks to you." Recently arrived from New Jersey, Sheila struggled with her own outsider status. "A lot of the people I waited on were high-class, snooty, monied college kids who treated me like shit," she recalled. "That stuff would hurt me. When Maynard and Kjiirt came in, they balanced that off."

They lingered over coffee and bread warm from the restaurant kitchen, the *Globe* turned to the comics pages and the day's *Zippy the Pinhead* cartoon, forgetting for a while the pretentiousness that characterized the city.

"Maynard was quiet," Sheila would recall. "You didn't hear too much from him, but he was a funny, sly, quick-witted kid, and so accepting. He must have been going through his own Michigan withdrawal and being out of his comfort zone. I was out of mine, but we found each other and got through those years."

Maynard remembered well the icy squalls that blew in off Lake Michigan, the deep snows that had kept school buses from their appointed routes, the mufflers and sturdy boots and thick gloves he'd worn while shoveling drifts from Mike's driveway. But nothing could have prepared him for the relentless Boston winter. Pedestrians stumbled single-file down snow-choked sidewalks, and commuters shivered while they waited for trolleys delayed by the storms. A day of warm rain was a welcome but short-lived respite that left ankle-deep pools of slush in the gutters—pools that froze overnight to treacherous, slippery sheets. The cycle of deep freeze and snow, rain, and thaw might continue until April, creating along the streets mountains of ice black with exhaust and studded with yellowing cigarette butts and tattered Dunkin' Donuts cups.

For a time, Maynard and Kjiirt braved the bitter winds that swept across the Mass Ave bridge and continued their nighttime visits to Lansdowne Street. But after weeks of snow and cold, even the prospect of discovering a new punk band wasn't enough to lure them from their apartment. "Boston has the most miserable winters in the world," Maynard would recall. "It's cold and wet and miserable and you start to read serial-killer books."

AND JUST WHEN HE'D GIVEN UP HOPE THAT HE'D EVER SEE SPRING AGAIN, rainy April made way for sunny May, warm with lilac breezes and blossoms pink against the brownstones on Marlborough Street. Folk musicians claimed their spots beneath the greening oaks in the park, and Sheila and Mario arranged umbrellaed tables on the patio under the grape arbor.

A change of apartments would mean new windows looking out over un-explored squares, where untold possibility might unfold. Kjiirt's small flat on Cherry Street was plenty big enough to store his Bianchi 10-speed, and Maynard signed the lease for a room in a shared triple-decker only a few blocks away on Pearson Street.

"When he came to look at the place, I thought, 'Who's this freak?'" Steele Newman would recall. "If somebody had told me he'd gone to West Point Prep,

I would have been, 'What are you smoking?'" But Steele and his housemates, recent graduates juggling student loans and electric bills, overlooked the leather and the outgrown Mohawk in exchange for Maynard's rent check.

He stowed his audio mixer in a far corner of his closet and set about creating an elaborate habitat for the zebra finches and fishes and salamanders and lizards he'd selected at the pet store. He arranged in his room potted plants and cages and an aquarium and installed a screen door so the birds could safely fly about. "If you're talking per capita, those birds had some pretty big-ass spaces to fly around in," he would recall.

> I needed some kind of calm around me. Boston has its share of parks, but to get to them I had to travel through the chaos of traffic and busyness. And I felt like my home was a frat house. I needed to create an oasis where I could shut the door and disconnect. I turned my room into our front yard in Michigan.

Maynard found himself the odd man out on Pearson Street. Steele and Todd and Peter dressed each morning in Filene's Basement suits and ties befitting their entry-level positions with investment companies and PR firms downtown. Even John Pashalakis, whose at-home wardrobe was limited to a selection of denim shorts in various states of fray, played by the rules and reported to work on time—and properly attired—at the Store 24 he managed.

But it was Maynard's aviary, the unconventional hours he kept, his habit of quietly observing as if he were recording impressions for some future use, that the others found the most perplexing.

In the morning, he rose late, leisurely poured himself a bowl of Cheerios, and was in no hurry to join the others in their rushed commute to the office. "We thought, 'What planet is this guy from?'" Steele would remember. "'Why doesn't he conform to what's expected? Isn't he going to get a nine-to-five job?'"

Only during the Pearson Street parties did they appreciate Maynard's wit. The almost weekly blowouts were legend in the neighborhood, replete with multiple kegs of Budweiser and a steady stream of guests arriving all night long. Their dancing and laughter spilled into the yard, and inside, they bent over rolling papers and open gatefold albums. "It was an animal house," Steele would admit. "All we cared about was how big our next party was going to be."

Somerville police appeared so regularly in response to noise complaints that a coffeepot and an assortment of mugs were kept near the front door especially for them.

A genial host, Maynard replenished through the evening artistically arranged plates of dog biscuits he'd set about the apartment, and bowls of tiny dried fish, the sort customers bought at the pet store for their gobies and tangs. "That was when we bonded most with Maynard," Steele would remember. "When it was party time and we were letting loose and we all had drinks in us, we were like, 'What a sense of freaking humor this guy's got!'"

Intolerant of the smoke drifting blue across the living room, Maynard stood well apart with his White Russian and watched the others, overcome with the munchies, scoop up the tasty if unorthodox party treats.

His housemates may have questioned Maynard's unusual schedule, but he considered it the chief perk of his job. The tarot readers in Grand Rapids had repeatedly advised him to pay closer attention to talents he'd ignored: They'd spoken again and again of his inner voice and urged him to make it heard.

> Many of the tarot readers Ramiro and I went to told me the same thing. They said it was like I was looking at a wall or a window, almost like a puppy display, but the light wasn't on. I just had to turn the light on and see what I was supposed to be doing. They used words like *arrangement* and *presentation*, and said it might take a while to figure it out, but that there was something I was meant to do.

At Boston Pet he could channel his artistic sensibilities, incorporate the principles of design and feng shui, and ensure that the shop's form indeed determined its function. "We did something we'd never done before," Alton explained in a 2015 interview. "We created an overnight merchandising crew, and Maynard was in charge of the receiving crew."

The schedule freed him during the day to enjoy the sunshine he'd so missed all winter long. But despite his passion for the finches and macaws in the shop's aviary, Maynard felt a prickle of discontent. Surely he hadn't studied and observed and filled sketch pads with architectural drawings simply to arrange catnip and doggie sweaters.

Early on summer mornings, he arrived at North Station just as inbound commuters descended upon the city from Concord and Salem and Newburyport. He held Harpo's cage in the crook of one arm and pushed past the parade of secretaries and CEOs, their faces fixed in permanent scowls as they marched in lockstep to their offices.

The Rockport train inched past the railroad yards and strip malls just outside Boston, then picked up speed and made its way through the forests and salt marshes of the North Shore. Maynard watched from his streaked window the piers crowded with lobstermen hoisting their traps over the gunwales, the marinas where masts glinted in the sunshine, their rigging ringing. And just beyond the hills and wetlands of Beverly Farms, the train stopped at the tidy Manchester-by-the-Sea depot, steps from the wooded path that led to Singing Beach.

Bounded by rocky outcroppings, the beach sloped to the water's edge in a sheltered crescent. The silica sand whistled beneath Maynard's bare feet and the aroma of seaweed drifted pungent on the salt air. He opened the door of the cage, and Harpo flitted out and perched on his shoulder, turned a questioning, beady black eye toward him, and then flew off and disappeared over the waves and the sand.

Maynard settled in a secluded cove, opened his package of Twizzlers, and gazed out over the water, a deeper blue and green the farther he looked. Glistening salt spray dashed against the nearby rocks, and in the distance, a sailboat glided slowly toward the Manchester harbor.

It wasn't as though he'd never seen the ocean before. He'd spent hours at the Jersey Shore, distance training beside Sarah Llaguno past throngs of tourists at Asbury Park. He remembered the shrieks echoing shrill from the Circus Fun House, the honky-tonk music of the midway, the Ferris wheel a gaudy silhouette against the sky.

But the Jersey Shore was different—wasn't, at any rate, an ocean like this one. Here, sky extended an uninterrupted blue over waves that gathered far from shore, broke, and receded slowly over the white sand. All but empty on a weekday morning, Singing Beach was the serene setting he required, a place of sand dollars and shells of the moon snail, forked tracks of seabirds, and shimmering dragonflies amid the beach grass.

Never a swimmer, Maynard lay back in the shallows, letting go his nagging concerns of what the future might hold. He closed his eyes and watched the play of color beneath his lids. For a long time, he submitted to the chilly water, tuning himself to the rhythm of the sea, to the silence broken only by sharp cries of gulls and cormorants swooping overhead.

At last he opened his eyes to the cloudless sky, to the small speck that was Harpo growing larger and larger as he flew straight and sure back to his cage.

Maynard paused in his walk back to the depot and knelt beside the tide pool. Colonies of blue mussels sent out their silky byssal threads and anchored themselves to the slick rocks against the rush of waves, the water and seaweed and foam a green, glittering mix in the bright sunshine.

ENERGIZED, HE RETURNED TO BOSTON in time for the night shift and washed salt and sand from his neck at the sink at the back of the pet shop. When their schedules coincided, he and Kjiirt met for samosas and korma at one of the Indian restaurants in Central Square and hurried through their mango ice cream to make the show at the Cantab just up the street.

The two were welcomed with smiles and greetings by the regulars who frequented the smoky, gritty jazz club. Host Little Joe Cook began the evening with his signature "Welcome to the show, all you hamburgers and cheeseburgers!" and no matter their background, the crowd bonded over inventive moves on the dance floor and a delight in Nancy PhD and James Brown Jr. and Jose Jose, psychologists and accountants by day who masked their daytime identities and became soulful funk performers by night. But theirs was the compartmentalized sort of association that Maynard had by now come to expect. The rigid boundaries between them never opened in portals that led to deeper friendship.

Maynard and Kjiirt hummed Little Joe's "Lady from the Beauty Shop" as they walked to the T, laughter from the Cantab growing fainter behind them, the orange moon floating fat and full over Mass Ave.

IT WAS ONLY ON KJIIRT'S CHERRY STREET ROOF DECK that the borders dissolved. His weekend barbecues drew his sister from the North End, Elias from the apartment downstairs, Jane and Ian, Hope and Lorri, and Harold, his coworker from the wine room at Martignetti's. A disparate group to be sure, but a select group able to provide the sense of connection Maynard longed for.

While Kjiirt tended the crackling duckling on his grill, they shared updates on poems they'd written, the set of watercolors they intended to buy come Monday, the necklace they planned to fashion from beach glass and seashells. They offered advice as if confident the dreams might one day come true and, for a few hours in the company of like-minded compañeros, came to almost believe that they might.

Their stories were small chapters in the larger story, the combined tale of friends on a sunny Somerville rooftop sharing laughter and desires, the Prudential Building and the Hancock Tower hazy in the distance, Public Enemy blaring from Kjiirt's tape deck.

> I had no frame of reference for such a thing. It was this intimate setting of good food and wine and good people. Something really resonated with me on that roof. It was just cooking and eating, but it was so powerful. It was like coming home.

Maynard gamely sampled the Shirazes and Valpolicellas Kjiirt chose to accompany the meals. He wasn't confident enough to comment on complexity or terroirs or acidity, but when Kjiirt and Harold analyzed a particularly nuanced first-growth Bordeaux, he leaned back against the deck rail and listened.

Maynard and Kjiirt had formulated their adventure in February, when spending one more evening in their snowbound apartment had become unthinkable. Returning late from Lansdowne Street, they braced themselves against the storm and recalled stories of endurance Boots Newkirk had told in his American history class. The voyageurs, they reminded each other, and the pony express riders, too, had survived far more brutal weather than this, those intrepid pioneers without even accurate maps to guide them. Halfway to Somerville, they congratulated themselves on their fortitude, their ability to press on through driving snow and rutted slush. And four miles really wasn't that far, they realized, not nearly as far as Michigan, say. Why, if they could walk across Boston during a nor'easter, a trip to Scottville under a clear summer sky would be a cinch.

Kjiirt began his training regimen soon after moving to Cherry Street, biking each morning to Walden Pond, toning his muscles and building his stamina in preparation for ten days on the road.

Not to be outdone, Maynard resolved to forgo transportation entirely. If on some fine morning he set out from Massachusetts, put one foot in front of the other, he knew it wouldn't take long at all to reach Scottville—a mere 800 miles away. He'd gone that far every seven months in his daily walk to and from the high school—farther if he counted his track and cross country miles. He'd give himself a head start, begin walking a few days before Kjiirt pedaled off, and meet him in Scottville in mid-August.

If they were ever to undertake such a journey, 1989 seemed the time. They'd begun to notice that summer more and more synchronicities, coincidences they called "Kashmir" moments, curious alignments that pitched them to a heightened awareness. Kjiirt's father turned 75 that year, Mike would soon be 50, and they'd celebrated their 25th birthdays in the spring. Perhaps the patterns they recognized were only illusions, no more meaningful than the shapes that showed themselves in clouds or the grinning faces among the roses printed on the wallpaper in Grandma Gridley's living room. But traveling home under their own power to honor such milestones just might tap into whatever energies lay deep in the mathematical symmetry of the quarter-century marks.

One more anniversary added another dimension to the geometric precision. The year marked Scottville's centennial, 100 years since its incorporation as a village and a coin toss between lumberman Hiram Scott and banker Charles Blain had given the town its name.

IN LATE JULY, MAYNARD'S FRIENDS GATHERED to toast his departure in longneck Buds at the Cantab, where he added his name to the open mic sign-up sheet. He jammed his hands in the pockets of his bib overalls and took his turn on the small stage. It had been a long time since he'd sung in public, but only a few words into "King of the Road," the old confidence returned, and with it the familiar wish that the music might continue long after closing time.

His friends looked from one to the other in stunned silence, then at the Cantab regulars who leaned forward expectantly as he began his encore, "Margaritaville." Kjiirt knew of Maynard's talents of course, but Ian and Jane and Sarah and Elias were astonished by his strong, sure tenor, his control, his inventive nuances. "I didn't know anything about his Grand Rapids bands," Steele would recall. "I'd never heard him sing in the apartment and had no idea he had any interest in music at all."

His birds and fish in the safe care of friends, Maynard set out not long after for South Station, accompanied by Sarah, his send-off committee of one. He carried in his backpack the essentials—plenty of extra socks, a wallet of American Express traveler's checks, a road atlas, his Walkman, a tent, and a bedroll. Only a few early risers stood at the bay in the Peter Pan terminal, tickets in hand and awaiting the first bus of the morning that would take them to Pittsfield, the westernmost stop in Massachusetts.

Just before he boarded, Sarah pressed into his hand a fat paperback, its cover a colorful collage of angular topiary and arced rainbows and spiraled nautilus shells, its title a bright block of flourished Edwardian capitals. "Take this," she said. "Open it only after you start walking."

WHEN HE REACHED PITTSFIELD, the sun was high in the sky, the mild day ideal for a stroll, but one that would not begin, he realized with a sudden panic, as he'd planned. Pedestrians, he was told, were barred from the route he'd chosen, the interstate marked in a thick green line in his Rand McNally. He ran his finger along the narrower red line that represented the secondary highway running parallel. Traffic would be light here, the locals in family sedans and pickup trucks in no hurry to reach Albany or Syracuse or Buffalo. The detour might mean more time on the road, but it might be more pleasant, he reasoned, and he adjusted the straps of his pack over his shoulders and stepped across the border.

Ahead lay the whole of New York, Ontario, southern Michigan, Scottville—a trip one could make in 14 hours if one drove straight through, but one that would take him two weeks, one tuft of windblown blue chicory after the next, one night under the open sky after one more sun-splashed day. The map showed a long, straight stretch ahead, and, confident of his immediate course, he turned his eyes from the road, opened *Little, Big*, and began to read.

> On a certain day in June, 19—, a young man was making his way on foot northward from the great City to a town or place called Edgewood, that he had been told of but had never visited. His name was Smoky

A Perfect Union of Contrary Things

Barnable, and he was going to Edgewood to get married; the fact that he walked and didn't ride was one of the conditions placed on his coming there at all.

The book's cadence drew him into John Crowley's tale just as his steps carried him forward along the graveled shoulder. Edgewood or Scottville, the destinations blurred as Smoky's story merged with his own. It seemed that Crowley described the very road Maynard walked, the maple groves he passed, the insect-buzzing fields, the spicy scent of hawkweed and Danish carrots along the highway's edge. He walked on, buoyed by the sense that others had walked here before him.

By that evening, Maynard suspected that his undertaking might be more grueling than he'd bargained for. His legs cramped when he stopped to rest, and his insteps tingled where his shoelaces crossed over them. Twenty miles behind him and 780 yet to travel, and he feared he'd assumed a challenge he might not after all be up for.

A challenge, yes, but not a chore. His father had explained the difference in the echoing halls of the high school while the wrestling team ran practice laps up and down, up and down. His course might be longer than the one he'd run with the cross country team, but the rules were the same: Sprint quickly when the road opened clear and easy, fall into a relaxed amble in hilly terrain or when he grew tired.

He'd vowed he would walk, and walk he would. He kept an eye on his watch, determined to spend more time on foot than in the cars of friendly strangers, and in the end, hitchhiked no more than a half-dozen times, and then only when weather or weariness trumped his need to meet the one condition he'd placed upon himself.

I soon recognized that the kind of person who is going to pull over and pick me up is probably a fuckin' mess. Even if they're not going to kill me, they're going to make me feel pretty uncomfortable, because they're probably a weirdo to begin with if they're willing to pick up a stranger. It's not like they're just being a good Samaritan. As much as I wanted to be engaging with these strangers, I had to be 100 percent on my guard.

One time, a guy picked me up and it got weird pretty quickly. He resembled

> the guy driving the car in *Repo Man* with the weird sunglasses and aliens in the
> trunk. That gets your Spidey senses not tingling, but going off like a fire alarm.
>
> He kept wanting to stop for pie. "Pie? No, no. I'm good." I'd noticed a
> couple of motels up the road, and that's how I got away from him. I went, "OK.
> Just drop me off at this motel," and as soon as he dropped me off, I went to the
> other one a half a mile back and stayed there so he wouldn't find me.
>
> I never told people I was sleeping in a tent, because I didn't have a locked
> door between me and the fuckin' cuckoo-bird Pie Guys.

"The trip wasn't about survival or endurance or foraging for food," Maynard would later explain. "The whole point was to walk as much as I could, and that was the fun part. It was about being outside my element."

He soon came to understand the rhythm of the road, the distant hills dotted with red barns and spotted Holsteins, the Optimist and Lions Club signs that meant the next tidy town was just ahead. Then came the clusters of low white motels, the Sleepy Hollow and the Bird's Nest and so many named the Starlite that he soon lost count, portals on the way from here to there where strangers paused for a night and then moved on in the morning to wherever it was they traveled.

When the road ahead extended long and straight, he read. He waited out sudden and brief cloudbursts in the old diners that replicated themselves all along Route 20, Jack's and Leo's and Burger World, their fading billboards boasting the bottomless coffee cup and homemade lemon meringue pie. Perched on a revolving red stool, he lingered over his meat loaf and rice pudding, *Little, Big* open on the Formica counter beside his plate.

"As I read, I thought the book might just be a metaphor of me walking from Massachusetts to Michigan," he said. "But on some other level, I knew it was about my journey toward something even larger."

It was certainly unlike any book he'd read before, a tale of worlds within worlds, its many-layered plot mirroring the house Smoky came to live in, its stairways and hallways and porticos branching and circling in an infinite progression of ascending forms. The story diverted like a trout stream, forking off into sidebars and tangents and vignettes, in the end regaining its course as it spiraled in an ever-widening, ever-rising pattern of repetition.

He turned often to the family tree printed opposite the title page, struggling to keep straight the generations of characters as he read of their paths, their step-by-step contributions—however insignificant—to the story's outcome.

When evening came, Maynard pitched his tent just off the highway and consulted his map. The course he'd begun in Pittsfield had, if not reached its end, grown noticeably shorter, and, content, he lay back in the weedy undergrowth until it grew too dark to read. To the south, he knew, Kjiirt made his parallel journey beside Pennsylvania rivers and past the busy industrial centers of Ohio.

Maynard gazed at the moon he knew Kjiirt saw too, the moon nightly more round in the summer sky. Crickets chirped from the tall grasses, their song a chant-like chorus filling the silences between his Swans and Joni Mitchell, and he drifted, bone-tired, to sleep.

He dreamed then of whorls and turnings, expanding designs like the ones he'd created long ago with his Spirograph, their seemingly random curves and rays and loops determined nonetheless by some unseen laws of geometry embedded in the toy's plastic rings and gears and templates.

ACCORDING TO PLAN, THEY RENDEZVOUSED on Darr Road, their schedules coordinated even in those times before GPS and smartphones. Mike's gardens were lush with August, buzzing with bees and dragonflies, and Maynard and Kjiirt walked among the sculpted shrubbery and day lilies and compared adventures. Their stories overlapped in a spill of words and laughter until Jan called them in for breakfast.

Just before noon, they completed the final leg of their journey. Maynard strode beside Kjiirt as he pedaled across the Pere Marquette River bridge, among streets named 100 years before—Elm and Main and Crowley—then over the railroad tracks and past the livestock barn at the edge of the parking lot.

They arrived tanned and glowing and grinning at the Scottville Café, where they found awaiting them a small group of family and friends and a somewhat bewildered reporter sent by the *Ludington Daily News.*

Their welcoming committee was oddly silent, as if unsure just what questions to ask about this unusual journey. Most of them couldn't fathom walking the 60 miles from Grand Rapids, much less Massachusetts, or why Ian and Jane and Kjiirt's sister had traveled—albeit by the more conventional plane and car—all the way from Boston to celebrate their feat.

Maynard knew they'd be most interested in hearing of the eccentric characters he'd ridden with, mishaps he might have encountered, where in the world
he'd slept when it rained. On the one hand, he was bursting to share the wondrous independence and freedom he'd felt along the road, the pitched pure
reliance on his own intuition mile after mile. But unless they'd done what he
had—looked up into the wash of stars outside some nameless village, watched
for weeks the earth's curve roll toward him at the horizon and then walked on,
not precisely sure where his steps would take him—they'd never quite understand.

"I let go of the need to translate these experiences to people," he would
recall. "Kjiirt and I ultimately did this for ourselves."

The *Daily News* photographer snapped their picture as Scottville's mayor
ceremoniously presented them with commemorative centennial T-shirts, and
the reporter dutifully asked what had inspired their journey. "I think it was
the night we learned they put strawberry filling in Twinkies," Kjiirt answered,
resorting to his signature humor and sarcasm. "We decided if they can actually
improve perfection, we can do anything."[1]

Maynard and Kjiirt had set a goal and reached it. The secret to their success
was as simple as that, and when the reporter turned to Maynard, he said, "I did
it because I could walk and have the feet to walk with."[2]

> If you have your sight and your speech and your hearing and you're able to
> move and walk, you're able to grab things, if you don't take advantage of that,
> it's probably because you haven't watched somebody lose it. I'd witnessed
> people that can't do that—or were able to do that and then became unable
> to do that, and that instilled in me a sense of responsibility to use my talents,
> not bury them.

He'd return to Boston with renewed belief that his way would reveal itself
there as it had along the road to Michigan. But not before he curled on his old
bed at Mike's house, his window open to the familiar sounds of night birds and
tree frogs in the woods outside, and finished reading *Little, Big*.

It was in the end a story of hope despite its heartbreaking turns of events.

---

[1] "Former Residents Return," *Ludington Daily News* (Michigan), August 14, 1989, 2.
[2] Ibid.

Maynard's walk had changed him in ways he couldn't yet articulate, and whether he realized it or not, *Little, Big* had, too. Its characters had contributed what they must to the plot, then vanished in the next chapter to far hills or tenement apartments, just as the farmers and truckers and short-order cooks had appeared throughout his walk and done their part in the day's unfolding. They'd passed as briefly through his life as he through theirs, and there was no telling what idle conversation, which nod across which restaurant counter, would be the word or gesture they'd remember forever.

The road that Smoky walked at the book's beginning had become by the last chapter a winding path that led inevitably to another turning and another, the way the New York highway had opened to Maynard around each shadowed bend. He remembered gazing at night into the vastness of the galaxy and feeling not insignificant, but secure, crucial. As crucial as any minor trump in the tarot spreads that fanned through *Little, Big*, each card altering the reading and creating one more dimension to the story.

He and Kjiirt would carry their experience back to Boston, sustain the heightened consciousness they'd relied upon during their long journey, keep a watchful eye trained for the opportunities and challenges that surely awaited them there.

"That's how it was that summer," Kjiirt would later recall. "Between work and the beach and the Cantab and cookouts on my deck and the Michigan trip, we burned the candle at both ends 24 hours a day. We seemed to have tapped into a strange confluence of energy, the belief that anything was possible. What could get in our way?"

Maynard arrived at Pearson Street to find his birds and fish just as he'd left them, and he shared with his housemates the clipping from the *Ludington Daily News*. "It didn't surprise me that he'd made it all the way," Steele would recall. "It was just an example of the quirkiness of Maynard."

The freedom and elation they'd experienced on the road left them impatient with their friends. Their lack of spontaneity annoyed them, their complacent acceptance of daily routines that left little energy for anything but curling on the couch after work with another movie from the rental store.

"The walk to Michigan planted the seed of OK, that felt right. Let's go further," Maynard would remember. "It wasn't a case of the grass being greener on the other side. It was more like, how was I going to apply the things I'd learned in a place like Boston? I sure wasn't going to apply them riding the T."

"That's the shadow side of living for experience only," Kjiirt explained in a 2013 interview. "If the big plan doesn't show up on the radar and nothing happens for months, you get self-loathing. You're in the middle of the ocean and there's nothing you can do but make friends with the jellyfish. The experience you're dealt is the one you have to live with."

The hand Maynard held—one he had perhaps himself drawn in an access of faith—was a straight flush of go-nowhere romances, guarded friendships, and a job that grew daily more repetitive and unrewarding.

> I was committed to Boston Pet, but I started wondering what it was preparing me for. Kjiirt and I had learned a few things about ourselves, but we realized if we continued the way we were, we'd just be going in circles. We were embracing life, we were drinking in our bliss, but it seemed like there should be a next level to it all.

His one redeeming relationship was with Gloria, a fellow Midwesterner who'd come east from Libertyville, Illinois, and whose intelligence and warmth helped him forget sometimes his loneliness and the vision of plodding Ravenna laborers, their dreams abandoned under the dismal Ohio sky.

IN LATE SEPTEMBER, Maynard took the train north through forests red with autumn to Rockport, the Cape Ann town empty now of summer tourists. He passed shop windows sparkling with beach-glass jewelry and glossy metal sculptures like the ones he'd made not so long ago at Kendall. At the town center, he turned a corner and saw it, a red-shingled house set back from the sidewalk, a black and white placard suspended over the door: PSYCHIC READINGS. WALK-INS WELCOME, and he walked in.

A cheerless woman sat in shadow at a small table, its surface draped in a bright red cloth, curls of incense rising from a tarnished brass bowl at her elbow. She motioned Maynard to sit opposite and arranged her worn cards in a pattern across the table—the magus, the hanged man, cups and pentacles, and a figure eight resting on its side. She studied the spread for a moment, then looked up at Maynard and spoke. He'd be moving soon, she told him. Los Angeles or Chicago, yes, that was it. One or the other was his destiny, though she couldn't tell which, and even her cards couldn't divine what he'd find there.

> I believe in magic. Well, I don't believe in crystal magic and I don't believe somebody can take a photo of your aura that shows the color of your emotions. I don't believe in any of that stuff, but I do understand some people's attachment to the zodiac. You have to acknowledge the pull of moon on tides and how such a huge energy could leave a residual pattern on you the day you're born, because you're an electromagnetic being.
>
> Whether that continues, whether nurture ends up amplifying nature or muting nature, I don't know. I don't think we're even capable of understanding that.
>
> But the power of tarot cards just goes back to the storyteller. It wasn't like that reader in Rockport was some spirit guide. She was doing a cold reading on a person she'd never met, and if I thought about what she said, it might help me clarify things.
>
> You go to psychics and tarot readers not to have some miracle ghosts speak from beyond and tell you what to do. You go for clarity, almost as a meditation. The answers are within you, and if you get out of the way, you can hear them. You answer your own questions.

Her analysis was as vague and disappointing as all the others, and he left the little red house shaking his head, no more enlightened than before. Surely his future wasn't in Los Angeles or Chicago. He had no ties to either city, no reason to move to the other side of the continent, and he certainly wasn't about to trade Boston's snow and cold for the even more intolerable lake-effect winter.

WINTER SWEPT IN FAST AND RESOLUTE and by November brought rain and temperatures in the 20s. Maynard walked with Kjiirt toward Central Square, the streets and sidewalks veiled in ice. He bounded over the deep puddle in the gutter, leapt to the curb, slipped, and came down hard on the wet concrete. He staggered to his feet, knowing this was only the beginning. It would be months before he'd walk in the sand at Singing Beach, months before he'd see from Kjiirt's deck the Boston skyline shimmering in the heat. He glowered at the deep tear in his jeans as if it symbolized all his life had become. Cold rain dripped from his long hair and under the collar of his black leather jacket.

Sometimes when he entered the aviary at Boston Pet, he imagined the parrots there squawking from stands of sugar-apple and mangrove, their bright plumage camouflaged among passion flowers and orchids. The birds, he knew, had been wild things once, snatched from the sunshine and blissful humidity of the Amazon, and brought here to live in this cold, gray city he suspected they found as hateful as he did.

Elsewhere, a coworker told him, humane birders bred macaws and cockatoos and conures and tenderly hand-raised them from hatchlings. Her friends in Los Angeles, she said, nurtured parrots in a climate as warm and sunny as their native rain forest, and the birds grew trusting and accustomed to humans.

She told him something else, too. Her colleagues had recently embarked on an extensive redesign of their stores, a long-term project and one requiring the same expertise and vision he'd applied at Boston Pet. Might he be interested in flying to L.A. to investigate and perhaps apply for the job?

There'd be no harm in interviewing, Maynard decided. At the very least, a few days in the California sunshine would lift his spirits. And Gloria was certain her old high school classmates Tom and Jack would make room for him in their apartment just off Sunset Strip.

Maynard's work ethic and track record at Boston Pet won over the project manager. He'd be happy to bring him onboard, he said, contingent on his performance during a six-month probationary period that would begin as soon as Maynard wished.

Letter of hire in hand and two days remaining of his California visit, Maynard enjoyed the company of his hosts and their friends, passionate artists willing to live in a cramped studio in the name of working toward their goals. They talked long into the night of Tom's plans for his fledgling band, Lock Up, of the screenplays Jack would write, of the ambitions and desires that would surely be realized by these Libertyville transplants who'd come west to follow their dreams—Andy and Vicki, Joel, an aspiring puppeteer, and Adam Jones, a guitarist who spoke of one day forming a band of his own.

THE DECISION WOULDN'T BE MADE by anything as arbitrary as a coin toss. If a single influence led to Maynard's departure from Boston, it was John Crowley—or, more precisely, *Little, Big*, the book he'd read as he'd walked toward Scottville and consulted for direction as often as his Rand McNally.

He'd go to California, then, just as the fortune teller had hinted he might, doubtful as he'd been sometimes along the road to Michigan, but trusting in the destination just the same. His time at Boston Pet might lead to his working with the bird breeders, or it might come to nothing. No matter. The friendships he'd made in New England would surely endure, marking like bread crumbs his path should he need to retrace his steps and come home.

Maynard left without fanfare, without so much as a goodbye, with little more assurance than a faith in his own decision. He returned the fish and finches to the pet store and loaded a U-Haul with his belongings, his salamanders and lizards and plenty of crickets and lettuce, should they get hungry along the way. He placed Harpo's cage on the seat beside him and drove across Cambridge to Soldiers Field Road and the entrance ramp of the Mass Pike, westbound.

7

Tinsel stars hung from utility poles all up and down Sunset Boulevard, glittering in the sunshine, and plastic sleighs and reindeer stood on green lawns as if abandoned mid-route, Maynard imagined, during a sudden thaw.

He moved his belongings into a corner unit on the top floor of the Haven-hurst, a 1925 pastiche of architectural styles, its spiraled columns and ornate fleur-de-lis frieze seemingly tacked on as decorative afterthoughts to the otherwise solemn white stone building. His windows admitted a gentle cross breeze and the traffic sounds of Hollywood Boulevard, and outside his French doors, a small balcony overlooked the palms and red tile roofs along Whitley Avenue.

One long wall would be the perfect expanse to display his Kiss memorabilia, he determined—posters and photographs and ticket stubs he'd amassed over the years. He'd have plenty of time to arrange the collage later, but just now, he was eager to return the U-Haul and explore his new neighborhood.

His first order of business was a visit to Tom and Jack's apartment, where he left a magnum of Mumm champagne at their door in thanks for their recent hospitality and to announce his arrival. "We were young, and it seemed both extravagant and a remarkably adult thing to do," Jack would later recall of his gift. "It was as though one of our peer group was acting like an actual grown-up."

The afternoon was warm as June, the streets crowded with tourists and locals and abuzz with the energy Maynard had missed in Boston. He passed the Whisky a Go Go and the Palace and the Palladium, clubs shuttered and silent at midday, but topped with marquees promising light and sound and music come evening. Handbills littered the sidewalks, colorful flyers printed to their edges with drawings and grainy photographs and announcements of the punk and metal and grunge of the Dickies and Helmet and L7. He stopped to read message boards layered with leaflets three and four deep, outdated notices of appearances by Jane's Addiction and Soundgarden and the Pixies stapled over with news of upcoming concerts: Celebrity Skin, Hole, and the Imperial Butt Wizards, whose act, he would learn, often included setting fire to the stage.

Los Angeles waitresses weren't really waitresses, he discovered. Short-order cooks and bank tellers fancied themselves frontmen of the next hair metal band, and tour bus drivers had higher aspirations than forever transporting gawkers to stars' homes in the Hollywood Hills. They scheduled their day jobs around rehearsals and casting calls, gigs and costume fittings, and rushed to lessons in guitar and voice and the Method in their relentless determination to become the best in a city of bests.

Maynard approached his duties at the pet store with the same commitment, the unquestioning work ethic he'd learned by necessity in Scottville. "In Michigan, you don't shovel snow to build your biceps. You shovel snow because you need to get the car out to go to work," he would explain. "You lift weights and work out because you want to win the wrestling match and the track meet. Working hard in order to reach a goal, to finish the job, always felt to me like a natural, human-instinct thing to do."

Finishing his Petland project would entail three or four days at each of the chain's stores throughout the region, his supervisor told him, dismantling shelves and endcaps and reconfiguring aisles. But if it were to be done properly, his assignment would take longer than that. Stock boys and cashiers must be trained to take advantage of the new layout, and it fell to Maynard to teach them the secrets of the upsell, the chew-bone pickup he'd so successfully instituted at Boston Pet.

THE LITTLE BLACK SCHIPPERKE COCKED HIS HEAD, his dark eyes following Maynard's every move as he rolled a pallet of dog chow toward the back of the store. Maynard paused before the puppy's illuminated cubicle. It would take time, he knew, to establish a faux family like the one he'd formed in Boston, and in the meantime, the devoted and curious Zippy would be companion enough.

And with so much to discover in the city of excess and possibility, loneliness was the furthest thing from Maynard's mind. His holiday gift to himself was a choice seat at Devo's Christmas Day show at a club just up the street, and a week later, he took the short flight up the coast to attend the B-52s' concert at San Francisco's Civic Auditorium. The next night, accompanied by longtime friend Kathy Larsen, he rang in 1990 at the Psychedelic Furs' Berkeley stop on their East of Eden tour.

It didn't, after all, take him long to find his social niche. By virtue of his relationship with Gloria, the Libertyville transplants—his hosts Tom Morello and Jack Olsen and their classmates who'd followed their passions to L.A.—accepted Maynard as one of their own. Theirs was an instant friendship that nearly didn't happen at all.

> Gloria had called them explaining that I was coming to town for a job interview and needed a place to stay. Tom checked their machine and wrote down her message for Jack to find. On it he wrote, "Tell her no." But Jack never saw the note.

"When Maynard showed up at our door," Jack would recall, "Tom and I looked at each other like 'Who is this guy?'"

The close-knit community provided a sort of psychological ballast as its members struggled to gain a toehold in the entertainment world. Their relaxed gatherings helped ease doubts about their careers: whether Jack's entry-level position as a script reader was the first step toward his becoming a writer, what new music venture Tom would embark upon after the imminent dissolve of Lock Up, whether Adam Jones's studies at the Hollywood Makeup Academy would bring success.

"The group was a good grounding element amid the insecurity of trying to make our way in our creative endeavors," Tom would remember. "It was good to maintain all these friends from the 'old country,' much like immigrants would do when they came to America. We were really charmed by Maynard. He came across as a good Midwestern dude, and he was a welcome addition."

Like Maynard, the Libertyville expatriates were bright and talented, had excelled in high school dramatics and found inspiration in heavy metal, and their Midwestern warmth and sense of humor equaled his own. On Saturday afternoons, Maynard joined them in touch football games in the park, and, despite his lackluster skills, he became a member of their midnight bowling team.

> When you first get to L.A., it's very romantic, but it's huge. It seemed like everybody had some connection with somebody else and everyone was one-upping each other with cool stuff that's going on.
>
> The Libertyville crew took the sting out of the move. So many people were trying to suck your blood in that town, and here was a place with no agendas. I didn't give a fuck about how well they could play guitar and nobody cared about Jack's chiseled chin. We were just bowling.

Before long, Maynard was a fixture at the weekend barbecues, cookouts attended by as many as 25 Libertyville alumni. They brought potato salad and six-packs to Tom and Jack's pool or Adam's loft, where they reported on the week's auditions and job offers and reminisced about high school escapades and Electric Sheep, the garage band Tom and Adam had formed when they were sophomores. And they introduced Maynard to the Libertyville song written by Tom and Electric Sheep vocalist Chris George and Adam, a silly campfire song they called "Country Boner."

They were as impressed with Maynard's accomplishments as he with theirs, eagerly viewing the Polaroids he shared around the picnic table of his arrangements of Habitrails. "He was the most successful person we knew," Tom would recall. "He had a career and a company car and he was very proud of his work."

"Here was a guy who could walk into a Petland and decide where everything should be put," Jack would echo. "As quirky as that sounds in retrospect, at the time, it seemed like a genuine, actual job to us."

Committed to one day finding his true place in contemporary rock, Tom kept his finger on the pulse of the L.A. music scene, learning all he could of cutting-edge sounds and industry trends. "I went to shows six or seven nights a week," he explained. "In those days, you went to your friends' shows, you went to shows of people you didn't know. I just lived rock."

MAYNARD WAS A MORE-THAN-WILLING COMPANION in Tom's darting from club to club, elated to explore with him the many and varied venues scattered about the city—Club with No Name, English Acid, Raji's beneath the old Hastings Hotel, and the Coconut Teaszer, with its sawdust-covered floors and complimentary barbecued hot dogs on Sundays. Established musicians mingled during set breaks with unknown hopefuls, with A&R reps and ardent groupies alike, in a convivial and spirited atmosphere that encouraged a healthy competition among performers.

"We met Gene Simmons at Club Lingerie one night," Tom would recall. "He would often come to club shows, and Maynard told him excitedly, like a fan, about his hallway covered with Kiss collectibles."

"That was the beginning of my living high on the hog—for a minute," Maynard would remember. Perseverance and unexpected turnings had brought him inexorably to this: enviable and satisfying work, a sudden circle of supportive friends, the diner near Tom and Jack's apartment that welcomed him among its breakfast regulars. And blocks from his door, a vibrant music milieu where chance encounters with longtime idols were a matter of course.

At night, he stepped from his French doors to his balcony. Zippy lifted his nose to the warm breeze, and Maynard sipped his tea, looking down across the white city where lights extended bright beyond Wilshire Boulevard all the way to Culver City.

Despite Maynard's track record in Boston, the higher-ups at Petland couldn't quite see the value of his strategies, much less understand how to implement them. As far as they could tell, he did little more than move products from one aisle to another, relatively pointless work, they thought, that didn't justify his top-dollar salary. Two weeks before his probationary period was to end, they took back the keys to the company truck in exchange for his final paycheck. "Everybody has moments of doubt when they think, 'What the hell's going to happen next?'" Maynard would explain. "And then you find out."

With six months remaining on his lease and no job prospects in sight, he panicked. His career path hadn't been exactly focused, and without a college degree, his chances of receiving another offer seemed unlikely.

Early every morning, he and Zippy walked to the bus stop on the corner and rode the five miles to Adam's apartment in the Valley. The big backyard would give the energetic puppy plenty of room to play and explore while Maynard crisscrossed the city in search of work, his pockets stuffed with bus tokens and a map of the Metro system. Out Sunset, along Santa Monica Boulevard, as far as Culver City, he pressed buzzers and knocked on doors and followed the blind alleys listed in the classified section of the *Times*. And after a particularly discouraging day of interviews, he returned one evening to discover a freshly dug tunnel below Adam's fence and Zippy gone.

I walked up the street, trying to figure out where Zippy might have run. I asked some people if they'd seen a dog and they said, "Yeah. He went that way."

I went in that direction until I saw a couple guys doing construction and I asked them, "Have you seen a little black dog?"

Then the cops pulled up. I went straight to Officer Butts and said to her, "I'm looking for a small—"

"Hands on the car."

What? "I'm looking for a small—"

"Yeah, sure you are."

"No, just ask those people. My dog got out of a backyard right over here on Willowcrest."

"Yeah. You're looking for drugs."

"I'm not looking for fucking drugs. I'm looking for my dog."

Turns out I had some parking ticket I didn't know about on that pet store truck, so they arrested me and took me to the station. They handcuffed me to a bench and took me to a cell and locked me up overnight because of the bullshit warrant I didn't know I had.

Adam and his buddy Sean came down and bailed me out. They waited for hours, and at three in the morning, they asked, "So, could we have our friend?" And a guy comes out from the back and goes, "Oh, yeah, your friend was processed out like three hours ago."

Now I've got to pay Adam back for bail and I don't have any money. And if I'd had any chance of finding Zippy, it was gone now.

The path that had been so clear after he'd read *Little, Big* seemed now impassable, shadowed and forked in nothing but dead ends. John Crowley's book had resonated with his deepest belief, his certainty that taking one step after the next could propel him toward his deepest desires. But as with any mountaintop experience, the elation faded in the face of the demands and disappointments of everyday life.

Had Maynard read *Little, Big* with a more analytical eye, he would have noticed in the final chapter Crowley's hint of that inevitable sense of loss. "One of the central feelings of sophisticated modern people is that they somehow missed out on participating in a magical world," Crowley explained in a 2014 interview. "We only find traces of it in songs and stories and poetry. But we're always disappointed, because we're not really *in* it. And experiencing that magic through movies and books is worse than never having it, because we get exiled when the book's over.

"There's an acknowledgment of that at the end of *Little, Big*, and if the book affected Maynard that much, he's got to have felt that same sadness of exile from the magic."

Maynard's feelings were more profound even than that. "I was freakin' the fuck out," he would remember. "I lost my dog, lost my apartment, lost my job, lost my car, all within the space of three months. I went from having a little extra money to play with to nothing."

MAYNARD HAD REACHED AN ENDING, YES, but one he had the power—in fact, the duty, he realized—to alter. He could return to Boston, yes, would be welcomed back at Boston Pet with open arms. "I was not happy at all when he moved to California," Debra Alton would explain. "That was the end of the overnight crew and the beautiful merchandising."

But it wasn't time to turn back yet. As long ago as junior year in high school, Maynard had vowed to take advantage of every opportunity to write and draw and sing, and surely his passion for art and understanding of its practical application were all the magic he needed.

Hollywood's production companies depended on the out-of-work actors, the between-gigs musicians, and the L.A. newcomers to perform the minimum-wage grunt work that brought their films and commercials to Technicolor life. Artistic vision was necessary to succeed even as an art-dog temp, the ability to craft scenery and props on the fly, to assist the art department with set dressing for Boyz II Men videos and movie trailers. "And, God help me," Maynard would recall, "a Cinderella video."

He quickly learned the tricks of his new trade, tricks not so different from foraging scrap lumber from Mike's workshop to construct a stand for his stereo. Resourceful as always, he fabricated illusion from the most mundane of materials. Nailed just so to the studio floor, he discovered, inexpensive paneling from the discount aisle at Home Depot would easily pass for costly oak under the flashing strobes of a dance video.

A shoot might last from dawn to dusk, 16 hours or more, a job interrupted time and again when the director realized a part of the set must be rebuilt or a prop hadn't yet been acquired. It was Maynard's job to create glamour and opulence from wood and brads and tape and backbreaking manual labor.

> On one project, they needed riding crops for an R&B video. The scene was an alley, wet like after a rain and with steam coming out of manhole covers. Dancers were supposed to do a Michael Jackson–type routine, all of them dressed in black leather and carrying riding crops. But somebody had forgotten to get riding crops.
>
> It would take too long to go out and find real ones, and time was money. So I just jumped in the dumpster, found some long, semi-flexible things and wrapped them with black gaffer tape. With all the action and the lights, nobody would figure out what they really were.

The unpredictable schedule might mean two long days of work, four at the most, followed by a week of waiting for the phone to ring. And when the call finally came, Maynard rose early and wasted a precious hour in a circuitous bus route to the studios.

Before long, the commute became tedious—and costly, given his meager pay. Sharing Adam's apartment would do until he was back on his feet. And sleeping on his floor wouldn't be so bad if it meant an extra few minutes in his bedroll in the morning before walking down the block to catch his ride with a fellow set designer.

By now, Adam had found work creating special effects for films, and his companionship was a welcome break from the grueling hours in the studio. Maynard looked forward to hearing of his plans for his fledgling band, Mother, and of the stop-motion film techniques he was learning. And fascinated, Adam listened to the cassettes Maynard popped into the player, bands he'd never before heard of, TexA.N.S. and C.A.D. and their driving lyrics about stalking butlers and paths of "must we."

And in the mornings, Maynard checked behind the cushions of Adam's chairs for the nickels and dimes that must stretch until payday, and left at sunrise for the studio. "It was a bitter time," he would recall. "I'm working 15-hour days, but I'm still fucking broke. The money isn't steady, and it isn't much—maybe $100 for 24 hours. It's long days, but at least I know I'm going to have food on the table."

In the short time Maynard had lived in L.A., the city's music scene had undergone a sea change. Leaflets no longer cluttered Sunset Boulevard and the tattered flyers still posted outside the clubs announced performances long past.

The Seattle grunge scene had spawned by the late '80s scores of garage bands across the country, underground and heavy metal and alternative groups that, with a little help from friends willing to share studio space, formed on a shoestring a cottage industry of independent recording companies. Every week had seen the release of countless indie albums and EPs, vinyl and cassettes that overflowed the bins at Music Plus and Tower Records, a smorgasbord of experimental sounds and lyrics and subgenres to satisfy the most discriminating of audiences.

It didn't take long for established recording companies like A&M and Geffen to recognize the gold mine just within their reach. They had the resources and infrastructure to promote and market the handful of albums sure to be million sellers and the deep pockets to pay for ads and performance space and radio play. They engaged in frantic bidding wars to sign the most promising bands, the handful of rap and alt and rock groups guaranteed to outsell all the rest. And by mid-1990, the customer-driven music model had been turned on its head.

The record-buying public had been as autonomous as the bands, but the new model directed their tastes and their wallets toward the industry favorites. The indies found themselves head-to-head with the likes of Soundgarden and Alice in Chains and Nirvana and, without the means to compete, receded further into obscurity.

Only a few clubs were willing to even book under-promoted acts—acts that might never come close to filling the house. The Whisky a Go Go remained, and the Rainbow, the Gaslight and Al's Bar and the Central, where unknown bands were still welcomed and assured of a first-time public performance.

On many nights, Maynard and Tom could be found at one or another, in support of Mother, of Tom's musician friends, of the bands that refused to play the corporate game. They made their way from Club with No Name to Raji's, up the moonlit blocks to the pub hosting Green Jellö, the quirky spoof-rock band formed in Buffalo some years before.

Leather-jacketed friends might go their separate ways halfway through the night and reassemble later at another club across town, their entourage growing larger and louder at every stop: Adam and Sean, Joe and Curt and Kyra, and Caroline, who knew the Green Jellö members well. And Maynard, who sat in the shadows sipping his White Russian, observing the shifting scene and wondering all the while where he might fit in.

THE SQUAT, WHITE BUILDING ON HOLLYWOOD BOULEVARD was renowned for having been during the film industry's earliest days the Cecil B. DeMille production studio, and now continued the tradition of creative innovation as home base of Green Jellö.

The group's founder, Bill Manspeaker, lived there, Caroline explained when she introduced the band members to Maynard, and drummer Danny Carey had a loft nearby. The neighborhood sounded to Maynard like a microcosm of Hollywood itself, a vibrant place, energetic and devoted to unbridled creativity. And although the space was already home to Manspeaker, his wife, and old friends from Buffalo, a vacant room could certainly be Maynard's if he'd like to move in.

The building's topmost floor was taken up by the enormous open loft with small bedrooms partitioned around its periphery. DeMille's projection booth had been converted to a kitchen, and a window still opened onto the living area where his crew had gathered to view dailies of *The Ten Commandments* or *Cleopatra* after a day's filming.

One more roommate would hardly disrupt life at the loft. The space was stacked with couch cushions salvaged on trash night from Hollywood sidewalks, foam squares and rectangles that would see new life once Bill fashioned them into the heads and body suits of the Green Jellö characters: Cowgod and Rock 'n' Roll Pumpkin and Shitman. Deep into the night, the loft jangled with the sounds of arcade games—buzzers and bells and metallic beeps of Space Invaders and Operation Wolf—a counterpoint to the Ministry Bill blasted as he bent over his worktable assembling the band's outlandish costumes.

On weekends, the loft became Party Central. Friends and friends of friends came and went sometimes until four in the morning to mosh with the latest L.A. bands who performed at one end of the room, much to the chagrin of the neighbors on the other side of the common wall.

"I built the loft so that people could come here and do whatever they wanted," Manspeaker explained in a 2014 interview. "And here was Maynard. He was kind of quiet and shy and grumpy. I believe that loft was a door for him. All of a sudden, he was in this place where it was OK to be weird."

If he sometimes needed a break from the pandemonium, Maynard walked across the lot to Danny's building, the old DeMille livestock barn where under the carpeting, traces of feed troughs could still be seen in the concrete floor. Danny had fashioned from the space a compact apartment and adjoining rehearsal room where Green Jellö explored their routines. On the nights he didn't perform with Carole King or Wild Blue Yonder or Pigmy Love Circus, he set up his drum kit and worked on new numbers with the band. And Maynard listened, delighting in the characters and costumes, the music, the masks.

EVEN AMID THE CHAOS AND COMMOTION of the loft, Maynard managed to re-create his oasis, a retreat amid the comings and goings and Bill's heaps of papier-mâché, glue pots, and bolts of fabric. Against one wall of his room, he built a sleeping platform high above the floor to make space for potted plants hung with tiny nests for Harpo and the other finches, for aquariums stocked with geckos and chameleons, for an elaborate ecosystem of waterfalls and ferns and luminous goldfish.

Across a 4-by-8 length of plywood, he constructed embankments and valleys molded with Quikrete over a chicken-wire frame and painted in soft greens and browns. Water spilled from the reservoir atop the highest hill down into the fish pond and, through a system of pumps and hoses, circulated again up the hill, gurgling gently.

Late at night, the sounds of arcade games faint behind his door, Maynard gazed down from his bunk at the dozing animals, the tiny gray birds settling into their nests, the fish gliding slowly among the aquatic plants. Lulled by the bubbling waterfall and the soft chirping of his menagerie, he drifted toward sleep, imagining sand dunes and stars, snow across some faraway bridge, stories shared around a campfire.

On Friday and Saturday nights, the streets below Maynard's windows echoed with shouts and raucous laughter, car horns and the pointless revving of souped-up engines. Those were the nights suburban youths descended upon the city to cruise the boulevards, to see and to be seen. Along Hollywood and Sunset, traffic was at a dead stop in a gridlock that stretched from Western all the way to La Brea, car stereos blaring a cacophonous medley of the Pogues and Motörhead and the Alarm.

> On more than one occasion, I stood on the roof and watched women go from one car to another and rabbit-punch each other in the face. I guess these girls recognized rivals in the car behind them or some chick who'd looked at their boyfriend wrong. Who knows.
>
> The girls would get out of one car and swoop in on the other car. They'd open the doors and grab a handful of hair and start punching the shit out of some other girl.
>
> Watching this, I started wondering how extensive my atrium had to be and how thick I needed to build my walls.

The stream of customers at the discount Regal Liquors next door only added to the mayhem and tense atmosphere. Vagrants and derelicts stumbled all night long into the shop to trade their begged, borrowed, and stolen change for off-brand strawberry schnapps and nickel nips, then claimed the nearby stoops and alleys as their weekend turf.

"Our neighborhood was a war zone," Danny would recall. "We had to fend off bums and cretans and criminals and all these people that came back into the parking lot and slept on our doorsteps, urinating and defecating everywhere. But there was strength in our numbers." Maynard's street smarts, honed in the anti-punk neighborhoods of Grand Rapids, served him well. "He had good survival skills and knew how to get rid of these people," Danny said. "We bonded over that from the beginning and made the best of an ugly situation."

When Maynard noticed particularly disruptive activity in the lot, he shouted from his bedroom window to Danny, and the two met outside, baseball bats in hand. "We'd make them pick up their doody so I didn't have to do it," Danny explained. "It was just painful."

MAYNARD HAD KNOWN WHEN HE'D COME TO L.A. that his choice would bring both benefits and consequences, but the swaying palms and balmy afternoons and even living in the center of a vibrant music scene couldn't offset his despair. What had been promised had turned to its shadow side, a no-man's-land of insecurity and wariness.

His set work was satisfying enough—his last-minute cleverness when the art department panicked over missing props. When halfway through the shooting of Tom Petty's "Into the Great Wide Open" video they found they were short a microphone, it was Maynard to the rescue. "Running down to SIR to buy or rent one would cost them two hours," he would explain. "I told them to hold on. I could take care of it." A length of duct tape and an empty toilet paper roll was all it took to fashion the realistic-looking mic Johnny Depp held in his nightclub scene.

But quick thinking and ingenuity didn't pay the bills, nor did the quarters and dimes he found scattered on the sidewalk outside Regal's on Sunday mornings. He'd seen the flyers posted throughout the city calling for background extras in films and television shows, and now he began to read them more closely. Nonspeaking actors could earn $50 a day, he learned, and if their appearance was especially unique, they could command even more. Perhaps his long, wavy hair, wiry frame, and studded leather were unusual enough to land him a role or two.

Jack Olsen, he realized, might serve as a mentor of sorts, a film industry professional with insider insights, and Maynard arranged a lunch meeting to discuss his possible entry into show business. "Here was a guy thinking about working as an extra talking to a guy who read screenplays," Jack would recall. "We couldn't have been anywhere closer to the absolute bottom of the enter-

A Perfect Union of Contrary Things

tainment pyramid, but we proceeded with great seriousness. Maynard always had a kind of adult focus."

Working as an extra, Jack told him, sounded even more unreliable than temping as a set decorator. But Maynard was determined to piece together whatever odd jobs he could to make ends meet, and he spent his evenings calling the numbers printed on the strips he'd torn from the flyers. He left countless voice messages that disappeared into the AT&T ether. Once in a great while, he reached a recruiter only to learn the roles had been cast days before. By spring, he'd appeared in only two or three crowd scenes in unremarkable films, films forgotten almost before their release, his roles undistinguished and uncredited.

Clearly, finding film work would require more than a studded jacket and tight black jeans. Maynard had put plans in place before, seen them through step by step to completion, and surely he could do it again. "Here I was in Hollywood, so I thought I might as well take advantage of classes and workshops and learn to do shit," he recalled. "As soon as my paycheck was spent, I could barely feed the animals, but I mapped it all out. If I could work X number of set gigs, I could pay my rent, buy food, and take some acting classes."

BY NIGHT, HOLLYWOOD BOULEVARD'S 6100 BLOCK was dominated by Raji's, the smoky, jam-packed club where strung-out junkies consorted with the queens just back from nearby drag bars. Concertgoers clustered in the shadows behind the club, passing joints and convincing the sympathetic bouncers to allow them back inside for the closing set of the Nymphs or Thelonious Monster.

But by day, the block was serene, the destination of committed actors and ingénues who dreamed of joining Brando and De Niro and Candice Bergen as alumni of the Stella Adler Academy. One of the many such schools throughout the city, the academy catered to the steady influx of hopefuls whose boundless faith in the courses and workshops kept their dreams of stardom alive.

Maynard walked the three blocks from the loft to his classes in scene preparation and character analysis, voice and movement and visualization techniques he'd need to bring convincing realism to his roles. "No matter what your scene is," he explained, "it has to be about your mother being run over by a truck. You make it real by making an emotional investment, by going to the memory of something that puts that 'look' behind your eyes."

Until the day his acting training would pay off, Maynard rationed his animals' food, replenishing it when his next paycheck arrived, and in the meantime, closely monitoring what remained. "One day," Danny recalled, "he ran low on crickets, so I gave him a ride to the closest pet store to get buckets full of them to release into his bedroom. As soon as he jumped in my beat-up BMW, he expressed his interest in getting a band together." Stunned, Danny glanced across the console toward Maynard, the set decorator with the curious menagerie, the neighborhood defender adept at wielding a baseball bat.

Danny had passed many a free evening in the Green Jellö loft, challenging Bill to a round of Space Invaders and sharing stories with Maynard of their high school accomplishments on the wrestling mat and track practice along muddy Midwest roadsides. Maynard had told him of West Point Prep and the frame shop in Boston, but until then had never hinted of musical talents or an interest in performing.

"Then he popped a tape in the cassette deck and played me some of his favorite songs," Danny continued. "Industrial '80s things and Nirvana, which nobody really knew about yet. And I was like, 'Well, this sounds kind of cool.'"

Intrigued as he was with the songs on Maynard's mixtape, Danny ignored his hint of a musical collaboration. Between Green Jellö and his other gigs, he had no time—or intention—to even consider becoming involved with another band.

But Maynard was restless. Participation, he knew, could be a partial remedy for his financial and employment anxieties. A headlong plunge into the punk-club world would be at least a distraction, at most a step toward regaining a modicum of self-confidence.

"HE WAS THE WEENIE GUY," Jack would recall. "We used to joke that his part-time job was as a performer—throwing hot dogs to the crowd."

Maynard had become by now an established member of the movable L.A. music feast, mingling from club to club with friends of friends and audiences often made up only of members of the next band on the bill—Green Jellö or Lock Up or Electric Love Hogs, or the ubiquitous angry bands competing to become the next Red Hot Chili Peppers. "They were funky metal, bonky-bonky snap-snap guys," Maynard explained.

Before long, Love Hogs fans looked forward to Maynard's antics as eagerly as they did the band itself. He toted a 12-pack of hot dogs to English Acid, the underground club on West Pico, and slipped over his head a white apron—SATAN'S WEENIES printed across the bib. In the shadows at stage left, a toque atop his head, he warmed the hot dogs in a microwave, then meticulously slathered them with ketchup and mustard and wrapped them somewhat securely in Baggies. Guitars blazing and drumsticks a-blur, the Love Hogs snarled their lyrics, tossed their heads, and leapt across the stage, while Maynard, with a leaf blower from the nearby Home Depot, propelled the hot dogs into the delighted crowd.

His role, albeit peripheral, was like a tonic, as intoxicating as the long-ago days of lip-synching to the Jacksons in his Ohio basement. Forming a band of his own seemed increasingly far-fetched in a city where new talent emerged overnight and disappeared just as quickly. Suggesting he join Adam's band was out of the question. Mother's vocalist and musician lineup was complete. But if Maynard wished to test his music mettle, he realized, the opportunity was at his fingertips.

"Green Jellö looked like a perfect fit," he remembered. "Bill had an open-door policy, meaning I could come and go as I pleased. I was like, OK, if I want to get involved in any of this, this might be the way."

Green Jellö's rotating cast of characters was an ever-changing array of costume and mask, a group whose job it was to provoke, to amuse, to tell stories. As part of the troupe of shifting personas, Maynard could explore just what his place in the entertainment world might be and develop a stage presence as he portrayed rock idols and nursery story characters and a mustachioed, white-haired redneck he called Billy Bob.

Manspeaker had from its inception dubbed Green Jellö the World's Worst Band, the band with the sole purpose of being mocked. "Whoever was in the band was encouraged to do that thing the teacher told them was dumb or their mom told them they couldn't do," he explained. Serious vocalists and musicians joined the troupe for the chance to let their hair down, to forget for a little while the constraints of their profession, to experiment and explore and make all the mistakes they wanted.

"You don't have to fear being bad, because you're already saying you're bad," Manspeaker said of its members. "You're the best at being the worst. That's what Green Jellö's about."

APRIL 13, 1991, MARKED THE MOST WELL-ATTENDED GREEN JELLÖ SHOW TO DATE. "It seemed like there were a thousand people there," Danny remembered. "That was a really fun show. The punk energy was definitely in the air."

The evening in the Hollywood High gymnasium was as eclectic as it was electrifying. A more conventional dance band would perform for the school's junior prom in only a few weeks, but the April show was the antithesis of pastel gowns and wrist corsages. Punks and moshers crowded the gym floor, their cheers and screams reverberating from the high ceilings when the opening act, the punk rock Dickies, made their entrance.

A power outage interrupted their performance, and the audience began filing, disappointed, from the auditorium. But the lights came back up just in time for the somewhat incongruous second act, Tiny Tim, who strummed his ukulele and grinned through his signature "Tiptoe Through the Tulips" and "America."

Next on the bill was headliner Celebrity Skin, the secondhand-store version of glam rock. A maniacal revolving jack-in-the-box clown announced their arrival in keeping with their theme of the evening, "Under the Big Top."

And then it was Green Jellö's turn. Guitarists and vocalists filled the stage, their costumes and masks crowding the small space. The long latex spider legs attached to Danny Longlegs's back bounced with his every beat, his cymbals glinting under the spotlight. As emcee, Maynard announced the performers as they morphed from character to character in a variety show treatment they called "A History of Rock 'n' Roll According to Green Jellö."

"The premise was this bad version of the history of rock 'n' roll," Manspeaker would explain. "We started from the beginning of time and went through the present day, and when we got to the future, the idea was that all the '90s would have to offer would be Green Jellö—and they suck."

Their chronicle began with Maynard's flawless and urgent embodiment of Ted Nugent, his strong, sure voice rising in "The Great White Buffalo." In loincloth and wig, he told the lyrical tale of mythologies and magic, of Indian lore and the white man's destruction, of ultimate salvation.

He transitioned from Nugent to Johnny Rotten, delivering a driving rendition of "Anarchy in the U.K." that brought the audience to its feet. Verse after verse, his intensity increased, his growl deepened. Just as they'd instructed in the Stella Adler workshops, he remembered—and remembered again: endless Boston winters, a rainy Grand Rapids street, a lead pipe tucked in his sleeve, coins collected from a gritty sidewalk, red lights like a strobe against a split rail fence. The Sex Pistols' lyrics became his own, his scream of anger, his bitter resolve to at last have what he wanted, his long-repressed wish to destroy.

"Here's Maynard," Manspeaker would recall, "this shy, quiet dude who's kind of grumpy sometimes. Then you gave him a microphone and he turns into fuckin' Johnny Rotten."

His song segued into Green Jellö's adaptation, "Anarchy in Bedrock," and the cast joined his lyrical desire not to annihilate, but to become Fred Flintstone. Their shrill "yabba-dabba-doos" echoing through the gym, Bill and Gary Helsinger, skinhead versions of Fred and Barney Rubble, chased each other up and down the aisles, shattering the fourth wall and drawing the eager audience into the performance.

If the future of rock 'n' roll was to be Green Jellö and Green Jellö only, the Hollywood High crowd wasn't one to argue. The penultimate piece, "Obey the Cowgod," was a crowd-pleasing extravaganza featuring Manspeaker in an oversized bovine head, his red eyes flashing as he strutted across the stage, demanding submission.

When the lights came up on Green Jellö's closing number, the audience stood and shouted as one. The stage was set for the band's newest piece, "Three Little Pigs," complete with miniature houses of straw and wood and brick. Moshing pigs accompanied the bullying wolf in updated lyrics to the old tale, their long latex tongues lolling from massive latex heads. In a frenzied finale, the stage erupted in clashing cymbals and droning guitars and faux machine-gun fire trained on Manspeaker's Big Bad Wolf as he burst among the pigs in defiance of Maynard's falsetto "Not by the hair of my chinny-chin-chin!"

Becoming an onstage little pig or bewigged Ted Nugent satisfied Maynard's dramatic urges and provided a pleasant diversion from his long days building sets. His involvement with Manspeaker's band gave him entrée into the wider music world of rehearsals and creative comrades and the chance to observe bands that shared the bill with Green Jellö at venues throughout L.A.

After the clubs closed at night, Tom Morello often accompanied him back to the loft, where they discussed Devo's innovative time signatures and the blues roots of Led Zeppelin. They loaded the tape deck with music a step beyond the mainstream, the obscure and innovative music Maynard had always appreciated the most. "I remember he played for me a Swans album, which was way outside my comfort zone," Tom would recall. Maynard explained the group's minimalist chord structures, the emotional effect of their snarling vocals, their primal interpretation of heavy metal, and Tom took careful note.

Now that Lock Up had officially dissolved, Tom focused his energies on laying the groundwork for a new band he planned to call Rage Against the Machine, a group he envisioned would push the boundaries of metal and challenge political complacency. Determined that Rage would be a cut above the fledgling bands he and Maynard saw at Coconut Teaszer and Raji's, he set about learning all he could to avoid the missteps that had doomed Lock Up. "Maynard taught me drop D tuning," Morello would recall.

The two sat on the park bench that completed the aviary's décor. Maynard cradled Tom's Fender Telecaster and tuned the low E string to D to create the Seattle sound, the heavy resonance that gave bands like Soundgarden and Nirvana and Pearl Jam their signature sonic quality.

Tom had recruited the best of the best to populate his new band: longtime musician Tim Commerford on bass and backup vocals and Greta drummer Brad Wilk, who'd contribute his extensive percussion skills. He had only to identify a suitable lead vocalist to round out his ensemble. By now, he'd attended plenty of Maynard's Green Jellö performances, had heard the C.A.D. cassettes, and respected Maynard's vocal talents as highly as his ability to analyze complex arrangements. "There was sort of in the air an idea of us working together," Tom would recall. "Brad and I had been jamming with both Maynard and Zach de la Rocha. We really liked playing with both of them, and Brad and I had this long phone call to discuss who we should ask to the dance."

In the end, rapper de la Rocha proved to be the most logical partner. His hardcore band, Inside Out, had gained a substantial underground following, and his success would help validate Rage. It would be only a matter of time,

Tom told himself, before his band would be noticed by one of the labels scrambling to be the first to sign distinctive and serious acts.

Even Bill Manspeaker, whose group included clownish farm animals and a moped zipping across the stage—and little apparent talent save Danny's drumming—came home one evening and announced Green Jellö's 11-song video deal with BMG affiliate Zoo Entertainment.

"When I saw them perform, they got up there with stuff they'd collected from the garbage, the foam they made these costumes out of," Zoo founder Lou Maglia recalled in a 2014 interview. "I thought, 'Yeah, they suck, but they've got something going.'"

MAYNARD'S MINIMAL GREEN JELLÖ ROLE hardly warranted a recording contract, and he'd written nothing new since his Grand Rapids days. No guitarists or drummers were on deck to perform even his C.A.D. songs, and he'd prepared no business plan or artistic manifesto. But he had one thing most other bands lacked.

From his table in the shadows at the back of Club with No Name or English Acid, he cast a jaundiced eye on the performers who cavorted about the stage. "I'm at the back of the room watching those bands and criticizing everything they did," he would remember. "They clearly *wanted* to be up there. But they didn't have a *need* to be up there."

> These bands were just there to dance around and be popular, to get into the club without paying or to get laid, to catch the attention of A&R guys who might be in the audience, or whatever it was that they were trying to do. They're wearing stupid hats and hopping around and not telling any story. And they're not even bonky-bonk-snapping very well. The whole scene was just vapid.

If he were ever to take his place in the spotlight, Maynard knew, his act would involve more than superficial leaping about. He had stories to tell—decades of stories—and an aching need to tell them. His was an instinctive drive to transform pain and loneliness to riffs and chords, an imperative to translate fear and disappointment and plans gone awry to words and rhyme until sadness and anger dissipated in pulsating sound that beat in rhythm with his soul.

"Even if you don't know what your endgame is or what you're trying to do, if you fuckin' mean it, I can feel it," Maynard explained. "When Brando did a scene, he meant it. When Dee Dee Ramone hit the stage, he meant it even if it was the one millionth time he'd done it. I wasn't seeing that in L.A."

Maynard's frustration only grew when he realized he'd become an appalling cliché, just one more jaded L.A. hipster living hand-to-mouth and finding fault with the soulless posturing of bands whose sense of teamwork was as out of tune as their thrift shop guitars.

"Eventually, people got tired of overhearing me being a judgmental asshole," he would recall. "They finally started saying, 'Well, if you think you can do better, why don't you?'"

8

"Imagine a table with only one leg." Boots Newkirk's class never knew what life lesson he had in mind when he began his lectures. He stood a copy of the 11th-grade history text on end and laid his grade book off-center across its top. The class burst into nervous laughter as his shaky construction collapsed across his desk.

His message that long-ago day had been on the importance of friends— or, more precisely, on the absurdity of depending upon one best friend, one girlfriend, one significant other whose inevitable abandonment would result in locker slamming and tears.

Better to build a community of support, Boots advised, a more complex framework with enough components to withstand change and uncertainty. He illustrated his metaphor by standing two books, then three, then four on his desktop, at last setting the grade book atop the secure base. It was a matter of simple geometry, he explained, the axiom that stability increased as forms progressed from point to line to triangle to square, the notion that the strength of a whole depended on a sufficient number of parts, each in place, and a counterbalanced tension among them.

MAYNARD HAD THOUGHT FROM TIME TO TIME about forming another band, but he'd never taken the whim seriously. He'd watched C.A.D. dissolve as its members focused on the rush of popularity to the exclusion of details that might bring success: sensible spending and attractive flyers, commitment to creative advancement, and a shared vision of the band's future. Like the L.A.

groups he criticized, C.A.D. had toppled into oblivion under its own imbalance.

He remembered enough guitar chords to write at least a few new songs until he could find suitable bandmates. "When the challenge came to shit or get off the pot and show what I meant by 'You suck!' the Irish side of me was like, OK." Maynard would recall. "I'll show you how to do this better. Not forever. I'll show you how it's done so you can do it yourself."

The madcap chaos of Green Jellö was a safe environment in which to explore his art, but with his own band, he could dig deeper into his frustrations and anger. The lyrics were ready to be written, lyrics that would address the discontent and resentment simmering just below the surface—and perhaps incorporate a bit of dark humor to spice things up and keep his listeners guessing.

On too many nights, Maynard lay alone in his bed while his menagerie settled into their nests. He watched the moon rise in the Hollywood sky and brooded over disappointments and hurts he should have laid to rest long before: the view from his mother's VW of the Indian Lake house growing smaller in the distance; his wary walk, armed and cautious, down dark Grand Rapids streets; his grandmother's scorn over his punk attire. Maybe she'd been right all along. Had he accepted the West Point invitation, he wouldn't be scrambling at week's end for change to buy crickets for the iguanas. An art degree might have meant by now a supervisory position at the studio, higher pay and regular hours.

The wrong turns had led to a dead end, a dissatisfaction and questioning of his every decision, the weighty sense of exile from the magic he'd believed in when he'd left Boston. As it was, he'd wasted nearly a year at the studio, marking time.

He'd ambled long enough. The time had come to sprint.

> The frustration I felt at that time is definitely what got this project off the ground *then*. I'd had good friends in Boston and I'd been successful at the pet store and I believed I was on the right path. Then I lose everything and I'm living on $400 a month. I needed to destroy. I needed to primal scream and I needed to be loud enough to make people go, "What the fuck was *that*?!" I needed to get it out. It was that tipping point where you either become a serial killer or a rock star.

Meeting the challenge would not be a chore, but a joy, he discovered. The familiar sense of accomplishment returned as he tuned his guitar and worked out a tentative smattering of melodies and lyrics. Writing in tandem with Tom as he worked to establish his own new band energized and motivated them both.

"I was jamming with different people as Rage was beginning," Tom would recall. "One day, Brad Wilk, a bass player named Noah, Maynard, and I were jamming and pairing riffs. Maynard was developing a brand-new song called 'Part of Me.'" Back and forth, the two played, creating by turns a counterpoint and a harmony of Maynard's piece and a song Tom called "Killing in the Name."

"It was pretty clear right away that the songs fit together," Maynard would explain. "We didn't actually create a song. We were just having fun." But discovering together the segues and intervals where their music meshed was encouraging, a validation that he was on the right creative track.

Adding musicians to his lineup would add levels and dimensions to the music, Maynard knew. He understood the interplay of guitar, bass, and percussion, the gestalt a solo act could never yield, and he began to look at musicians who passed through the loft and the clubs with a more discerning eye.

Over midnight breakfasts at Canter's Deli, at the picnic table at the Libertyville barbecues, in the back corner of Raji's, Adam had hinted for months that he and Maynard should collaborate. He'd heard the C.A.D. cassette, seen Maynard's Green Jellö performances, and upped his urging after Mother fizzled. But Maynard had remained resistant. "I hadn't seen what Adam was capable of," he would recall. "I knew he was a successful special-effects makeup artist at Stan Winston Studio, but I wasn't sure what he could do musically."

He'd observed Adam's slow and meticulous process in assembling Mother—slower at least than that of Maynard, who once he embarked on a project, whether an aviary or an 800-mile walk, worked obsessively to complete it to perfection. And he wasn't about to deal with the same lack of commitment he'd seen in the Grand Rapids bands. Unless his new bandmates shared his hunger to succeed, he knew the group would stay together for no more than one or two loft parties.

But Adam was persistent, and Maynard began to take his interest seriously. "It didn't matter who I got into the room," Maynard would explain. "The band would have a different vibe with the different people, so it didn't make much difference at that point who it was. Any reservation I had about working with specific people was irrelevant. I had an idea and I was going to see it through."

It was up to Maynard to communicate his vision—the pure simplicity of the arrangements, the minimalist sonic approach, the archetypes of pain and redemption underlying the lyrics, the raw emotion reflected in guitar and clashing cymbals. Once the others agreed on the parts that must be in place, individual differences would take care of themselves. "The geometry of this table we were building was very basic," Maynard explained. "It wasn't Victorian. It was four legs with a top on it, a very simple structure. If somebody was going to start doing guitar solos and noodling everywhere, this just wouldn't work."

Maynard invited Adam to jam on a basic song structure and recognized immediately his rhythm skills, his methodical pace that reflected commitment to his craft, and he had no doubt he'd lay down a firm base for his words and fury. Adam was no noodler.

Adam brought one afternoon to Danny's rehearsal space a new Stan Winston coworker, a Spokane transplant who spent his days creating special effects until his dream of working in film might come true. Paul D'Amour's skills at the pool table were matched only by his proficiency on bass. A member of a number of Washington bands that had never quite gotten off the ground, he was eager to audition for a part in any new group with even a whiff of success about it.

Maynard leaned forward when Paul began his aggressive picking, a style he immediately imagined enhancing the song he'd been working on that morning. Paul was an ideal candidate to fill in on bass, Maynard told Adam—at least until a full-time player might turn up.

Identifying a suitable percussionist was another matter altogether. The Green Jellö loft was a revolving door of artists and musicians, an ever-replenishing talent pool if one were assembling a pickup band for an impromptu show or a party—unless one needed a drummer.

"In Hollywood at that time," Bill Manspeaker would explain, "everybody wanted to be a singer or a guitar player, and that's it. Next was a bass player. But a drummer? Forget it. That was the hardest thing to find."

The drummers Maynard and Adam met failed to appear for their auditions, or if they did, couldn't grasp Maynard's plans for the band. They came through

Danny's loft—past his foosball machine and high school basketball trophies and under the inflated pterodactyl suspended from the ceiling—and never once commented on the décor. Their apathy only reinforced Maynard's fear that his venture would be a repeat of Grand Rapids. He waited for no-show after no-show, calculating Danny's rental fee while the rehearsal space sat unused.

"I felt kind of bad when their drummers weren't showing up," Danny would recall. "And I really wasn't doing anything, so I decided to play with them since my drums were already set up there."

WITH ADAM AND PAUL AND DANNY ONBOARD, Maynard breathed a sigh of relief. Their combined expertise and experience would surely get the band off the ground. With any luck at all, they'd remain interested long enough to help discover its potential, or at least its direction.

Before they'd played their first number, Maynard began to plan the practical aspects of their partnership. He assessed the venture in the same way he'd assessed a pet store layout or a video shoot.

> When I was on the high school cross country team, I'd walk or run the entire course before the race. I'd identify the hills, the pitfalls, the puddles and mud, the choke points and the opportunities. I'd make the courses my own, even though I'd never set eyes on them before. And that's what I'd do now.

He'd make sure the pieces were in place—the budget, the equipment, the devotion to a common mission—and set out with military precision the rules they must keep if they were to succeed.

Five days a week, he told them, rehearsals would begin at 11 a.m. sharp. "I wasn't going to accept any excuses," he recalled. "No 'I gotta do laundry' or 'I'm too drunk.' If I was going to do this, I didn't want to be fucking around. We were gonna do this right or we weren't gonna do it at all."

The new band would need new songs, of course, and rough melodies were there to be refined, half the lyrics, too. For years, Maynard had harbored anger and annoyance, been misunderstood, and had watched himself helplessly backslide when a goal was just within reach. If songs must be written, he had plenty of fodder.

But the lyrics must reach past the personal if they were to resonate beyond the walls of Danny's rehearsal space. "In order to write effectively, you have to write from the spot you're standing in," Maynard would explain. "You have to tap into the pure emotion of where you are, but also the broader picture, the Joseph Campbell of it all."

His collection of Campbell and Jung held a prominent spot on his bookshelf, and on the rare nights when the parking lot was quiet, he lay in his bunk and read of the characters that populated dreams and legends: kings and peasants, giants and gnomes, gods come down to earth in the guise of serpents and great birds. He'd come to recognize the Shinto priest and the African Bushman, the ancient Pima Indians and Noah and his sons as no different from the leathered punk in the mosh pit or the hipster who sulked in the shadows of English Acid. They must all in the end come to terms with love and sacrifice, death and resurrection, and great floods, actual or allegorical. The great equalizer was the story repeated across time and borders as each embarked on the same hero's journey, faced the same perils, suffered the same heartbreaks on their way to enlightenment.

The L.A. youth of 1991 might not have been threatened by fire-breathing dragons, but they had their own monsters to slay, and they hungered for stories that would resonate with their fears and anger and healing quest. "Every step of that journey is an entire story in and of itself," Maynard would explain. "Every five minutes of a life is a story if you tap into the archetype that transcends the individual and connects to everybody." And songs could do that, he knew, distill a story to its metaphorical essence, provide a useful allegory to spark understanding and a safe distance from which to work through one's dilemmas.

He knew, too, that he must exorcise the judgmental voices that echoed in his memory, voices of his third-grade teacher, the short-sighted supervisors at the pet store, old friends threatened by his Mohawk. A journey of his own through music might silence them at last.

"And I needed to yell my head off," Maynard would admit. "You can't just run down the street breaking shit."

ACCORDING TO PLAN, THE FOURSOME MET EACH MORNING in Danny's rehearsal space, windows closed against the May breezes and the traffic sounds in the street below. They wasted no time with small talk. All that mattered was the music, their chance to dig deep into their own discontent, their frustration with dead-end jobs, and their annoyance with the derelict camp on their doorstep.

Maynard envisioned the new band's sound arising at the intersection of Born Without a Face and Joni Mitchell, and used as a foundation his old C.A.D. songs. The music must depart from expected 2/4 and 4/4 time signatures, he told Adam and Paul and Danny, must break conventional boundaries, take harmonic risks on the way to revealing the band's style.

On a typical morning, Danny might improvise a groove while Adam and Paul jammed a free-form interpretation. Then they picked up the pace, infused the melody with a sudden brutality and then a balancing vulnerability, until the song culminated at last in the solid rhythms that formed the framework for Maynard's spare lyrics.

"I felt the band was something special from the very first time the four of us played together," Danny would recall. "The hair on my arms was standing on end. It had a power I could feel instantly, the flame of those guys. I told them I wouldn't charge them rent anymore and that I would play. I'd do this for myself because I loved playing that kind of music."

Within the parameters Maynard insisted upon, the group nonetheless discovered freedom, a creative leeway to experiment at will within the messy disorder of half-memorized guitar riffs and in-progress verses in a true punk atmosphere of egoless collaboration.

Not that individuality was compromised for the sake of the collective. Quite the opposite. The band members not only respected their own strengths, but, attuned to each other's every nuance, drew instinctively from the collective energy to complete fully formed songs sometimes in as little as a day, a week at the most. "Everybody was really open about letting an idea go and just be drawn and quartered and turned into something else," Danny remembered. "It was a healthy process and really inspiring because the possibilities were endless."

The members of C.A.D. had never quite understood Maynard's vision, his emphasis on trimming the music to a sonic minimum. But Danny and the others seemed to intuitively grasp the concept. Maynard played for Paul the *da-da, ch, da-da* riff that opened "Burn About Out," the C.A.D. song Chris Ewald had urged him to pursue. Paul spontaneously broke in with a funky wave of sound that buoyed Maynard's lyrics just as he'd always imagined. Then Danny fell upon his drums at the precise interval where Maynard had felt the need for deep bass. He created reverberation that shattered the song into a cubist version of the original, a slowed, chunky rendition that reduced it to its primal simplicity.

And Maynard added the most primal sound of all, the deep, throaty scream, the sustained cadence of birth and new beginnings.

> We were four people listening to each other and making songs that were based on the *songs*, not on a hat. It wasn't like, "Chili Peppers and Nirvana are popular now, so let's wear flannels and funny Cat in the Hat hats." How about no flannels, no Cat in the Hat hats?
>
> Get rid of all the fluff, don't worry about all that shit. Focus on the point of the story and the sounds and energy that drive it home. The primal scream was the key to making it sound sincere.
>
> This thing needed to punch you in the face, back up, extend a hand to hug you, and then punch you in the face again.

"It did have a different sound," Danny said of the band's music. "I just didn't think it would ever have any commercial possibilities."

ONE LAST PIECE OF THE PUZZLE REMAINED, one final detail to bring the concept to reality. The band needed a name.

It must be catchy, brand-new, not in the least derivative or gimmicky, an intriguing name that suggested a backstory, a name they could live with for a long time should the band actually succeed.

While they riffed and jammed and jotted down lyrics, one of the four might spontaneously shout out a word or a phrase, a potential candidate dismissed often as quickly as it was proposed. Nothing seemed to quite hit the mark, until one or another of them flippantly suggested a word that silenced the guitars and cymbals.

"Toolshed" seemed entirely fitting, a name that brought to mind the shadowy outbuilding where a menacing uncle might bring a young charge for a beating—or worse. It implied the mystery and terror of the themes that wove through the emerging songs, the recurring motifs of violence and outright horror, the pain and tears necessary for healing to begin.

Less was more when it came to a name, Maynard knew. His merchandising work at Boston Pet had taught him that much. Paring the name would lend space where multiple meanings might arise. Lop it in half and the word could mean whatever one wished: the right gizmo for the job or a blind and unquestioning follower. It might evoke the image of an implement digging deep to touch a nerve or a midnight spin down Sunset Boulevard in a Corvette ragtop. And if the name was a double entendre, it couldn't hurt.

Maynard spoke the word aloud, whispered it, sketched it in his notepad. It was a fine name for a band, they all agreed, a name with pleasing mouth feel and eye appeal, its elongated open vowels bounded by sturdy consonants. A one-syllable name that left room for interpretation. A hard-to-forget name. A solid name. Tool.

"GREEN JELLÖ JUST GOT SIGNED," Manspeaker would recall. "Of course we've got to have a party." And of course Tool would perform.

If past parties at the loft were any indication, this one was sure to be an event, complete with revelers spilling to the roof deck and the parking lot and sure to annoy the neighbors who operated the design firm on the other side of the common wall.

Musicians and writers and aspiring painters descended upon the squat white building on Hollywood Boulevard that mild June evening, toting Heineken and Corona and SunChips and sidestepping the vagrants who'd begun to assemble outside Regal Liquors. They climbed to the loft, where they joined Adam's coworkers and the Libertyville crowd, friends of friends of friends, and Green Jellö pigs in their offstage blacks and leather. Tom Morello arrived, and tattooed young punksters befriended at Raji's and Club with No Name, and Kevin Coogan, who'd introduced Manspeaker to Zoo Entertainment.

One corner had been cleared of foam and discarded department store mannequins in various stages of dismemberment—raw materials for Green Jellö costumes—to make room for Danny's drum kit and a portable amp. Nearly a hundred guests crowded the loft, curious to learn just what this new band might offer.

At last, Maynard and Danny and Adam and Paul set down their drinks and took their places. It had been a long time since C.A.D.'s Top of the Rock show, a long time since Maynard had performed his own music. Adam took up his

Gibson Silverburst and Paul his Rickenbacker, and from the moment Danny began his staccato intro, Maynard's old confidence returned, and with it the surge of all that had brought him to this place.

He sang of the heady intoxication of dreams come true and the inevitable letdown, the urgency to begin again in the face of naysayers who dared dictate his thoughts and words. His words were his own now, his band's, and he sang.

The guests looked from one to the other, astonished by Maynard's sure, even voice, his control, the athletic contortions and menacing crouch that punctuated his guttural, sustained scream. Tool's music rose in a swell of offbeat tempos, then ebbed in quiet minimalism and mounted again, Danny's drumsticks a furious blur and Adam's powerful chords and chiming arpeggios echoing from the high ceiling until the plush Fred and Barney dolls suspended from the exposed beams vibrated.

The sudden clamor brought partiers down from roof. They listened, transfixed, to Maynard's lyrics of fear and sacrifice, shadows and empty promises and threats of violence—lyrics they suspected were about more than they seemed, as if their own fears were shouted beneath the canopy of twinkling white lights strung among the rafters.

It DIDN'T TAKE LONG for a report of the event to reach the other side of the continent. The next morning, Tom phoned Jack Olsen, who'd moved not long before to Connecticut. More than two decades later, Jack remembered well the note of wonder in his friend's voice. "Tom was shaken by the performance," he would recall. "What I heard was the expression 'fully formed from the head of Zeus.'" They'd shared hot dogs with Maynard and Adam at many a Libertyville barbecue, battled them in countless midnight bowling tournaments, but they'd seen no sign of the creative fury Tool had displayed the night before. "Adam and Maynard were two people who could not have been, it seemed, further from the world of rock," Jack would recall. "Adam was the special effects makeup guy and Maynard—Maynard was something we couldn't quite put our finger on."

But on that night in the loft, Maynard and Adam, and Paul and Danny too, had come together in a force that belied their placid demeanors, a force larger and more complex than its individual parts. Tool's debut performance had been a collective release of sound and emotion, a wave of contagious energy that swept the party guests in words and rhythms, driving and terrifying and familiar and continuing relentlessly into the morning.

Just before dawn, guests made their way down the narrow staircase to the street, calling over their shoulders approval and congratulations and a request that Tool entertain at a private party at the Central later that month.

"I've never been more surprised in my life," Tom would recall. "Tool was awesome from day one. It was unbelievable."

"There was Maynard, this kind of quiet dude, and all of a sudden, he's loud and he's singing these angry songs," Bill Manspeaker remembered of the loft performance. "This crazy guy with long hair screaming about shooting people in the fuckin' head."

Manspeaker had seen the video of C.A.D.'s 1987 cable television appearance, had noted Maynard's dramatic gestures, his strutting and head tossing and motions choreographed to mimic those of the idealized rock star. "You can see the musician in him, but he's playing the musician role," he would recall. "They're all trying so hard in that video. Then he joins Green Jellö and we're telling him, 'Don't try hard at all. Just be goofy. Be yourself. Be what you want to be, man.'" Brief as it had been, Maynard's stint with Manspeaker's band had freed him to relax into an organic interpretation of sound and words and message.

"The first loft party was the decision point," Maynard would explain. "I could be the actor in Green Jellö and play a part. I could keep doing this thing that was completely awesome chaos, or I could follow this opportunity to actually express my own ideas. Green Jellö was fun, but it would always be Bill's thing, and I would just be a performer in the circus."

THE CENTRAL ON SUNSET was acrid with the lingering aroma of stale beer and cigarettes. Danny struggled to fit his drum set on the shallow stage that ran along one wall, and the others crowded in beside him. The hundred or so birthday party guests hadn't come to hear the band. They were there for the free-flowing drafts, to fête the guest of honor, to socialize as best they could above guitar and percussion and lyrics of right and wrong and the wish to sleep forever.

Tool was still rough around the edges, but its power was undeniable, its sound too surprising, too full and heavy and insistent to ignore. "We just made their ears bleed," Maynard would recall.

Word of the performance reached the bookers at the Gaslight, the cave-dark club behind the Ivar Theatre where Maynard and Tom had not long before seen Dead, White and Blue and Liquid Jesus. Turnout was slight, not surprising at an early-evening performance by a brand-new group. But Tool took the stage like seasoned professionals, holding back nothing and executing the songs with the same forceful confidence they'd displayed at the loft and the Central. A few patrons looked up from their Budweisers, surprised to recognize the vocalist as the hot-dog shooter from English Acid. And the next day, they told their friends about the show.

Not a day went by that a musician on some L.A. street corner didn't hastily press a leaflet into Maynard's hand, a slip of paper he misplaced or tossed just as quickly. The quarter-page notices were covered to their edges with poorly reproduced photographs and amateurish cartoons, crazy quilts of myriad type-faces competing for attention on a maize or purple background.

But Tool's flyers were simple and elegant, the message understated. At the center of full-size crimson or snow-white sheets, Maynard placed one inch-wide, ink-black word: *Tool*. Across the bottom, in sharp, clear lettering, he listed the date, location, and cost of admission.

> People would complain and tell me I was wasting paper. I would show them the other flyers and ask what they were all about. Of course, they didn't know, because there was too much noise on the page for them to remember any of it. But ours sunk in.
>
> I was handing out flyers one day and Donita Sparks from L7 and her bass player Jennifer Finch came out of one of the clubs. I believe it was English Acid. They both took a flyer and went, "This is genius!" They were like, "Oh, dude, look at what you just did! This is awesome!" I was really into that band's fury. They were like the Ramones to me. It was great to be validated by them, of all the people I saw that day.

Within weeks, Tool had five shows under its belt, shows that drew ever-larger audiences to the L.A. dive bars that still booked unknown acts. A half-dozen devoted punkettes had appointed themselves the band's first groupies and faithfully followed Tool from the Gaslight to Raji's to Club Lingerie to Al's Bar downtown. "It was a surprise, I'm sure to all of us," Danny would say of the band's sudden popularity. "We had so many musician friends trying to make it, but we knew we had something really special. I didn't even care if we made it or not."

MAYNARD AND THE OTHERS KNEW it wasn't exactly time to quit their day jobs. Bookings were sporadic, and more often than not last-minute. They might be called to perform on a weeknight after a long day's work, but they schlepped their gear across town to take the unenviable first or second spot in the evening's lineup of six bands, a spot that paid nothing. Club owners believed exposure was compensation enough, that a draft on the house was sufficient exchange for 20 minutes on the stage.

Printing T-shirts and more flyers would cost money, money the band members did not have. But Maynard had been through this before and knew renting time in a studio wouldn't be necessary. In late August, the band invited Adam's friend Steve Hansgen to join them at the loft with his Fostex four-track to record the songs they'd completed only two months before. Steve, a bass player with punk band Minor Threat, invited the group to sit in while he put the finishing touches on the tape in his home studio in North Hollywood.

> It was one of those moments when you fall in love with a house. Oh my God. I had no idea there was something like this in L.A. It was a real home. It had a backyard and a front yard with a big tree in it. It looked like a gingerbread house. I felt almost excited enough to go look for the oven.

Adam sketched a striking logo to illustrate the glossy black J-card, a combination open-end and double box wrench that suggested strength and authority. His design displayed a certain salty innuendo as well, a hint of humor to balance the intensity of the six tracks on the self-titled cassette.

Business was business, Maynard insisted. There would be no freebies, even for those claiming to be record company reps. "If they wanted to be a part of what we were doing, they could pony up their six bucks and go listen to the tape," he would explain. "I didn't need their record deal. I just needed to be up here doing this." The goal of most new bands was the record contract, the golden prize at the end of the dive bar tunnel. Maynard had watched too many of them hand out demo tapes like candy tossed from a float in an Independence Day parade, hoping against hope their work would fall into the hands of an eager A&R rep.

"Their priorities were way out of line," he remembered. "The most important thing was to focus on the music. Make sure all the pieces are in place, do things properly and for the right reasons, and don't get sidetracked."

The A&R reps who prowled the clubs were indeed searching for the next Nirvana, the next REM, the next band that would bring to their label fortune and acclaim. But identifying the next big thing before it quite existed was a challenge, given that they weren't exactly sure what sound or message or even genre they were looking for. Of one thing they were certain: The band that would justify their investment would be the one that excited the public.

By early September, there was no doubt about it: The public's enthusiasm was centered on Tool. When Maynard and Danny and Adam and Paul appeared on the bill, the little clubs were packed.

Tool was the band that delivered exactly what they'd come for: furious aggression tempered by subtle humor, ambiguous lyrics that demanded attention, solid musicianship, and the shock of unexpected tempo. And a wiry, manic frontman with a piercing scream and an unrelenting stare he fixed on the middle of the captivated crowd.

The clubs Tool played that summer weren't the glittering, sold-out arenas rock star dreams are made of. They were cramped and dark, and their kinked mic cables were mended with fraying gaffer tape. A patina of grime covered the mismatched chairs and unsteady tables, and in some, like the Gaslight, water seeped onto the stage from the men's room upstairs. Taking a slot on their schedule was a rite of passage as aspiring bands ascended in the L.A. music hierarchy. "If you went on at 6 o'clock, you're a fuckin' loser," Bill Manspeaker would explain. "If you went on at 11, that means you're kickin' ass and soon you're gonna be playing on the Strip. Bands that weren't good enough yet played at places like the Coconut Teaszer, the clubs just at the edge of cool."

> A wrestler has to bring his best game onto the mat. You can't worry about whether your opponent is in tip-top condition and you can't worry about whether the audience is all open-minded and ready to like what you're doing. It doesn't matter if it's a shallow stage, whether there's two people or 200 in the audience, or if there's pee coming down on your head. You have to adapt, to morph to the space and command it.

Lou Maglia rarely ventured into the clubs. He left it to his reps to endure the stale cigarette smell and beer-sticky floors in their search for promising new talent. But in early September, he'd decided to join them at Gazzarri's, a fixture on L.A.'s waning hair metal circuit. That evening, the club would host Dumpster, the hottest band on Zoo Entertainment's radar, and Maglia welcomed the chance to see for himself what the underground favorite might bring to his label.

Kevin Coogan and his A&R colleagues Anna Loynes and Matt Marshall looked forward to the performance as well, but admittedly with an ulterior motive. Dumpster's show would end in plenty of time for them to reach the nearby Coconut Teaszer and Tool's 10 o'clock performance there. Kevin had told his coworkers all about the loft party, and when he'd played Tool's demo tape for Anna and Matt, they'd agreed that the band was destined for success. And they were determined that the label to represent them would be theirs.

But they played their plan by ear. "As good as Tool was, I was a bit nervous to have the president see them after seeing Dumpster," Matt would recall. "We figured if they killed it, it might not be the best night for him to see Tool."

The night, in fact, was not one of Dumpster's best. The band was unfamiliar with the club, and the early showtime drew a sparse audience. To make matters worse, only a few seconds into the opening number, drummer Kellii Scott came down hard on his pedal, plunging the beater squarely into his kick drum head. The group soldiered on as best it could until vocalist Robert English leaned into his mic and announced that their set was over. "After one song, they left the stage," Matt would recall. "It was absolutely crazy!"

Their evening needn't end, Maglia's team assured him. A new band was playing just down the street, a band featuring Danny Carey of Green Jellö. "I wasn't excited," Maglia admitted in a 2014 interview. "But the night was young, and it was over as far as Dumpster went, so I said, 'Yeah, let's go down there and see what's going on.'" And they made their way through the yellow L.A. twilight to the Coconut Teaszer, the club at the eastern end of Sunset, the point where the cool began.

A SMALL BUT ENTHUSIASTIC GROUP OF TOOL FOLLOWERS stood in a semicircle before the stage, the half-dozen young women who'd trailed them from club to club all summer long. Adam and Paul began their guitar intro and Maynard grasped his mic, crouched, and glared menacingly about the room. The stage burst in rush of raw energy, in Maynard's dark lyrics, his strut across the stage, his scream suspended in the smoky dark.

"All I could think was that Maynard was a musical Charles Manson," Maglia remembered. "He was frightening. He didn't have a shirt on and he had a big scorpion tattoo from his neck to his ass. When he sang, he tucked in his stomach like he was gonna throw himself up from inside himself."

The band had been forewarned of Maglia's possible presence, but they performed that night no differently than they did in rehearsal or a show on a too-small, urine-soaked stage. They dominated the space, made it their own, poured their passion and their fear and their need into every nuance, every anguished note. "That's what we did every night," Maynard explained.

It was Maglia's job to imagine. The Coconut Teaszer was just the Coconut Teaszer, the Hollywood night a night like any other, but he visualized the band in larger venues, bright venues with state-of-the-art sound systems and colored spots following Maynard's contortions across the stage, and his vision was already in the present tense. "My first thought was, Yeah, he's great in a club. He's very impressive when you're standing five feet away from him, but what about in a stadium?" he would recall. "Can he scare the shit out of people like he's scaring the shit out of me here?"

After the show, Maglia turned to make his way to his home in Beverly Hills, but not before leaving Anna with instructions—classic Hollywood instructions. "Tell them to come to my office tomorrow," he said.

MAGLIA SMILED ACROSS HIS WIDE DESK. Zoo Entertainment, he assured Maynard and Danny and Adam and Paul, would offer what other labels would not.

Should they decide to sign with him—and he sincerely hoped they'd decide to sign with him—they'd enjoy creative control over their work, and because his was a small independent label, they could always speak directly with him, free of the corporate chain of command. To be sure, he warned, they'd soon be targeted by other labels now that Zoo was interested.

He alerted them of the tantalizing tactics the reps would employ to divert attention from the risks: the dazzling future they'd offer, the Nova Scotia lobsters, the $400 bottles of wine. And after the band had heard it all, he promised, he'd be there waiting when they were ready to talk again.

Indeed, once word of Zoo's interest in Tool hit the street, ponytailed reps from Sony and Mercury, from Atlantic, Interscope, and Epic descended upon the group and pressed embossed business cards into their hands. They arranged lunch meetings at Sushi Nozawa, dinners at Marino Ristorante and the Palm, where they discussed funding and promotion and painted a future of spotlit arenas filled to capacity and slots on the *Billboard* 200 chart.

> It was exciting, but I was wary. I'd heard enough Hollywood horror stories, and I was very cautious. I immediately started looking for the escape route in case somebody tried to fuck me up. If I'm gonna run this cross country course, how do I know I can finish without them putting up construction halfway through? I needed to ask the right questions to find out how they might trip me up and interrupt the job I needed to do.

Certainly, filet mignon was seductive fare after months of ramen noodles and takeout from the Thai restaurant across the street. But the spellbinding haze cast by the A&R reps was no match for Maynard's long practice in remaining clearheaded in the face of empty rhetoric. He'd learned a long time ago the importance of thinking for himself, and as the sommelier brought another bottle of '89 Montrachet Laguiche to the table, he sat back on the upholstered banquette and offered his goblet. "I got a glimpse of what power was and how quickly it could be abused," Maynard would remember of the labels' over-the-top courtship rituals. "So you play with it. If you can pretend they're wearing bunny ears while you're eating their expensive food, it's the most exciting time in your life."

Ahead lay contract negotiations, discussions of album art and liner notes, foreign rights and royalties, a journey a band might be lucky to embark upon after months and years of performance and practice, but one he and Danny and Adam and Paul were beginning after only seven shows in second-rate clubs.

ONE AFTERNOON IN LATE AUTUMN, Maynard came home to a message from yet another bubbly club manager offering yet another unpaid gig. Tool should come play third in a six-band lineup, she urged. Danny would use the club's drum kit, of course, but the engagement would give them great exposure, great experience, and drinks on the house.

"I called her back," Maynard recalled. "I told her, 'Here's the deal. We'll play next to last on our own drum kit. And you'll pay us a hundred bucks. She snapped back, 'Who do you think you are?'"

"So I said, 'I'm the guy you're going to call back very soon when you realize that *you* need *us*.'"

And after discussions of branding and percentages, options and advances and exclusivity clauses, after luncheons rolled in on white-linened carts by white-linened chefs, the band came back to Maglia. Of the many label execs they'd met, he was the one who best understood Tool's message and methods, the importance of its creative integrity. "I'm not asking you to give me a budget for each video," he told them. "I'm asking you to do videos the way you want to do them, and I'll pay for it."

"I felt like the things I'd done all my life were finally leading up to something," Maynard remembered. "This was my chance to do it right. You can't keep building two-legged tables and bitch about them not standing up."

Working with the independent subsidiary of BMG would offer them nearly the same freedoms as if they'd remained independent themselves, the group realized. And, Maglia assured them, Zoo's energies and budget would be directed toward what mattered the most: live performances. "Not everybody said that," Maynard would remember. "What we heard from most of the labels was basically, 'We're a big machine and we can force you down peoples' throats.'"

Together, Maglia assured the band, they could surely create an artistically satisfying and financially sound agreement.

"It was very much a democratic process," Danny remembered of the negotiations. "At every meeting, all four of us fought tooth and nail for ourselves, kind of like musketeers, which was really a good thing for all of us."

Tool had formed out of curmudgeonly frustration, had burst with little preparation on the city's club scene, had unquestioningly responded to Maglia's request to meet with them. Signing with his label after only seven performances would be one more act of faith. "There's a sense that all this just fell into place," Maynard would explain. "But most of it was just dumb luck and trust. You step over the edge into darkness. The bliss finds you."

ON THE DAY BEFORE THANKSGIVING 1991, THE AGREEMENT WAS FINALIZED, an unusual deal considering that Tool hadn't yet recorded an album. Zoo would produce an enhanced release of the band's demo cassette, a six-song EP, and later, a full album, and, true to Maglia's promise, would provide greater-than-average tour support. The agreement granted the band creative control and provided for an advance to cover expenses and equipment until royalties began rolling in. "Tool was the only band I ever signed that had my complete trust and support whenever they needed it," Maglia would recall.

The deal included one more provision, a clause that wasn't set forth in the contract but one the band members considered as important as all the others. Maynard and Danny and Adam and Paul were committed to pastimes and passions discovered long before they'd come together as Tool, and they were determined their private lives would remain just that. Whatever demands and responsibilities they'd just signed on for, they promised one another, books and barbecues, magic and mythology, friends and family and finches would come first.

> I didn't want to be an animal on display. I needed to find a brake pedal to slow down elements of this opportunity and figure out how to emotionally process it. What was all this extra attention going to do to me? What would it do to my body—my emotional body, my spiritual body, my mental body, my physical body? I had goals, and being famous wasn't one of them.

The paperwork signed, Maynard and Danny and Adam and Paul stepped from the Zoo Entertainment office into a city that seemed spread about them like a stage set for a performance all their own.

Their first stop was the Palace, the vast art deco establishment on Vine already filled with a club crowd eager to begin the long Thanksgiving weekend. "We went in like we were hotshots, like we're a big deal," Maynard recalled. "And we proceeded to get extremely drunk." They roamed the main floor and the balcony, their shouts ringing loud above the music. A band could celebrate its first signing only once, they rationalized, and celebrate they would, until, in an access of exuberance, an upended tray of shot glasses shattered in bright shards under the spotlights and the bouncers requested they move their revels elsewhere.

They joined the crush of hipsters at the Frolic Room just around the corner, the narrow, dim dive bar where they fed the jukebox and sang along from their red swivel stools, ignoring their rising bar tab until the ceiling lamps flashed, signaling closing time.

They stumbled to the sidewalk, their stagger a disjointed victory dance up the boulevard to Regal Liquors and the cooler at the rear of the store. "We came back to the loft hooting and hollering," Maynard recalled. "We were out of our minds and just *free*." They drained their Coors and pelted the empties about the parking lot until their shrieks and laughter and clattering brought the neighbors to their window with the promise of a visit from the LAPD.

They scattered into the Hollywood night, Danny to his loft, Paul to his apartment, and Maynard, Adam, and Manspeaker to a nearby cab and its reluctant driver. Adam's apartment in the Valley would be safe enough haven until the fracas blew over.

> We could have had integrity and been nice, but we chose to be dickheads because we were young and we were suddenly empowered. We were flexing. And everything you grow up seeing, you assume that that's how a rock band is supposed to act.
>
> There's no excuse for any kind of violence. I just don't do that. Our actions weren't directed at anybody in particular. But we'd been so beaten down, and finally there was light.

In the morning, they searched in hungover stupor for a market open for business and returned to Adam's apartment with strong coffee and one of the last Butterballs to be found in the city.

And Maynard and Adam and Manspeaker—newly signed performers with every reason to enjoy their holiday in style—passed a cold and windy Thanksgiving Day searching cupboards for a pot big enough to hold the bird and for ingredients of a passable turkey soup. "Adam had failed to mention that his oven didn't work," Maynard remembered. "It was a dreadful fucking day."

NEWS OF TOOL'S RECORDING DEAL elevated the band's status almost overnight. Club managers who only weeks before had relegated the band to 6 o'clock shows called to offer choice spots in their New Year's lineups. And Maynard's demands that had seemed baseless hubris a month before were now perfectly justified. Tool would headline, he told the bookers. The band would use its own gear, and their rate was now $500, more-than-fair remuneration for a group surely destined for stardom.

Sensible as his requests were, Maynard didn't mind when they were refused. Tool had New Year's Eve plans of its own.

Weary of Manspeaker's blowouts, the neighbors had at last relinquished their lease. Their departure meant an expansive addition to the Green Jellö space. Maynard and Manspeaker brought out hammers and saws and opened the common wall to create a home theater complete with projection room and doubling the space for parties.

On New Year's Eve, the loft was packed as any club on Sunset. Punksters and rockers arrived, and actors and artists and curious passersby were drawn up the narrow stairway by the music that blared down into the street. Quantities of schnapps and Corona and Kahlúa glimmered beneath the colored lights strung from the rafters, and a mobile sound truck was parked in the lot to record the night's performances.

The Green Jellö troupe reprised its little-pig antics, and then Tool took up its guitars and drumsticks and mics and filled the new space with driving lyrics of fury and fear, right and wrong, sacrifice and shadow and pain.

Maynard's scream rose that night with new intensity, a deeper sincerity born of elation and triumph. His was a cry of retaliation for a lifetime of misunderstanding—a wall of defiance against hurdles that might lie ahead. And his strong, sure song continued into the first gray dawn of the New Year.

M aynard's announcement of the recording deal came as a surprise to old friends who'd only sporadically received news of his L.A. adventures. "Sometimes a long time would pass, but we wrote letters and talked," Kendall instructor Deb Rockman would remember. "He would call late at night and we'd be on the phone for a couple of hours. Sometimes, we wouldn't even talk. He'd play music and I'd listen. Then the next thing I knew, he was making it big with Tool."

But those who knew the full story recognized that his was no overnight success. "Everyone in the band had paid their dues in multiple disciplines," Matt Marshall explained. "Therein lies part of who Maynard is and what Tool is. They took all their influences and molded the music into something completely unique. By the time they got together, they were just instantaneously better than almost anybody."

Maynard may have seen his destiny long before had he paid closer attention to the cups and wands and empresses the tarot readers had fanned across their tables.

> I hadn't realized the readers might have been talking about singing. They'd always used the words *voice* and *presentation*, and I thought they were talking in a metaphorical sense. I thought pet stores and sets were the stages they were speaking of. I'd never considered that they meant *band* and *music* the whole time.

NINETEEN NINETY-TWO WOULD BE A TIME OF BEGINNINGS—and of letting go. The tedious and ill-paying art-dog days were behind him, and little Harpo had lived out his good long zebra finch life. It was time, Maynard knew, to step from the familiar path and open himself to this new course, and, his other birds and iguanas and fish in the safe care of his loft mates, he was free to discover where it might lead.

Zoo's marketing strategy had included a professional pressing of the Tool demo and given it a tongue-in-cheek label number—72826, digits Maynard chose to correspond with the letters S-A-T-A-N on the telephone keypad. Matt and his colleagues had sent cassettes to bands whose style and message complemented Tool's, and by spring, they were performing up and down the California coast, opening for the fusion-punk Fishbone and heavy metal Corrosion of Conformity in clubs renowned as testing grounds for the most promising of new groups.

Tom Morello's band was now ready to perform publically as well. Rage Against the Machine had followed a track parallel to Tool's all winter long, and its music had become a solid blend of punk and hip-hop, a sonic rant in opposition to corporate greed and government oppression.

Opening for Tool was a fitting debut, a continuation of the creative alliance begun months before. The riffs they'd explored had at last found their proper places in Rage's "Killing in the Name" and Tool's "Part of Me," and their pairing on Jabberjaw's stage only strengthened Maynard and Tom's faith in the other's talents. "There was a healthy competition between the two bands," Morello said. "We really sharpened each others' knives early on."

Just as Lou Maglia had imagined, Tool's shows created the hoped-for groundswell of interest. Audiences were captivated by Maynard's hunched creep to the edge of the stage, his curious Mulhawk, his penetrating gaze, his confrontational delivery.

Early reviewers were at a loss when it came to categorizing the band's music, calling it everything from grunge to metal to alt, but the audience didn't trouble itself with labels. Tool's was music that mattered, whatever its genre. After more than a decade of conservative politics, conformity, and complacency in the face of oppressive dogma, they were primed for change, and they found their anthems of rebellion in the countercultural songs of Smashing Pumpkins and Dumpster, Dead, White and Blue—and Tool, whose harmonic complexities and multidimensional lyrics set it apart from the rest.

> Our songs were telling people to wake up, stop living in hypocrisy, be true
> to themselves, but that message had to be tempered. There's an element
> of humor in all the songs. A friend might say something really funny, and
> we'd include a verse based on what they'd said. Satire helps push through
> heartfelt emotions and serious issues. That's how you punch the big ideas
> through.

EVER SINCE HE'D SPECIAL-ORDERED FROM SOUNDS GOOD the Pretenders' 1981 *Extended Play* album, Maynard had understood the power of the EP, the reverse chew-bone pickup, the tease to whet audience appetite for high-ticket albums and concerts. Recorded at Sound City and released in March 1992, Tool's EP, *Opiate*, would bring to the band widespread attention, he was sure. Better yet, touring with a nationally known act would be the first step in building a coast-to-coast fan base.

If ever a group complemented Tool's raw sound and message of noncon-formity, it was Rollins Band. Its *End of Silence* tour had begun that spring, and thanks to Zoo's efforts, its opening band would be an ideal match. Selections from *Opiate* would provide a fitting counterpart to the themes of integrity and self-reflection, Tool's sound a perfect pairing with Henry Rollins's forceful an-ger and the fury of Andrew Weiss's bass and Sim Cain's percussion.

Three months on the road with Rollins Band would give Maynard the chance to observe in action the man whose musicianship and work ethic he'd long admired and to learn from seasoned musicians the ins and outs of touring. "Andrew Weiss gave me great advice," Maynard would recall. "He helped me understand that the working man is what makes this shit happen. He told me, 'We're just these rock dudes who show up late and leave early, but it's the crew who really gets things done. Treat them well. Respect the guys who actually do the work.'"

Their Atlanta stop included a rare evening of freedom before their gig at the Cotton Club. After investigating the many bars along Peachtree Street, the band members stepped into the mild springtime evening, and the conversation turned to the dedication necessary to excel amid fierce competition. Maynard shared with Cain his memory of Black Flag's 1986 Grand Rapids show and the lasting influence of its opening band. He couldn't quite recall the group's name, but the energy and passion they'd displayed even before the embarrassingly sparse audience had been a glimpse into a world of professionalism he'd dreamed even then of inhabiting.

> I get uncomfortable when people give me weird accolades. So I had no intention of boring Henry with the story of this thing I had once witnessed. But I felt comfortable talking to Sim, because he loved music so much.
>
> I told him about this amazing show I'd seen years ago and how it had just blown me away. My heart was racing after the show, I told him, and it impressed me so much that it basically shaped the way I approached my performance with Tool. I'd learned that night that if you're professional, if you *mean* it, it doesn't matter if there's five people in the audience or 500,000, they'll feel it. That honesty translates.
>
> And Sim said, "That was me. That was me and Andrew Weiss in Gone. You just described our performance in Grand Rapids."

MAYNARD SOON CAME TO UNDERSTAND the rhythm of the road, the daily routine of packing the Ryder truck, the club parking lots often the only glimpse of the city he would see. He mastered the fine art of unrolling his futon over the equipment cases in the back of the truck and napping a bouncy nap before the next show.

The monotony of the highway was tolerable, he learned, if he took comedian Bill Hicks's advice and embraced the journey. En route to Omaha and Austin and Providence, Hicks's cassettes were in frequent rotation in the tape deck, his satirical monologues an echo of Maynard's impatience with mediocrity and apathy—and belief in redemption.

> Behind all the dark humor, Bill was talking about the same things I'd read in Joseph Campbell. If you look at things, really look, if you lift the veil, you start to recognize that light is love, is infinite, is unconditional. Bill was saying that once you understand the nature of nature, you can let go of difficulties and sign on for the ride—knowing that it's just a ride.

And Maynard grew familiar with the Holiday Inns that replicated themselves across the landscape and the occasional Motel 6 on the outskirts of town. In city after city, he walked from stage doors all alike, crossed yet another parking lot, and watched the last of the club-goers depart into the night, leaving him at the other side of the low fence, alone in the darkness.

FAMILIAR FACES ALONG THE TOUR ROUTE balanced the anonymity of weeks on the road: Kathy Larsen at New York's CBGB, Ramiro at Bogart's in Cincinnati, and at Tool's one-off show at the Reptile House in Grand Rapids, DJ Steve Aldrich.

Art students and alt rock aficionados wedged into the club on Division to experience the garage punk of Michigan's own Soiled Betty. Then the headliner took the stage, and the space vibrated in a fury of tempestuous rage, in the complex rhythmic force that was Tool.

"The Reptile House wasn't ever supposed to be a live venue. It was supposed to be a dance bar," Aldrich would explain. "The building was all hard surfaces, tile and concrete. Shows normally sounded like crap in there. But when Tool played, it was just like they'd put the CD on. It sounded incredible."

Aldrich recognized in the music familiar echoes. Tool's atypical time signatures, its subtle nuances, its hint of Swans minimalism blended in a mature rendering of the C.A.D. tracks he'd featured on his *Clambake* radio program. And Tool seemed to him the fulfillment of the band abandoned for lack of a suitable vocalist, the realization of the sonic space and experimental chords he and Maynard and Chris Ewald had explored years before. "As soon as I heard Tool, I thought, 'This is the final version of what was supposed to happen a long time ago,'" he said.

And in Boston, Lansdowne Street was just as Maynard remembered. Most of the crowd had come to Axis to hear Rollins, but a steadfast half-dozen were there for Maynard: friends from the North End Thanksgiving table, and Kjiirt, who'd loyally flown from Seattle to back his buddy at the club they'd so often visited together.

When Tool took the stage, the crowd responded as if it were the headliner. They filled the dance floor and moved in time to the music, leaned forward and strained to decipher Maynard's every word, and not a few women shouted suggestive invitations from the mosh pit—the very women perhaps who'd not long before ignored the advances of a lonely pet store merchandising manager.

A lone manic mosher thrashed convulsively through the pit, hurling himself against the others, oblivious to their angry glares. "He was a big dickhead punk," Kjiirt would recall. "It was totally uncool. If he was going to roughhouse during the show, he had to go, but nobody on the staff was noticing. Finally, he ran into me and I grabbed him and pushed him away as hard as I could." The commotion brought the security crew at last from the shadows, a pair of stern bouncers who reached for Kjiirt's arm.

Despite the spotlights shining into his eyes, despite his concentration on the job at hand, despite his inability to tell one slammer from another in the dark pit, something caught Maynard's glance. Perhaps it was the flash of Kjiirt's white Tool-logo T-shirt. Perhaps it was his blond hair distinct in the darkness. Perhaps it was synchronicity or chance or coincidence, but he looked out into the crowd and saw his friend.

Maynard stopped singing. He stepped to the edge of the stage and raised one arm. The guitars fell silent, Danny's drumsticks were still. The crowd was quiet, too, disoriented by the sudden shift in energy. Maynard pointed toward Kjiirt and spoke, his voice steady, firm. "He stays."

Then he stepped back, and the music resumed as abruptly as it had ended. Danny and Adam and Paul picked up the beat and Maynard's cry rose on key. The troublemaker was led to the door, and Kjiirt joined the crowd as it closed in a swaying semicircle before the stage, the driving rhythms drawing them deeper into the mystery of what this group might be all about.

Maynard's 1993 Day-Timer showed few breaks in an itinerary that would take the band three times across the Atlantic and to no fewer than 29 cities on the summer's Lollapalooza circuit.

> You wake up and you know you're on the road, but you don't know where you are. It wasn't like I was drunk the night before and woke up and couldn't remember anything. But you had to remind yourself what's happening today and where you were yesterday. There were so many people profiting from our being on the road that half the time, you didn't have any control of where you were going or when.

A month in Europe early in the year included stops in Paris and Copenhagen,

Zurich and London in a performance schedule that left no time for sightseeing. Given the minuscule per diem, even cab fare for a quick jaunt from their hotel to a castle or a museum was out of the question. A day off meant an excursion no more exotic than a walk to a nearby pizzeria, where Maynard and his bandmates pooled their kroner and weighed a life on the road against its all but invisible rewards.

> I'm hoping that I'm not out here for nothing. You're looking for acceptance in whatever form it might take, whether it's a young German lady smiling at you, or some guy who's excited because a song blew his mind, or an older dude who came to the show with his younger brother. You didn't expect he'd like this music, but somehow it resonated with him. You're looking for any sign that you're doing something right.
>
> You wanted a roomful of people to walk away going "Holy fuck! Yes! That was what I hoped it would be!"

The release in April of Tool's first full-length album kicked off a two-month promotional tour up the California coast where audiences discovered in *Undertow* a study in contradiction, a balance of heavy metal and soft cadence, a lyrical paradox that not only demanded attention but invited participation.

The album's immediate success was due as much to Zoo's respect for the band's creativity as to its marketing efforts. "When you have a band that is so thoroughly evolved, the smartest thing to do is to support it and get out of the way," Matt Marshall explained in a 2014 interview. "The best marketing a record company can do is be as invisible as you can and let the artwork and imagery and music speak directly to the fans. To do that full package as well as Tool did right from the beginning is rare."

With the release of *Undertow* came the official Tool biography, an out-of-the-box departure from the standard just-the-facts-ma'am press kit. The two-page backstory credited the band's mentors whose work had impacted their own, including first and foremost American lachrymologist Ronald P. Vincent. Tool's ideology was at last explained, to the relief of journalists and music critics struggling to understand the band. Its approach, the document explained, was a musical testament to Vincent's principles: the imperative to fearlessly face both joy and sorrow in order to transform personal pain into healing and enlightenment.

Radio stations across the country soon added the audience favorite "Sober" to their programming, and the video was regularly featured on MTV's *Headbangers Ball*. And word of mouth played its part in bringing the album to the attention of listeners who'd otherwise not have associated Maynard with the latest rock sensation.

"A friend of mine told me about the album shortly after it came out," Steele Newman would recall. "He told me about this great guy on vocals, this Maynard Keenan. I'm like, 'Not Maynard James Keenan!'" Steele remembered Maynard only as the housemate who'd sat quietly on the Pearson Street couch eating Cheerios and was hard-pressed to imagine the man who'd fed fish food to party guests as a frontman. But when he placed the CD in his player, the voice he heard was unmistakable. "I listened to it, and wait a minute! Yes! I loved the music, and not just because it was my old roommate singing."

Maynard, always insistent on giving credit where credit was due, listed as an inspiration in the liner notes comic Bill Hicks, whose recordings had made bearable the long hours in the Ryder truck the summer before. "We sent him copies of the album," Maynard would recall. "He wrote back and thanked us for the music. I called him and pointed out that we'd mentioned him in the liner notes. He hadn't noticed. He was just thanking us for the CD."

The call began a dialogue that by the time the band returned from Canada in early summer had turned to the topic of collaboration. "We were both excited about working together on a mixed media presentation," Maynard would explain. "Maybe he could do a comedic stand-up between Tool sets. Maybe he would open for us, or we'd do half a set and he'd come out and do a bit."

But the more they discussed their plan, the less confident they were. Hicks had no trouble captivating a crowd in a comedy club, but as much as his in-your-face material complemented Tool's, holding the attention of keyed-up slammers would be another matter. "We realized a show like that would have to be presented in an unfamiliar forum," Maynard explained. "Given the expectations of a Tool audience, we'd have to take it out of the rock club they're used to so they could appreciate the whole experience. We spent a lot of time trying to figure out how we'd calm down a bunch of skinheads to listen to jokes."

EVEN IN THE WAKE OF *UNDERTOW*'S SUCCESS, Zoo Entertainment hadn't forgotten its commitment to Bill Manspeaker. *Cereal Killer*, the 11-song Green Jellö video

Manspeaker had begun nearly two years before, had wrapped recording at Sound City and was at last ready for distribution. Zoo had sent copies to a handful of outlets including Seattle rock station The X KXRX.

The Seattle DJ was appalled by *Cereal Killer*'s low artistic quality and high degree of inanity. "He said it was the worst degeneration of music that could possibly be happening," Manspeaker remembered. The assessment only confirmed what Manspeaker had said all along, that the history of rock 'n' roll had culminated in the world's worst band and its song about pigs. The DJ cued up the track to demonstrate to his listeners the sort of drivel he received from recording companies and prefaced the song with an exasperated discourse on the lamentable breakdown of the music industry.

Then a curious thing happened. The request lines flashed with calls from Seattle listeners begging for more—more Big Bad Wolf, more machine-gun fire, more falsetto chinny-chin-chin. And "Three Little Pigs" became the most requested song in Seattle radio memory.

When the news reached the Zoo office, they scrambled to press enough CDs to satisfy the sudden demand of record stores and radio stations from California to Maine whose listeners had learned of the little-pig phenomenon and insisted they, too, air the song. "All of a sudden, this weird pig song's playing everywhere," Manspeaker said. "The next thing I know, we're on MTV." To his amazement, the song rose to Number 17 on the *Billboard* Hot 100 list and Number 5 in the U.K. And in May, "Three Little Pigs" was certified gold by the Recording Industry Association of America.

"That was Maynard's first hit song," Manspeaker explained. "Of all of his incredible songs and all the gold and platinum records, that was his first. The guy that everyone is so serious about, it all started with 'not by the hair of my chinny-chin-chin.'"

IN 1993, AMERICAN YOUTHS HAD MORE ON THEIR MINDS than cavorting pigs. L.A. still reeled in the aftermath of the Rodney King incident and the ensuing riots, and tensions were high following American attacks on Iraqi intelligence headquarters and the attempted bombing of New York's World Trade Center. They welcomed a summer of release in the third season of Lollapalooza, the movable feast of music and dance cofounded two years before by Tool manager Ted Gardner.

All summer long, they descended upon stadiums and fairgrounds and amphitheaters as the festival made its way from Portland to St. Paul to Raleigh and across the South. Thousands strong, they came in search of grunge and alt rock, of earsplitting, angry catharsis to reflect their discontent and deflect their anxiety. They crowd-surfed in the mosh pits and visited the ethnic-food tents and vendor booths, and despite the heat and overpriced Evian, they dedicated their days to their mission: a surrender to the dark metal of Alice in Chains, the funk twang of Primus, the passionate melodic screeds of Rage Against the Machine—and the discovery of bands on the second stage, groups like Sebadoh, Royal Trux, Mutabaruka—and Tool.

Tool was low band on the totem pole and its tour bus only a step above the Ryder truck. "It had kind of a better bed," Maynard would recall. "If a coffin is a better bed." At dinnertime, he took from the small cooler another can of Coors Light and watched band managers and promoters and accountants share fine Rieslings and Gewürztraminers. Faint guitar riffs and shouts of the crowds drifted over the grounds, and he thought of whole ducks crackling on a grill, goblets of first-growth Bordeaux.

But Lollapalooza was the realization of dreams he'd never imagined on those Somerville evenings: an invitation to join Alice in Chains's Layne Staley in a stirring duet of "Rooster" on the main stage, and best of all, taking the stage following his friend Tom's act. "Many a show, Tool would get the better of us and we were like, 'We gotta go write some more songs,'" Morello would recall. "It was great. People were getting the shows of their lives."

The enthusiastic audience response to Tool allayed any lingering fears Lou Maglia might have had about Maynard's appearing in a venue larger than Club Lingerie. "The band was killing it," Matt Marshall would recall—so much so that in mid-July, Tool was elevated to a slot on the main stage.

The tour was a chance for friends and family along the Lollapalooza route to discover exactly what Maynard had been up to since he'd moved to L.A. "We were surprised," Jan would admit of her day with Mike at Maynard's July performance at Chicago's World Music Theatre. "We thought he was just saying he was in a band."

WHEN THE TOUR REACHED ITS FINAL STOP in Irwindale, California, in August, Maynard and Bill Hicks tested their idea of collaboration. Hicks announced the band, and then, deadpan serious, told the crowd he'd dropped a contact lens in the mosh pit. Impatient as it was to hear "Swamp Song" and "Flood" and "Prison Sex," they obediently knelt to search the dusty lawn.

Maynard returned to L.A. for a two-month respite before he must do it all again. And his dream began, the dream of a place welcoming and safe and somehow familiar, the dream that stirred in him a nostalgia for green valleys and canyons and creek beds he'd never seen, of mountains red with sunrise, of the spangle of stars in a sky he'd never known.

> I dreamt that I was flying over a vast desert. I'm flying through the air, and I come over a crest into a valley and hover over a small town on the side of a hill. I turn toward the west, and I see in the distance a huge wave cresting and just completely annihilating this large city on the horizon.
>
> About a month later, I got a package from Bill Hicks. He was in the middle of editing his third album, and he sent me a cassette of the music. He had some questions for me about whether the music fit with the comedy or not. It was called *Arizona Bay*.
>
> I thought about my dream, and I had an idea that it had to be Arizona I saw. I'd spent time in Phoenix, and the dream didn't look anything like that. But I knew that it was definitely Los Angeles getting its ass kicked.

With the new year, Maynard was off again for performances in Atlanta and D.C. and Toronto. "A normal, going-home lifestyle? You don't want to let your mind go there," he would recall. "Touring is what life is now."

Between gigs, he'd found time to move to the Tudor bungalow in North Hollywood he'd admired when he'd visited Steve Hansgen's sound studio there. When the house became vacant, he was first in line to sign the lease and transported his boxes and his black trunk, the finches, two parrots, and a brand-new water bed to the little house where gingerbread cornices curled beneath the eaves, a shade tree overhung the front lawn, and the porch light would be on when he came home.

The windowed wall in his bedroom looked out over the gardens and the wide backyard where squirrels and chipmunks scampered through the ferns, and hummingbirds and kinglets and the occasional raven settled among the purple flowers of the jacaranda tree. Once the touring schedule settled down, he imagined, he'd tend the rosemary and bougainvillea and trim back the ivy that crept up the side of the house. "A Zen garden always includes a water feature, so I built a pond in the backyard and stocked it with koi," he would recall. "I needed to maintain that sense of where I came from. You've got to have some sort of oasis to stay grounded."

He'd have no trouble writing there in the productive company of Hotsy Menshot and Pepper Spray Jerry, housemates as committed to their work as he. Hotsy was Gary Helsinger, a Green Jellö member and a savvy A&R rep for Chrysalis Music Group. Guitarist by night and businessman by day, Jerry Phlippeau spent long hours hunched over his desk developing his credibility and his contact list and working to legalize the public sale of pepper spray.

A frequent visitor was Tim Cadiente, a self-styled entrepreneur whose talent behind the camera was equaled only by his passion for rock 'n' roll. If there was a band to be photographed, Cadiente was there with his Nikon, and after shooting Tool's Palladium show in January, he and Maynard had become fast friends. As marketing consultant for Oakley, Inc., Cadiente was ever on the lookout for opportunities to promote its sunglasses and visors and ski apparel, relying on social networking long before his competitors had heard the term.

> The word *marketing* had always left a bad taste in my mouth. But Pepper Spray Jerry and Tim weren't in a stuffy office coming up with clever catchphrases to trick you into buying carcinogens. They were growing their businesses by working with friends. It was my first glimpse into the positive side of marketing. They made it look like fun.

Maynard's own work had reached an awkward and worrisome impasse. His *Opiate* and *Undertow* lyrics had come easily, the words and motifs he'd translated from his own anger and frustration and sadness, but his new efforts seemed forced and uninspired. Tool's next album should transcend what had come before, he knew, but nearly two years on the road could only inspire an industry cliché, the legendary and doomed third album. "In the '70s and the '80s, it seemed like the first two records of every band were exciting collections they'd worked all their lives to write," he would explain. "Then there was the third record they wrote on a tour bus or in a hotel room. There's no life in it. It's the fuckin' road album. I didn't want that for us."

But the house on La Maida, six miles from the commotion of Hollywood Boulevard and the unpredictable comings and goings at the loft, might be his haven, the peaceful setting where he would regain the psychic balance he seemed to have lost.

GOLD RECORDS AND HIT SINGLES and international acclaim cast about Maynard an aura irresistible to the groupies and aspiring performers who imagined fame-by-association when they appeared in public at his side. If they weren't the trusted sisters of the long-ago beach days, their adoration and intimacy was, for the time being, satisfying enough.

> My biggest concern was to get laid. My priority was to be validated, to be desired. This was my ticket to undo all of the dismissive behavior from family and teachers and the army of people that had ignored my potential. It was my chance to have somebody who I didn't even know and who didn't even know me give me *everything* in a moment, without question. Just surrender. I'd never had that. That power was new.

There was no dearth of attractive young admirers eager to share his life and his bed, and he became expert at subterfuge and split-second timing, often returning from a night with one woman seconds ahead of another pulling into his driveway.

The women brought to the relationships dysfunctional patterns of their own, coping mechanisms and habits that perfectly dovetailed with his. The borders between their performance personas and their offstage lives were porous, their dramas enacted in suspicion and disparagement and angry outbursts. The criticisms and manipulation were subtle at first, but escalated over the weeks into irrational demands and attempts to control his every coming and going, into slapping and pummeling and windows broken in jealous rage.

"I didn't understand this weird abusive dynamic," Maynard would recall. "My parents never hit me when I was a kid, and none of the women I'd known in Michigan or Boston ever acted this way. I was trying to be open to whatever might happen and just embrace whatever came, but much of the time, the relationships went in an ugly direction."

He explained and cajoled and struggled his way from one tumultuous amour only to find himself in another just as destructive. More than once, the violence and confusion led him to retaliate with passive-aggressive tactics of his own: abrupt and unexplained breakups and restraining orders against women he'd once believed he loved.

"When I look back, I'm not happy with a lot of my behavior," he would admit. "I was gaining understanding on a lot of levels, but on quite a few more, I was doing things I wasn't proud of. I'm not ashamed, and I don't regret anything, but I felt like I was losing myself to weird desires."

So many seemed unaware of such concepts as commitment and fidelity, and Maynard, caught up in the addictive cycle, succumbed to their allure and their attention, however superficial. And then he'd turn, as if just over his shoulder someone might appear to understand his unspoken joke, ask to hear his story, and be there to help rewrite it.

On a morning in mid-January, Maynard awoke to find CDs and books spilled across the floor and the pictures on the walls askew. He'd slept through his first California earthquake, the Northridge quake centered in Receda only 12 miles away. He found only a broken saucer or two on the kitchen floor, but he soon learned of collapsed apartment complexes and parking garages and whole sections of the Santa Monica Freeway. Reporters called it one of the most powerful urban quakes in U.S. history, powerful enough to damage Gazzarri's on Sunset so irreparably it would be demolished. The old Hastings Hotel would close, too, and with it Raji's.

He spent the morning putting his house in order and reflecting on Bill Hicks's cassette and his prescient rant of fault lines and of L.A. slipping complete into the Pacific.

Over the winter, Maynard had noticed in Hicks a shift in focus and enthusiasm. "I sensed something was off," Maynard would recall. "I told him we had a short tour coming up in February and that we should talk about him joining us." But Hicks was hesitant to commit to the project he'd embraced only months before. "He was like, 'Yeah, we'll talk about it,'" Maynard would remember.

Hicks had always answered Maynard's calls on the first ring, but now, without warning or explanation, the calls went unanswered. "Then I had another dream," Maynard recalled. "Bill's girlfriend Colleen and his manager Duncan and a lot of other people were at a motel, and everybody was crying. And Bill wasn't there. So I called Duncan, and I said, 'Man, I just had the most fucked-up dream, and I haven't been able to reach Bill. What's going on?'"

Hicks, Duncan told him, had told only a few close friends about his diagnosis of pancreatic cancer. The weekly chemo treatments had had little effect, and in January, after a final show at Carolines on Broadway, he'd moved from New York to his parents' house in Little Rock.

"We talked many times after that," Maynard remembered. "He was still hopeful like, 'Well, maybe if I can beat the unbeatable cancer, we can still do this show.' I felt like he just wanted to talk." And they talked often, Maynard listening patiently as Hicks struggled to articulate his increasingly incoherent thoughts. The calls continued until Valentine's Day, when Hicks—the man of unstoppable wit, the man with still so much to say, so much to teach of consciousness and compassion—could not speak at all.

LOS ANGELES CONTINUED TO LIVE UP TO ITS REPUTATION as a new age hub, its mediums and seers and self-proclaimed oracles peering into cards and tea leaves and crystals to bring insight and guidance to their anxious customers. Worried for his friend and frustrated by his own creative inertia, Maynard turned to a psychometry practitioner in the Valley, a woman who claimed the gift of reading magnetic energy patterns in metal. Allowing her to see what she could see in a piece of jewelry certainly couldn't hurt and might offer some new perspective.

He'd searched for a suitable object for analysis and chose at last a silver ring he hadn't worn in years and with no particular significance. The reader held the ring between her palms and closed her eyes, channeling or meditating or perhaps only acting. "Then she asked me who Paul was," he remembered. "And she goes, 'Yeah, that's done.'"

Her words took Maynard by surprise. This Paul she sensed in the ring's aura might be anybody at all, he reasoned, and surely not Tool's bass player, who seemed as devoted to the group as he'd ever been. But he wrote the name on a slip of paper and asked what his next steps should be.

"She goes, 'I don't know. Something about London,'" he would remember.

He added *London* to the piece of paper and put it in his pocket, no more enlightened than he'd been that morning, but armed with a cryptic map, at least, should he ever need to consult it.

IN EARLY FEBRUARY, THE BAND'S SHORT TOUR HAD BEGUN AS PLANNED, a three-week barnstormer up the East Coast and through the Midwest that included an evening at the Orbit Room in Grand Rapids.

"I saw Maynard firing up a lot of disenfranchised and disillusioned young people," art instructor Deb Rockman would recall of the sold-out show. "He had to be really loud and scream this stuff to get through to that very angry generation." She'd watched the crowd sway in trancelike attention before the stage, watched them lip-synch his lyrics. "The music was very mature," Rockman said. "It wasn't all about fucking and drinking and partying. Maynard was telling people to look around, to notice what was wrong. That was always his intention."

The Grand Rapids stop included a day of freedom before he was due in Detroit for Saturday's show. Maynard walked with Steve Aldrich and Ramiro through the downtown, hearing the latest news of Aldrich's radio program and Ramiro's paintings and noting the changes to the city since he'd lived there. The amphitheater was empty of skateboarders on the subzero afternoon, and they stamped their boots against the cold and darted into the welcome warmth of a coffee shop, where record bins lined the walls and a narrow staircase led to the tattoo parlor downstairs.

"And there," Aldrich explained, "we find a Grand Valley art teacher." The man sat alone with his design binders, his graph paper and ink bottles, the instructor who six years before had severely critiqued an assignment Maynard had believed was especially well-executed. "It was a metal sculpture that Maynard loved," Aldrich would recall. "This guy had hated it and just ripped it apart, and now he's departed the university and is working in a basement tattoo shop."

The professor looked up from his sketch pad at Maynard's Mulhawk and faded jeans and asked what he'd been doing since he'd left school. Maynard's response was matter-of-fact, emotionless. "Well, my band and I did a show at the Orbit Room last night for 1,500 people," he explained, extending toward the astonished teacher a copy of the day's *Grand Rapids Press*. "And here's my picture on the front page of the paper."

"You have no idea how happy this made Maynard," Aldrich recalled.

With time to spare, his friends delivered Maynard at the stage door of the State Theatre, the Beaux Arts performance space that dominated Detroit's Grand Circus Park. Once more, Tool pulled out all the stops, its energy drawing the crowd to its feet in frenzied appreciation of "Prison Sex" and "Sober" and the enigmatic "4 Degrees."

Exhausted, Maynard went to his hotel afterward and fell into a troubled sleep. "I sat up in my bed not long after midnight, full upright like somebody just punched me," he remembered. "It freaked me out. I'm wide awake in this room going, 'What the fuck was that?'"

He went to the window and looked out over the city. Cabs moved slowly through the streets below, and in the distance, the lights of the Ambassador Bridge reflected white against the dark river. All was well, he told himself, and set his alarm to be sure to wake up in time for breakfast with Danny.

In the morning, his pager flashed, alerting him of some urgent message left while he'd slept. Perhaps his manager had called with last-minute schedule changes. Maybe Danny had phoned to tell him of the perfect bacon-and-eggs diner he'd found nearby. Maynard dialed his 800 number, and in the gray dawn quiet, listened to Duncan's message. At 11:20 Little Rock time, he reported, Bill had died.

Maynard powered through the evening's show in Cleveland, his performance as professional and controlled as any other. The night flight to London would give him plenty of time to sort out his feelings. One thing was sure. He would not mourn.

> Bill and I had always talked about how life is just a ride. If you really believe that, then death shouldn't be seen as an awful thing. But at the same time, I don't think he was ready. His career was so right on the edge of exploding.
>
> I would imagine most people's tendency would be to get obliterated, but I didn't. My reaction wasn't to get drunk on the plane. My reaction was to get some sleep so when I got where I was going, I could do what I do. I felt like the best way to remember Bill was to keep using my talents.

He lay his forehead against the window and looked down at sea stretching dark in every direction to the horizon. And he slept, the sky brightening as the jet flew toward sunrise.

THE LONDON SHOW KICKED OFF A SUMMER ITINERARY as rigorous as that of the year before with stops in the Netherlands and France, a nonstop blitz across the U.S. and Canada, and a second European tour. In late July, the Shepherd's Bush show opened with U.K. band Peach, a progressive metal group whose experimental melodies and daring psychedelic style complemented the Tool sound. Maynard was impressed by the inventive whammy work of Peach bassist Justin Chancellor, so much so that he and the others invited him to sit in for Paul on the evening's performance of "Sober." Chancellor's growling low-end interpretation brought an unexpected depth to the song, and if this was all the metal reader had seen in her vision of London and Paul, it was enough.

Nearly five months of downtime would be just the break Maynard needed to come to terms with Bill's death, to think or not think at all, to laze away his afternoons, a package of Twizzlers beside him on the water bed and a supply of VHS tapes stacked nearby.

It might be time to revisit *Wings of Desire*, or *Bliss*, but he was curious about the collection of Drunvalo Melchizedek lectures a friend had dropped by some months before.

Peculiar as Melchizedek's backstory was—that an otherworldly spirit had stepped into his consciousness to promote ancient esoteric teachings—Maynard was fascinated by his theories. The Egyptian pyramids, Melchizedek maintained, weren't in fact tombs, as anthropologists had long claimed, but initiation chambers where a chosen few had been granted an understanding of sacred geometry.

Melchizedek had accepted his mission, he explained, to enlighten twentieth-century minds of the power of mathematic principles underlying everything from spiraled nautilus shells to the structure of DNA to the arrangement of leaves on a long-stemmed rose, the recurring patterns that give order to the physical world.

> A lot of what Melchizedek talked about rang true. Never mind all the "I'm a walk-in spirit who existed back in Egypt and the god Thoth taught me geometry." What I took from it was all the things that can be explained by geometry.

> It went back to what Boots Newkirk tried to teach us about a table with only two legs. Is it gonna stand up? No. Three legs? OK. When you do a transit survey, two points don't tell you anything. Your target could be either one. But if you have a third point, you can calculate center lines and meridians and trajectories to pinpoint the artillery's location and the direction of enemy fire. The geometry of three points makes things stable.

Maynard lay back on the water bed and thought of the honeycombs his father had kept in a far corner of his garden, their endlessly replicating cells each the same, of fugues and canons, of the spiderweb hanging lacelike and precise in the cornice over the front porch, of the apple he'd sliced at lunchtime and the way its halves had fallen across his plate to reveal the shape of a star.

HIS READING LIST THAT SUMMER branched from novels to folklore to ethnographies, spiraling in an ever-widening study of fact and myth that, no matter the genre, came to the same striking conclusion: There was, it seemed, more than one history of the world.

"Sober" had become a hit single in March, and in September, *Undertow* was certified gold by the RIAA. "I was absolutely aware of having put the dominoes in a row and of making them fall in the way that I had hoped," Maynard would recall. But to take the next creative step and avoid the dread third album, he knew he must take the time to regroup, to revisit the concepts and notions that had first fueled his dreams.

"All this touring is eventually going to catch up with you," he would explain. "Now let's do some sit-ups and try to see if we can't maintain an edge. I needed to find a balance in order to bring structure to the art and still make it vulnerable and volatile."

He drew his blinds against the August heat and began to sort through the stack of books he'd accumulated during his time on the road. He turned first to his tattered volumes of Joseph Campbell and segued to the John Crowley novel he'd looked forward to reading for months. *Ægypt*, to his delight, was a tale even more fantastical than *Little, Big*. He read of a forgotten age when mathematics and magic, alchemy and astronomy weren't antithetical but faces of the same reality, of days when scryers gazed into their glass and communed with the angels they saw there, learning from them their lost language.

Accounts of those gone times weren't recorded in history texts, Campbell had written, but they hadn't entirely vanished. Their traces persisted across millennia in the symbols of the tarot, in rune stones and hieroglyphs and petroglyphs. They endured in the stories passed down from grandfather to father to son, tales of lead turned to gold, of giants and dwarves once as common as fruit flies, of gods and goddesses come down to live among men. They remained as parables and allegories, stories of transformations and transmutations that defied the laws of modern science.

On the other hand, maybe it had all happened just that way. Maybe, as Crowley suggested, the laws themselves had changed, the very axioms that explained time and space and life and death and love.

And perhaps another history determined Maynard's own path, a forgotten or deliberately denied story as crucial to his success as Boots Newkirk's lectures or maneuvers on the Fort Sill training ground. If he shifted his gaze, he thought, the details of his hidden tale would come into sharp relief, the way the picture in the *Highlights* magazine at the dentist's office had changed from an urn to smiling profiles when he'd tilted his head just right.

For a long time, Maynard had struggled to make sense of the hazy memories that returned sometimes when he least expected: the hours alone in the farmer's house in Tallmadge, his distant and taciturn stepfather no one dared defy. Perhaps he'd only imagined the furtive glances between the otherwise stern church members when they'd come to the Ravenna house, the sudden silences that even as a small boy he'd known he must never question, the not quite covert touches passed between the adults gathered in the living room on a Saturday evening. The oddly uncomfortable memories might not have been real at all, but fantasies he'd created to cope with Mike's departure, scenarios he'd dreamt to distract himself from Judith's infirmities. But fabrication or fact, his narratives had left their trace, a vague sense of confusion and mistrust, of trespass and violation.

His mother would remember more than he, he was sure, but drawing from her the details was no easy task, and their frequent phone calls that summer left him no more enlightened than before. "Judith was blocking things then," Maynard's aunt Pam would recall. "She was trying to forget the painful things that had happened when he was a little boy."

His unresolved bitterness and fear had inevitably found their way into his lyrics, but Maynard had for a long time sensed an untold subplot, a backstory that would explain his confusion and anger. It would take gentle prodding to reveal the truths that had gone unspoken for decades, truths that once he understood them, could only bring a deeper dimension to his art.

"Eventually, the whole story came out in conversations with my mother and my aunt," he explained. "It turns out the family included a classic inappropriate uncle. My mother was raped when she was a little girl. That's what the songs are really about, the cycle of denial and abuse—emotional and physical—that, for all I knew, had been going on for generations."

> When you're exposed to that kind of abuse as a young child, you carry it with you, especially when everybody else pretends it never happened. My mother buried the memory of what her uncle had done, and it came out in her own lack of boundaries. She invited people into her home who had questionable boundaries, because that's what she knew, that's what she attracted. Then I grew up seeing that, so I learned "no boundaries."
>
> Having that moral ambiguity could be the makings of a sociopath, but on the positive side, it could be that I think outside the box because I was never confined in one. I'd done some inappropriate things that I wasn't even aware were inappropriate. But that lack of conventional boundaries helped me push the envelope in other areas. It's the way I was wired.

THE PALMS THAT LINED LA MAIDA DROOPED in the heat, and the animals in the garden sought what little relief they could beneath the ferns and the rosemary bushes. When the temperature was at its record-breaking highest, Gary ventured to the market, and by the time he returned, Maynard's Mulhawk was no more. "It was so fuckin' hot," Maynard remembered. "I took scissors and a razor and shaved it all off."

The new look offered an unexpected benefit. Shorn, Maynard found he could go about the city incognito and fear no censure should his activities conflict with his public's expectations. As the band had become more and more well-known, fans and followers were quick to recognize on the sidewalk the wiry frontman with the long curls, and Maynard found the attention not only annoying, but limiting.

> I felt like this thing on my head had become some kind of a signature, and I
> needed to get rid of that so I could move about freely. On the one hand, being
> part of Tool meant people knew who I was, and that was cool. But the paradox
> is that that public image ends up stifling you. It slows you down and boxes
> you in.
>
> Back then, there was no Facebook to be throwing pictures at you. So if I
> changed my look, I could be anonymous and walk around unrecognized. That
> made it easier to move forward and discover new things.

At the gingerbread house, he rediscovered pastimes and passions he'd long
neglected. He brought out sketch pads and pens and recipes for quiches and
chocolate chip cookies, and invited in old friends and new, Tom Morello and
Brad Wilk and Moon Unit Zappa, and their camaraderie provided the connection and centering he'd so missed while he'd been on the road. They shared
stories and laughter, updates on the role they'd read for that week and the upcoming gig, take-out orange chicken and crab Rangoon.

"We connected intellectually and heart-wise," Zappa recalled in a 2014
interview. "Maynard was an extremely soulful person. There was such a difference between this mild-mannered Clark Kent type living in that funky little
house and his contained-electricity punk rock persona. The dichotomy was
fascinating."

And before they settled in for a screening of *Monty Python and the Holy Grail*
or *Dead Men Don't Wear Plaid*, Maynard led his friends to the backyard to greet
Butterball, the newest addition to his menagerie. The fat tom turkey stomped
and charged and fluffed his feathers and jerked his head toward Tom and Brad.

His L.A. family grew to include the waitresses at Millie's Café, the Silver
Lake diner fitted out in campy 1940s Hollywood décor. They greeted him by
name when he came in the door and served up his scrambled eggs with spinach
and toasted pine nuts and news of the day. "I felt like I'd finally found my
groove," he remembered.

And Maynard and Danny and Adam and Paul found themselves not so
much invited as expected at Lou Maglia's over-the-top feasts. "Every holiday,
I had open house," Maglia would explain. "The rule was, the line starts at
2 o'clock, and if you're late, you've got to put your food in the microwave
yourself."

There was always room for one more at Lou's house, one more musician whose schedule prevented their going home for Thanksgiving, one more song-writer with deadlines that kept them in L.A. at Christmastime. Before the day was over, 200 guests might circle the buffet table to heap their plates with turkey and ham, lasagna and candied yams, asparagus parmesan and garlicked green beans prepared by Lou himself.

Maynard and the others stayed as long as politely possible, prolonging their visit with another slice of pie, one more cannoli. Their laughter echoed long into the morning through the big house in the Hollywood Hills, this home where candles burned and no one need be alone.

BY MIDWINTER, MAYNARD'S WAS A FAMILIAR FACE at the city's premier comedy clubs—Beth Lapides's UnCabaret and the Diamond Club on Hollywood where Laura Milligan hosted her Tantrum shows.

He and Gary took their place at a table near the stage and escaped for an evening in the routines of David Cross and Bob Odenkirk and Jack Black, as-piring comics testing their routines and honing their timing. Maynard listened to the satire and send-ups of Craig Aston and Brian Posehn and began to imagine himself on the Tantrum stage. If ever there were time between Tool tours, he might just give it a try.

"I saw unlimited potential in him," Zappa would recall. "Maynard is a batch of raw materials. It's like those reality shows where they tell you to make clothing out of things you find at a recycling center or give you a bunch of ingredients and say, 'Make a meal out of gummy bears and mustard.' It's like he had too many talents."

At closing time, he might dart off to a romantic liaison, to his room to finish a new song or begin a new drawing, or to the airport to make the flight to Honolulu and the next night's performance there.

"It felt like he was running from something," Zappa would remember. But his was not a race against an opponent. He was determined to stay ahead of the thing that pursued him, the echo of dismissal and underestimation, as if the mediocrity he must outdistance were his own.

After his walk from Massachusetts to Michigan, Maynard was met by a welcoming committee at the Scottville Café, including Kjiirt's father, Viggo. *(MJK collection)*

Kjiirt Jensen and Maynard Keenan receive T-shirts from Scottville officials

Former residents return
Hike, bike back to Scottville

Two former Scottville residents wanted to participate in the city's centennial, but both lived in Massachusetts.

Jim "Maynard" Keenan and Kjiirt Jensen, both 1982 graduates of Mason County Central High School and currently residents of Sommerville, Mass., walked and bicycled their way from the east coast to Scottville.

Keenan, 25, left Boston July 20, and walked from Boston through Massachusetts, New York, and Canada.

"I did it because I could walk and have the feet to walk with," he said.

Jensen, 25, began his trip on July 24, bicycling through Massachusetts, New York, Pennsylvania, Ohio and into Michigan.

"I altered my original route as I went in an attempt to avoid a lot of hills," he explained.

They began their trip because they said they love their hometown and wanted to honor its centennial birthday.

The planning for the trip began about six months ago.

"I think it was the night we learned they put strawberry filling in Twinkies," Jensen said. "We decided if they can actually improve perfection, we can do anything."

Once arriving in Scottville, Mayor Glenna Anderson and Scottville Chamber of Commerce President Richard Cox presented a centennial T-shirt to the pair while friends and relatives watched.

The pair said they weren't going to return to Sommerville the same way they left. Jensen is planning on riding back with friends who followed him in their car and Keenan is planning on using a friend's car.

Keenan, the son of Mike Keenan of Scottville, is a merchandising manager and bird breeder for Boston Pet Center.

Jensen, son of Mr. and Mrs. S. Viggo Jensen of Scottville, is a manager for Bread and Circus Whole Foods Supermarket in Cambridge, Mass.

The August 14, 1989, issue of the *Ludington Daily News* featured a story of the 800-mile journey. *(Reprinted with permission)*

Zippy the schipperke would be the perfect companion until Maynard put down roots in L.A. *(MJK collection)*

Tom Morello (far right) was in the front row for Tool's performance at Raji's in early 1991. *(Photo by Bob Blackburn)*

The November 1991 show at Club Lingerie celebrated Tool's signing with Zoo Entertainment. After the party, Maynard hobnobbed with his longtime idol Gene Simmons and Matthew and Gunnar Nelson. *(Photo by Lindsey Brice)*

Maynard's understated announcement informed family and friends of his latest achievement. *(Sarah Jensen collection)*

Zoo ENTERTAINMENT

6363
Sunset
Boulevard
Hollywood
California
90028

TEL
213
468
4200

FAX
213
468
4207

IM IN A
ROCK BAND.

LOVE
MAYNARD

A Bertelsmann Music Group Company

When his son was born in 1995, Maynard began wearing wigs and costumes onstage in order to remain incognito in street clothes when he and Devo went to the park or the corner store. *(MJK collection)*

The ambiguous Perfect Circle logo invited a shift in perspective to decipher its layered meanings. *(Photo by Tim Cadiente)*

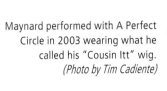

Maynard performed with A Perfect Circle in 2003 wearing what he called his "Cousin Itt" wig. *(Photo by Tim Cadiente)*

The idiosyncratic frontman takes the stage in a Tool concert. *(Photo by Tim Cadiente)*

The Rev. Maynard rocks it at the Coachella Valley Music and Arts Festival. *(Photo by Meats Meier)*

The Merkin Vineyard Judith block, named in honor of Maynard's mother. *(MJK collection)*

Maynard's work in the vineyard is hands-on, from operating the forklift to inoculating the fruit to racking and rinsing barrels in the bunker. *(MJK collection)*

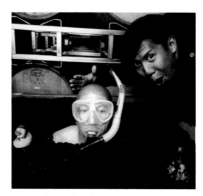

Tim Cadiente has been Maynard's photographer and partner in shenanigans since shooting Tool's 1994 show at the Hollywood Palladium. *(MJK collection)*

Maynard looked to Penfolds winemaker Peter Gago for advice and wisdom when he began his vineyard, and the two have remained friends. *(Photo by Milton Wordley)*

In 2015, Maynard attended a jiu-jitsu seminar with Rickson Gracie in St. Louis. They'd worked together since Maynard's early days in L.A. *(Photo by Ariel Amores Belano)*

Maynard reunited at the Neighborhood restaurant in 2012 with his childhood pastor Paul Grout. After 30 years, he had important matters to discuss. *(Photo by Sarah Jensen)*

Luca Currado of Vietti winery in Castiglione Falletto, Italy, set Maynard on the path to discovering his Italian ancestors. *(MJK collection)*

During their honeymoon in Italy, Maynard and Lei Li visited the Venaus house that had been home to four generations of Marzos. *(MJK collection)*

Maynard reprised his Green Jellö "Three Little Pigs" role during Cinquanta, his 50th birthday concert at L.A.'s Greek Theatre. *(Photo by Tim Cadiente)*

Lei Li Agostina Maria helped with the first Agostenga harvest on her first birthday in 2015. *(MJK collection)*

10

So much was still possible, Maynard believed, and nothing would get in his way. Few performances were on the docket, and no romantic entanglements, and with the departure of Pepper Spray Jerry and the arrival of a new housemate, Tool guitar tech Billy Howerdel, the La Maida house had settled into a comfortable domestic routine. He would take advantage of the calm and focus on the next album.

But the universe, he should have known by then, has a habit of bollixing the best of intentions. One telephone call, and his every certainty was replaced with doubt. Fatherhood was one piece of the puzzle that hadn't exactly been on his radar.

"My dad hadn't been around for me when I was young," he would recall. "Now here I was in a similar situation, which sucked. I didn't want to repeat that pattern. I wanted to break it."

Of his many doomed romances, this had been the one ended not in door slamming or restraining orders but levelheaded kindness. After only a few dates, the two had recognized their passion wasn't destined for the long term and had said their respectful goodbyes. "We agreed as adults that it wasn't working, and we parted ways," Maynard recalled. "I finally handled a breakup the way it should be handled."

A white picket fence and a two-car garage weren't entirely out of the question. The year before, he'd congratulated Kjiirt on his marriage and the birth of his daughter not with a little envy. He imagined that one day, it would be his turn to gather with family at the dinner table every night and spend Saturdays teaching his children to plant peas and lettuce in the garden behind the house. But not yet, not now. "I wanted all that, but I wanted to be with the right person," he would explain.

But whatever his fears, whatever his reservations and regrets, this child—his child—would never doubt his love, never twist in its car seat to catch one last glimpse of its father. If he and the baby's mother had managed a respectful break-up, he resolved, surely they could maintain that civility for the sake of their baby.

Maynard's demands were few but firm. He'd have a say in choosing the best schools and the best orthodontists. His child would spend Christmas with him, and together they'd sprinkle cookies with powdered sugar and create pinecone Santas and hang them on their real tree.

"IT'S JUST A RIDE," BILL HICKS HAD TOLD HIM often enough. No matter what, he'd said, things would always work out. Maybe so, but just now, Maynard was hard-pressed to reconcile instant family with his artistic ambitions, not to mention an increasing abhorrence for the city he lived in. "There are those moments when you feel like you're losing touch with your identity," he would later explain.

The Melchizedek tapes had only scratched the surface in helping him to understand cosmic order, and when he saw the announcement of an upcoming Flower of Life seminar, he drafted his tuition check and cleared his Day-Timer. A weeklong immersion in Melchizedek's teachings of pattern and structure might bring the clarity he needed.

Early each day, Maynard arrived at the house in San Fernando Valley and joined his fellow students in a meditation, visualizing the creative energies supposedly crackling in the instructor's living room. She lectured on tragedy and hope and the mathematical formulas that formed Melchizedek's teachings, while Maynard and the others sat on their pillows and exchanged smiles as if they shared in some great secret.

After lunch, the lights were dimmed, and Melchizedek's image filled the screen against one wall. Maynard watched rapt as the ponytailed guru enlightened the group about the earth's forgotten histories: of extraterrestrials who'd long ago come from the star Sirius and left their mysterious marks upon the land, of Stonehenge and the pyramids on the Giza Plateau, their designs suggesting some occult universal system of measurement.

In the evening, over IPAs in the backyard, Maynard updated Gary and Billy on the day's lessons. He reported on the cataclysmic changes to come, changes predicted for millennia by seers long separated by space and time. Any time now, Melchizedek had taught, great seismic shifts would heave the earth's plates and set them down again willy-nilly, creating a new landscape of ocean waves crashing over Arizona. As best he could, he told them of the new breed of humans beginning to populate the earth, a race evolved with not only the usual 46 chromosomes but an additional two, equipping them to usher in an age of cosmic consciousness—a race Melchizedek called Indigo Children.

"My friends thought I was fucking bananas," Maynard would recall.

> I don't care whether there's aliens or not. That's a great story and it makes for great movies. The more logical story, just like Crowley wrote in *Ægypt*, is that there are way more histories to the world than you can imagine and that records of them survived violent changes throughout time. But it's not aliens. It's just us leaving messages for each other.
>
> And I don't believe in psychic power stuff. I do believe in creative energies. I believe information is out there if you just tune to it. I don't think it's anything spiritual. It's just there. If all of a sudden people on different continents discovered electricity, it's not like they had some cosmic Internet and shared that information. It's just that on some unconscious level, people end up being at the same stage of readiness.

The seminar included somewhat more pragmatic topics as well. The principles of sacred geometry, Melchizedek claimed, manifest themselves in all things seen and unseen. The universe hums with the energy of the Fibonacci sequence—a series of numbers, each the sum of the two that precede it—the mathematical pattern that determines the shape of the spiraling galaxies, and hurricanes, too, and garden snails and cochlea inside the human ear.

The larger-than-life Melchizedek spoke from the screen, and Maynard scribbled notes, imagining sketches or even lyrics he might create based on this new knowledge. Every emotion, Melchizedek claimed—love and compassion, fear and anguish—has its unique sine wave signature, and neuro researchers had recorded and then converted them to three-dimensional polyhedrons, their angles and lines as predictable as the recursive patterns of a Bach fugue, as precise as a Midwestern highway grid.

"Those patterns have to do with consciousness," Maynard would explain. "They clearly have to do with art and music and how your body reacts to their structures. When artists figured out this mathematical proportion thing, they created paintings that vibrate in us at more powerful frequencies. The same with classical music. Beethoven could barely hear. He wrote music based on math, and that music makes you cry."

Even synchronicity and coincidence, Melchizedek explained, are natural and expected expressions of mathematical order. Nothing magical about them. Real magic happens with consciousness, the force that causes events and inventions to come into being in the first place.

Maynard sat forward as Melchizedek trained his laser pointer on images of circles, of angles and arcs and simple geometric forms. Any beginner, Melchizedek explained, can take up compass and straightedge and pen and draw triangles and squares, pentagrams and hexagons, and the star in all its variations: the cross and the star of David and the swastika.

But to reach the next level, to draw a form no compass, no Spirograph, no idle doodler can produce, is to enter into the divine. Participation and will are required to draw the heptagram, the star of seven lines, seven interlocking nodes, seven points. Seven: the number of chakras as the Buddhists count them, the number neo-pagans give to the entrance to the realm of Faerie. Seven: the holiest of holy numbers signifying the completion of God's creative act. When a man applies conscious thought and draws a seven-pointed star, he becomes with God a cocreator of the universe.

> If I built on Melchizedek's principles—not that I understood any of them—at least I could get something out of the classes. I wanted to do more, I wanted to create. I wanted quality of life and I wanted to take care of my child. I wanted to boil Melchizedek's story down to the basics and to understand the practical nature of geometry as it applies to emotions, to human behavior, to music, to architecture, to food, to wine.

When the final class was dismissed, Maynard pulled his battered four-track recorder from the back of his closet and experimented with vocal levels from whisper to scream. He replayed Bill Hicks's cassettes and considered the union of comedy and tragedy, the vibrations that might exist between them, the intersections that might produce in an audience deep resonance.

"Maynard has a very practical, logical side," Moon Zappa explained. "You can hear it in the complex point of entry where he brings a story to you. He can direct information. And you can only do that if you're working on yourself, discovering, and doing deep work."

And the orange moon followed its own geometric trajectory across the L.A. sky as Maynard curled on his bed with pen and ink and tried his hand at sketching seven-pointed stars.

If, as Melchizedek believed—as Bill Hicks had predicted and the Bible too—the end times were just around the corner, it would probably be a good idea to be prepared. "OK, I signed on for this ride, and if I couldn't jump off, I at least needed to be able to physically endure it," Maynard explained. "I had to be ready to defend myself or defend my space. At least, I had to become centered enough to stay calm in the face of whatever might happen."

Tool's local performances that winter had featured the innovative metal band Laundry, and over the months, its drummer, Tim Alexander, had become a frequent guest at the house on La Maida. He arrived one afternoon, updated Maynard on his work with Primus, paid the obligatory visit to Butterball, and presented to Maynard a set of VHS tapes of the pay-per-view Ultimate Fighting Championship.

This was geometric principle in action, Maynard realized. Long after he should have returned to his writing, he marveled at Royce Gracie, UFC founder and its three-time champion, as he bested opponent after opponent with his singular jiu-jitsu moves.

The Gracies, Tim explained—Royce, his father Hélio, and his brother Rickson—had made it their mission to revolutionize mixed martial arts, to incorporate into jiu-jitsu cross-training and new ways of applying leverage and sensitivity to turn an adversary's energy against himself.

In those days, every martial arts studio claimed theirs was the best and that they could teach you how to kill a man in under five seconds. I love to be part of a movement that's calling bullshit, and the Gracies were clearing up the

> mysteries and nonsense surrounding most of the other martial arts and all their dance steps. And these guys were actually fairly nonviolent. Half the time, they disabled their opponent without even striking.

Maynard was soon a regular at Rickson's L.A. studio, studying grappling and joint locks and chokes under the black belts there. He learned to transmute his body to fulcrum and pivot, to maintain a disciplined control of his torso and limbs, of line and leverage and angle. "That was the beauty of Brazilian jiu-jitsu," he would recall. "I was learning physical, practical skills that kept me grounded during a time when I was trying to figure out what really mattered and trying to maintain my center in this ocean of chaos in L.A."

Bill Hicks's death—at 32 and with so much yet to accomplish—left Maynard with a sense of urgency. He'd seen bands achieve sudden fame, receive accolades and awards and astonishing royalties. He'd seen the downside of success, too, the one-dimensional existence that came of the single-minded focus required to stay in the spotlight.

"Tool was moving in a direction that was keeping me from pursuing other interests and dreams," Maynard explained. "I felt I had to do something before we got to the point of no return."

THE DIAMOND CLUB ON HOLLYWOOD BOULEVARD offered an eclectic lineup from disco on Saturdays to Wednesday night comedy. Laura Milligan's Tantrum shows weren't the predictable stand-up monologues and timeworn mother-in-law jokes, but variety shows of mini-skits and offbeat humor, and Maynard and his friends made it their go-to spot to experience the new generation of comics: Kathy Griffin and Bobcat Goldthwait, Janeane Garofalo and Margaret Cho and Mark Fite, and David Cross and Bob Odenkirk, whose sketch comedy series *Mr. Show* would premiere in November on HBO.

He looked forward most to the recurring comedy-club-within-a-comedy-club routine featuring Laura's character Tawny Port, a former child star who'd descended into the shadow world of drugs and rock star romances and had only now begun her climb from the cycle of self-abuse. Recently released from yet another rehab program, Tawny had turned to comedy as her first step in reentering the limelight.

The skits always ended with the same gimmick. Tawny stood alone on the stage waiting for her down-on-his-luck boyfriend Vince to appear with his band and close the show. "He'd never show up," Laura explained. "The show always had this anticlimactic ending."

The disappointing denouement was humorous enough, but Maynard imagined taking the sketch further. What if, he suggested, Vince *did* show up, and not alone but with his ragtag band in tow? The attentive man with the shaved head, Laura had learned, might know a thing or two about music, and, intrigued by his idea, she agreed to offer him a few lines in the next week's performance.

"So I became the boyfriend," Maynard would recall. The disco bass that pounded into Tantrum from the main room only added to the realism of the routines. "It was perfect," Laura would recall. "The premise was that Vince's band was making this pathetic attempt to get industry people to come see their act on a weeknight, so the more that could go wrong, the better."

As Tawny wrapped her routine, Maynard and Adam and Sean took the stage in wigs and spandex pants, red suspenders and T-shirts, fedoras and Cat in the Hat hats. "Every time Vince's band showed up, it would be a little different, because they couldn't keep it together to last longer than a week or two," Maynard explained.

They took up their guitars in a parody of the wannabe bands he'd scorned when he'd arrived in L.A. Their music didn't much improve from week to week even as the band's name changed from Twisted Mister to D'Artagnan Canyon to Umlaut to Recreational Racist.

> My firm belief is that comedy—to quote Steve Martin—isn't pretty. Comedy is bound to offend somebody. It's self-deprecating or somebody else is getting thrown under the bus. We have to laugh at ourselves. Never mind that some guy writes a cool song and puts a nice video online. That's not what gets the traffic. "Fatty Falls Down a Hole in a Convenience Store," that's the one that goes viral. Somebody's the butt of that joke. Deal with it. I'm the butt of many jokes, but I'm not going to lose any sleep over it.

The audience sang along, clapped, and shouted for more when Laura, in cowgirl hat and boots, joined Maynard's Billy D character in leisure suit and wig and moustache in a bawdy performance of the old Tom Morello and Adam Jones song "Country Boner."

PERFORMING AS PART OF A COLLECTIVE freed Maynard to test new personas and material a frontman dare not explore. "There was less judgment in doing comedy than in music," he would explain. "I could go into that space with other comedians and be a side note. I wanted to pursue this and figure out how I could do more. This was fun."

By early summer, his role had expanded from member of the comedy chorus to creative collaborator. "We'd spend all week putting themes together," Laura remembered. "We'd come up with ideas and Maynard ran with them and helped produce a lot of those shows. He always got so excited talking about this stuff. His eyes would light up and it's almost like he was rubbing his palms together."

The players might don white lab coats and head mirrors and portray doctors-cum-waiters. The Diamond Club, according to the script, had been purchased by a restaurant chain, its theme a surgical practice complete with cocktails wheeled to the tables on gurneys. Until Tantrum's lease expired, the show would go on while Dr. O'Cuttahee's served its patrons. "Maynard made table tents," Laura explained. "Instead of regular menu items, he listed things like colostomy baguettes and tater cysts, just horrid medically themed appetizers."

"While some poor bastard like Craig Anton was up on the stage trying to do his bit," Maynard remembered, "the rest of us—David Cross, me, and a couple of other people—stood at the back of the room and whirred about 32 mixed-drink blenders."

Their working-class, fundamentalist backgrounds created between Cross and Maynard an instant camaraderie, the foundation for long hours of conversation on any topic at all—discussions at times heated but always ending in unexpected insights and laughter.

"Maynard's really an intense dude. That's probably the number one reason we connected," Cross recalled in a 2013 interview. "I knew early on that he deeply appreciates comedy, and more specifically, pointed comedy about cultural hypocrisy and politics and religion.

"The first time I hung out with him, he invited me to his house in the Valley.

He was conscious of the fact that we were doing man stuff," Cross recalled of Maynard's carefully choreographed evening of animal care, jiu-jitsu, and red meat. "He definitely appreciated the irony of saying, 'I just gotta feed my lizard and then we'll watch UFC and cook up these steaks.'"

And after their meal and after cheering on the Gracies, they sat over pale ale discussing the roles they'd take in next week's Tantrum show, the progress on Cross's upcoming TV program and Tool's next album, like-minded compañeros offering encouragement and support.

"Many comedians are mean-spirited and jealous and petty and want to see others fail. Maynard isn't like that," Laura explained. "He wants to uplift and he has really high standards. I think he feels let down when people don't measure up to their potential."

If Tool's fans recognized him on the Tantrum stage, Maynard realized, they'd no doubt fear his new ventures would dilute his commitment to the band. But he knew too that an infusion of comedy could only enhance his music.

> I still wanted to see if I could blend comedy and music in a way that made sense. I felt like I could offer another dimension. I'm not a drummer, so I wasn't going to move in that direction. I'm not a guitar player. I'm a storyteller. As I expanded my palette, everything would benefit from everything else.

This new venture wasn't exactly a parody band. It wasn't a country band either, or a shift to comedy or theatrical production. It was, if it must be named, a project, a project of many facets, each dependent on all the others. A project that would spiral in unexpected directions as its course became clear. A project he'd call Puscifer.

Maynard stood on one foot. Keeping his balance wasn't hard, and he tipped his head back and stretched his fingers toward the sky. A warm wind swirled around his outspread arms, then gently lifted him until he soared above the village. It didn't seem in the least odd that he could fly. He floated there, suspended in the sunshine, and looked down at weathered wooden buildings set along dusty streets, at roads winding in switchbacks and hairpin curves through green valleys and copper-gold mountains.

The dream came more often now, always more detailed, and each time, he awoke satisfied and content. He didn't question the source of the dream or what his subconscious was telling him. "I didn't feel like anything in L.A. resonated properly," he recalled. "It didn't feel good there."

Tool's royalties didn't yet provide the income required to enjoy the city in style, and he'd had his fill of gridlock and smog, ruthless competition, and relationships he couldn't quite trust. And the music landscape had lost not a little of its appeal with the demise of Raji's and Gazzarri's and Club Lingerie. Maynard needed only a place to lay his head when Tool was in rehearsal or recording, and he cringed when he considered his certain future should he remain in L.A. "I knew if I stuck around, I was going to get sucked into the red-carpet-at-the-Grammys scene," he would remember. "I had to get out and regain some connection with the land and with space where there wasn't a lot of noise and distraction."

He'd moved enough times to know that no matter where he lived, he needn't lose his friends, David Cross, Moon Zappa—or Tim Alexander, despite their inauspicious meeting during the Lollapalooza tour. "I remember him walking toward me backstage where all the buses were parked," Tim recalled. "He had a Mohawk at the time, and it reminded me of Robert De Niro's character in *Taxi Driver*. I didn't know who he was, so when I saw him headed in my direction, I became a bit concerned, not knowing what this strange person could possibly want."

The two had since become allies, and Maynard related to Tim his recurring dream and his suspicion that the place in his vision might be Arizona. He didn't particularly want to live there, he explained. When Tool had performed in Phoenix, Maynard had found it just one more congested urban maze crowded with secretaries and CEOs parading in lockstep to their cubicles.

But Tim told him of another Arizona, an Arizona of rugged mountains and wide skies, of sudden cloudbursts that eased the summer heat and cleared to bright, balmy afternoons, of a town that sounded to him very much like the village in Maynard's dream. "Tim said he needed to take me on a little trip," Maynard would remember.

THE BUCKSKINS AND THE HARQUAHALAS AND THE EAGLETAILS extended mile after mile across western Arizona, unbroken by forest or highway, their peaks and gorges resolving in sharp relief as the plane began its slow descent over the Phoenix airport.

Midsummer wasn't the ideal time for a road trip through the desert. July was the state's hottest month with temperatures expected that day to top 110 degrees, but Maynard was eager to visit the town his friend had described and ignored the thermometer. Tim lowered the top of the rental car, and Maynard ran his finger along the interstate marked in a thick green line in his Rand McNally. In two hours, he determined, they'd reach their destination, so long as they kept close watch on the fuel gauge and calculated the distance between the tiny towns along the way where trading posts might or might not sell gasoline.

Their northbound route took them through flatlands brown with scrub, the Johnson grass and mullein at the road's shoulder drooping in the heat. They passed Rock Springs and Turret Peak and Towers Mountain, and looming outcroppings barren of vegetation. At the horizon, the Weavers and the Sierra Anchas rose in purple-gray haze, and the cloudless sky reflected in the heat mirage that shimmered always before them across the asphalt. They drove higher, above the tree line, above the frost line where even cactus did not grow.

Through the foothills they climbed, their ears popping, until they turned at last from the interstate at Camp Verde. "We came over the crest into the Verde Valley," Maynard remembered, "and my heart started to race. What I saw was so familiar."

They'd reached a promontory nearly a mile above sea level, a place of green meadows and stands of Arizona elder, willow and walnut and sycamore. The gentle climb along the ridge paralleled the valley, the gorge bounded by towering mountains, a vista he'd never known but recognized all the same.

Not far ahead were Cornville and Cottonwood and the old highway that wound in switchbacks past billboards announcing Dead Horse Ranch State Park and a bit farther, Cleopatra Hill, the mountain formed nearly two million years before by a volcanic eruption beneath the vast Precambrian inland sea. Maynard and Tim looked out on the United Verde open pit, the 300-foot-deep reminder of the area's copper mining heyday at the turn of the twentieth century. And just up the road was Jerome, the tiny town of brick and wooden buildings perched on the mountain's face.

Jerome was a collection of antique shops and cafés, art galleries and boxy brick hotels, weathered storefronts like the television versions of Virginia City and Dodge Maynard remembered from evenings in the Ohio living room. None of the buildings were particularly square. They stood pitched at odd angles along the canted streets, victims of gravity and decades of settling mine shafts beneath the town.

The sidewalks might be crowded come the weekend, but just now, only a few pedestrians walked about, friendly enough strangers who nodded in greeting as Maynard and Tim made their way up Clark Street and down Main, streets arranged in parallel terraces up the mountainside and crisscrossed by steep flights of concrete steps. Maynard read the brightly painted signage advertising gemstones and pottery and pizza and looked out at the far ridges of the Mogollon Rim. And he knew again the sensation he'd known in his dream, the feeling that he had come home.

"We stopped at the Flatiron café," he would recall. "Brian and Alan, the managers, introduced themselves right away, and their amazing Italian espresso was the last piece of the puzzle. I said, 'I'm living here.'"

> My gut and my heart and my head were practically screaming in three-part harmony that this was where I was supposed to be. If you've ever met your soulmate, you've felt that. You just know. No one has to talk you into it. Your intuition and your instinct tell you this is the one. When we got to Jerome, I thought I was going to pass out, because it was the little town in my dream.

Fewer than 400 people lived in Jerome, and the town proper was less than a mile square. But as he walked its dusty streets, Maynard imagined the dreams of long-ago miners who'd built this town—and the Yavapai and Apache before them, and people from the cities more recently come to stay. And he knew that should he live the rest of his life in this small place, it would not be long enough to learn all its stories and secrets, its promises and possibilities.

In this mile-high town, borders dissolved in a vista of valley and mountain and sky. Maynard might turn down Hill Street, climb higher to Hull Avenue, but wherever he stepped, he would be a part of the vista he walked through, and as limitless.

Here he might discover the profound silences and sounds of the desert, turn to song its legends of hills and light, read the weather and the sky and the soil, and tend the things that would grow here.

The doctors had said his child would be born in the first week of August, but that was no reason to bow out of his commitments to Tool. The August 6 Big Mele festival in Oahu would put the band on the bill with Rancid, Down by Law, Face to Face, and Guttermouth, and Maynard looked forward to the final performance before starting work on the next album. Surely he'd be back on the mainland well before the baby made its appearance.

But when the plane set down at Honolulu International, he checked his pager and discovered that sometimes, babies paid attention to due dates after all. "I had to do the right thing and be there for the birth," Maynard recalled. "I sent the band on ahead and told them I'd try to be back the next night in time for the show."

He darted through the terminal, imagining the baby's mother—2,500 miles away—repeating the deep-breathing exercises she'd learned in Lamaze class. He'd never quite understood their purpose, but he practiced them now as he negotiated with the ticket agent and fidgeted during the flight delay and suffered the stop-and-start cab ride through the more-frustrating-than-ever L.A. gridlock.

He arrived at the hospital harried and exhausted, where the baby's mother lay upon her pillows, a cassette player at her bedside, the baby an hour old. The nurse nestled the child in Maynard's arms, and he moved the edge of the blanket back from his face, stroked his fingers, held his tiny head against his own. "I couldn't say anything," he remembered. "I just played 'Kashmir' over and over."

"Kashmir," the song that seemed a portal to connection and synchronicity, the song to welcome Maynard's son, the child with wide brown eyes and thick dark curls, the baby they named Devo.

Ticket holders were plenty disappointed when they found Tool missing from the Big Mele lineup. Another flight delay had kept Maynard from the island after all. But the no-show was forgiven the next year with the release of Tool's new record, the 15-song collection that would debut at Number 2 on the *Billboard* 200 chart and prove to be anything but the uninspired and stereotypic third album.

Before the critical acclaim, before the international tour and the Grammy award and triple platinum status, the band must resolve the creative standstill interrupting the album's progress. "We'd worked individually on a few lyrics and some music," Maynard recalled. "We met for long sound checks and practices and rehearsals, but we didn't seem to be getting anywhere." The teamwork that had come so effortlessly in the past seemed elusive, as if with maturity and new interests, the four had begun to lose sight of their common goals. By midsummer, it was clear that, like Maynard's, Paul's objectives had broadened. His taste in music had shifted from the heavy riffs a Tool song would demand, and he felt ready to realize the dream he'd abandoned in Washington and form his own group.

Paul's departure created another challenge: identifying the bass player whose learning curve would not further delay the band's work. "We were looking for someone with a wellspring of ideas and talent," Maynard would recall. "Two things were most important. They had to be a very competent player and they had to be somebody we liked."

Candidates were dismissed one after the other, flawless players who couldn't quite grasp the band's philosophies, personable musicians who arrived for their auditions unprepared, professionals with perfect execution and prior commitments. When Danny and Adam suggested they consider the Peach bass player they'd met the year before, Maynard agreed. Justin Chancellor's low end had brought to Tool a welcome complexity, and a transatlantic phone call later, he'd committed to join them.

"I pulled a dog-eared slip of paper out of my pocket," Maynard would recall. "I unfolded it and showed it to Adam and Danny, the piece of paper that said 'Paul' and 'London.' It kind of blew their minds."

WITH CHANCELLOR ONBOARD and the band's momentum restored, Maynard could forget his concerns and devote time to his new pursuits—at least until album production began in earnest.

Since Tool's earliest shows, Maynard had spoken with countless reporters who'd powered their way through their questions and allowed him only truncated responses before moving on to the next. "It was weird being interviewed," he would later admit. "Most of these people had already anticipated my answers, so they didn't even bother listening to what I said."

It was time to turn the tables and ask a few questions himself, to create the sort of interview he'd like to read.

Bikini Magazine was willing to accept a submission, and Rickson Gracie agreed to an interview as Maynard's first subject. If he wanted a deeper understanding of Gracie and his beliefs, perhaps readers would, too, and he guided his instructor through a candid exploration of jiu-jitsu philosophy, the mathematical principles his father had applied to the discipline, and the balance of body, mind, and spirit that guaranteed joy on the hiking trail and victory in the ring.

The piece would need a bit of editing before it would be published the next September, but in the meantime, Maynard received a second assignment. Editors at the San Diego publication *Hypno: The World Journal of Popular Culture* were impressed enough with the Gracie draft that they suggested he try his hand at a similar piece for their magazine.

His choice of an interviewee, he realized, was a long shot, but he was prepared. Maynard had imagined the things he would ask her for a long time, their conversation should he ever have the chance to speak with her. "I told them if I was going to interview anybody," he would explain, "I'd like to talk with Joni Mitchell."

His open-ended questions allowed Mitchell to speak at length of her unconventional chord progressions, her melodic structures and alternative tunings. Their dialogue branched in unexpected turnings and illuminating tangents from the synesthesia of color and sound to the mathematical basis of a Mozart composition to the way minor chords resonate with the rhythm of the soul.

"I think she was comfortable speaking to me because I was an artist," he explained. "I didn't come in with an agenda. She was able to just talk stream-of-consciousness about music and process rather than having to jam sound bites into a predetermined format."

Published in *Hypno*'s October 1995 issue, the three-page spread was illustrated with photos of Maynard and Mitchell, their hands clasped, their smiles wide as if caught by the photographer mid-conversation before a cozy fireplace as they shared stories and a fine Shiraz.

And in November, HBO aired the inaugural episode of *Mr. Show*, the series created by Maynard's Tantrum colleagues David Cross and Bob Odenkirk. Among the sketches was a nine-minute routine featuring Cross as Ronnie Dobbs, a trailer trash troublemaker catapulted to fame by Odenkirk's television program documenting his arrests. And Maynard—in a badly cropped wig and the blue and gold cross country T-shirt he'd worn in high school—made his own TV debut. Partway through the skit, he and Adam performed as the Dobbs tribute band, a band called Puscifer.

"Whatever Maynard did, there was always a lightbulb that would go off that he could meld comedy and music," Laura would recall.

HBO viewers knew what to expect of a variety show format and didn't question a rock band's sudden appearance in the middle of a comedy sketch. But audiences weren't so forgiving when it came to humor as part of a live concert. "In December, we brought Tenacious D to open for us in San Diego," Maynard explained. "They got fuckin' quarters thrown at them." They'd been audience favorites at Tantrum, but their clowning was lost on the Soma crowd, who pelted the stage in a rain of coins and silenced their routine with shouts of "We want Tool!"

THE BAND'S NAME WAS AS MUCH IN DEMAND AS ITS MUSIC. Social justice organizations and environmentalist groups seemed to believe that if their fund-raising events included a Tool performance, contributions would roll in and the rain forests would be saved, political prisoners freed, and puppies in South America rescued from starvation.

> It was heartbreaking to be in a position where people were coming to us saying, "We value your name enough to attach it to this event which will help somebody." I'm sure many of these organizations were legitimate, but you often find that a huge percentage comes off the top for people who set up the PA and the riggers and the lighting guys. They're not donating their time. And some artists are paid insane amounts of money to be part of a benefit and then promote themselves as benefactors.
>
> We had no interest in being part of that. That's not what I consider a true

> benefit. Yes, money has to go for basic infrastructure, for insurance and water and to make sure people are fed, but at the end of the day, everybody should be donating their time, and the cash should go to the actual cause.
>
> So much of the energy they put into these things seems misdirected. How about saving the guy who's dying in the alley right next to your house?

Maynard, true to form, recognized the comedic side of the fund-raising efforts.

He'd heard the rumors about Frances Bean Cobain, daughter of Nirvana's Kurt Cobain and Hole frontwoman Courtney Love. He'd read in the tabloids of Courtney's suspected heroin use during her pregnancy and of the investigations that had led authorities to remove the baby from her parents when she was only two weeks old. He knew of the parade of nannies assigned to her care, of the toddler's visits to her father during his stay at the rehab center. "I read this stuff and thought, 'That poor girl is stuck with a tornado of a mother,'" Maynard would recall. "'How will Frances Bean survive this crazy life?'"

Helping a four-year-old caught up in a world of drug abuse and family dysfunction was a cause he could stand behind. A run of T-shirts would raise awareness of the child's plight, T-shirts he designed and produced and distributed to whomever laughed, white T-shirts printed across the front with the message FREE FRANCES BEAN. "I thought it was appropriately rude," he would explain.

COURTNEY'S BEHAVIOR SEEMED TO MAYNARD just one more symptom of the madness that was L.A. He'd been there for melees in the parking lot and snail's-pace traffic on Wilshire, and for a tense and harrowing week in 1992, he'd watched the city erupt in riots and lootings in response to the acquittal of police officers responsible for the beating of Rodney King the year before. "L.A. was burning to the ground," he would remember. "I saw how quickly everything could go off the rails."

> By 1996, I'd had enough. I'd been listening to Bill Hicks talking about L.A. falling into the ocean. And in a way, I think I wanted it to, because so many people I met were negative and just kind of vampires.
>
> I felt like so much was polluting my ability to remember that it was all just

a ride. You get so worked up into thinking it's not going to work out that you can't imagine that it will. I had to get away.

"For a long time, Maynard talked about leaving L.A., getting off the grid," Moon Zappa would recall. "I'd never met anybody so convinced something was going to happen and that we had to get out of here fast."

On the other side of the Buckskins and the Eagletails were green valleys, wide expanses of rock and sky, quiet and space and dusty streets terraced up a mountainside golden in the sunset. And one morning in late summer, the new album completed and ready for production, Maynard loaded a rental van with his belongings. He placed a supply of strawberry Twizzlers on the seat beside him and drove across the city—past Sunset and Hollywood and Beverly Boulevard and to the entrance ramp of I-10, eastbound.

"I unpacked the van and put everything in the Jerome apartment," Maynard would recall. "And then I was on a bus again." The low-slung duplex stood at the eastern end of Jerome in a row of bungalows all alike, efficient units where mining crew foremen had lived years before. Maynard moved in cartons and bags and the black trunk, and, with little time to set up housekeeping, took a deep breath and prepared for another international tour.

He and Adam and Justin and Danny had found their groove. For the past year, they'd translated their shared vision to sound and story, to an ambitious album that would—as they knew it must—surpass their previous work.

They'd hung the walls of the loft with whiteboards and covered them with equations and formulas, geometric depictions of intervals and reversed beats and fractional time signatures. "As Tom would remark, a Rage song is easy," Jack Olsen said in a 2014 interview. "A Tool song is not simple by any stretch of the imagination."

Complex as it was, the music, as always, came first. Only after Danny and Adam and Justin had worked out melodies and motifs did Maynard put pen to paper. He drew upon all he'd studied: Jung's shadow-self archetype, Melchizedek's genetic theories, Joseph Campbell's battle of opposites and the redemption their union would bring, the angle of a jiu-jitsu stance. He counterbalanced lyrics of healing with acid rock dissonance, juxtaposed images of destruction with poetic Eastern rhythms.

And on September 17, 1996, the album was released, a sonic collage of metal and comedy, of Teutonic cadence and seagull cries, of wailing babies and the click of a skipping phonograph needle. The glittering cover art harkened back to the extravagant gatefold albums of decades before, and the dreamlike images on the picture disc and promotional posters were all Ramiro's. "The spiritual nature of Ramiro's art represented Tool in a good way," Maynard would explain. "It was a grounding factor." It was, then, an album of connection, an album dedicated to Bill Hicks, an album called *Ænima*.

It took only a bit of research for fans to discover the title's etymological roots: *anima*, the Latin term for the soul and the feminine force coupled with *enema*, a sophomoric allusion to the album's theme of spiritual cleansing. But as with most things Tool, the title's significance went beyond the obvious. "I chose the name partly as a tribute to John Crowley," Maynard would explain. John Crowley, whose fictional doors and pathways had opened the way for Maynard, whose multivolume *Ægypt* series told the tale of lost histories and the hum of creative energies existing between souls.

Every track was strong enough to hold its own, but *Boston Globe* music writer Steve Morse was among the first to articulate the album's larger artistic accomplishment. *Ænima*'s message, he pointed out in a November 15 review, could be best understood by a close listen, start to finish. This was no collection of random rock rants, no crazy quilt of sound effects and hidden meaning. *Ænima*, he recognized, was an experience, a CD with a message, a sonic vehicle "taking listeners on a journey."[1]

"They obviously have a lot of darkness on the surface," Morse said of the band in a 2014 interview. "But ultimately, there is an emphasis on communication and bringing people together."

Maynard's lyrics didn't disguise his growing dislike of L.A., and even when California disappeared from the map when the lenticular jewel case was tipped just so, it didn't mean despair. All would be well, the songs urged, if one at last learned to swim: remembered one's place in the collective unconscious, one's role in the co-creation of the universe.

---

[1] Steve Morse, "Sonic Evolution with the Use of Tool." *Boston Globe*, November 15, 1996.

"Maynard has that spiritual side," Moon Zappa explained. "He's doing something with that mind of his, and he's able to straddle being technically excellent at his job and taking you a little bit further. He's a philosopher with an audience and a microphone."

TOOL HADN'T PERFORMED OUTSIDE CALIFORNIA since early 1995, but now the band would more than make up for lost time. In mid-October, they'd begin a nearly nonstop tour through the U.S., Europe, and Australia that would keep them on the road for much of the next two years.

If the band's sound had reached a new maturity with the new album, Maynard's onstage moves had taken on new aspects as well. From their front-row seats at L.A.'s American Legion Hall in October, Tom Morello and Brad Wilk could see the detailing of the Enochian magic board suspended behind Danny—and they were close enough too to notice Maynard's stomps and struts, the sharp jerk of his head when he passed near. "He had a whole new repertoire of frontman behavior," Tom would recall. "It was turkey behavior."

THE ÆNIMA TOUR MADE ITS WAY THROUGH THE SOUTH and across the Midwest, on to Amsterdam and Paris and Auckland, and at every stop, audiences looked forward to what Maynard might wear nearly as much as they did the music. At first, his costume was no more outrageous than a Mulhawk or the red union suit he'd worn during the *Undertow* tour. In black sweatpants and Birkenstocks, he ducked and dodged across the stage, singing of boredom and burdens, of balance and nipple rings, his bare torso glistening.

But by the third show, he'd taken his look in a complete 180. His face was a Kabuki mask of white, his eyes rimmed in thick black liner, his stare more penetrating than ever. In December, covered in blue and white body paint and clad only in print boxers, he crouched and swayed in a sinuous interpretive dance against the triple meter of Danny's floor tom.

Just before the band departed for the Netherlands in January, Maynard temporarily abandoned dramatic attire altogether. When vocalist Tori Amos suggested he accompany her during her Madison Square Garden concert in support of RAINN, the Rape, Abuse and Incest National Network, he didn't hesitate. The two had long admired each other's art, and when they'd met the summer before, they'd become fast friends, baking cookies from Judith's recipe and spending hours on the phone in the lonely Los Angeles nights. And when he'd opened the 1992 Napa Valley Silver Oak she'd given him, Maynard suddenly understood what Kjiirt had tried to tell him about pairing a fine Cabernet Sauvignon with a good steak.

> Appearing with Tori was more important than my reservations about benefits in general. If my being there helped the cause, great. But it would also let people see what I was capable of. I was perceived as a metal dude, but that really isn't who I am. I needed to let out some of the more complex nuances that get lost in the sonic bulldozer that is Tool.

They sat close at the piano, their harmony creating of Tori's song "Muhammad My Friend" a passionate reminder of the feminine side of divinity. And that night, Maynard was the relaxed, smiling man in a gray crewneck, a singer more balladeer than bad boy.

FROM HOUSTON TO DETROIT TO GHENT, Maynard's costuming became increasingly outré, and ten months into the tour, he made his entrance at California's Concord Pavilion in flowing black curls, white face paint, and deep crimson lipstick, his floor-length silver gown slit up the front. He vamped across the stage, methodically stripping until he stood in the spotlight in only green panties and a scarlet bra and sang of sacrifice and chaos, of the black holes of memory, of the dead Ohio sky.

He and his bandmates had made it a point to focus attention on their art and had kept their likenesses from Tool videos and promotional materials, but with increasing fame came instant recognition. Too often, fans approached Maynard in cafés and airports and the corner store, expecting a few words of conversation as if they were old friends. In truth, all they really knew of him was what they'd interpreted from his gnomic lyrics, and that's the way he preferred it.

The wigs and gowns and makeup might create a necessary diversion, he realized, a smoke screen to enable him to travel incognito in street clothes to the playground with his son.

> Back when I watched the early REM videos, I liked not having a clue what Michael Stipe looked like behind his hair. And you only heard of Swans. There

> were very few videos of them. Kiss would be onstage with all their makeup and you'd wonder who they were, what they looked like. There was power behind the characters. And when they took their makeup off, they were able to go on their merry way.
>
> In art school, Deb Rockman had taught us that less is more. You don't have to have every structural line in place to get the general gist of a painting or a charcoal drawing. And I didn't need to be recognizable to tell a story. I felt like less was not only more, less was safer.

Silly costumes made it easier, he soon discovered, to at last bring humor into a Tool performance. During the summer's Lollapalooza tour, a new character emerged. Billy D—the mustachioed satyr from his "Country Boner" routine—had metamorphosed to the Rev. Maynard. Audiences had no trouble accepting the irreverent humor of the Southern preacher in a tan leisure suit. During breaks between "Pushit" and "Hooker with a Penis," the good reverend called for hallelujahs from the mosh pit and invited volunteers to come forward and be healed of the curse of fundamentalism—all in the name of the Church of Jesus Fucking Christ.

By Ozzfest '98, Maynard had adopted more effective camouflage than sequins and painted eyebrows and ball gowns. "For a multitude of reasons, I receded to the back of the stage," he would explain. "As the eye contact became awkward, I stepped back. It was partly a technical decision; the sound was spilling into my mic from the cabinets behind me. But it also helped get away from the 'frontman' label. I absolutely *hate* the phrase 'lead singer.' I'm not a frontman. I'm just part of the story."

THE LOLLAPALOOZA FAITHFUL WANDERED in clouds of patchouli across the festival grounds. They examined woven bracelets and tie-dye skirts at the crafts booths, visited body piercing tents, found cooling relief at the misting stations, and received, if they laughed, FREE FRANCES BEAN T-shirts.

When the opening bars of "Ænema" rang out across the grounds, they turned their attention from the taco and samosa stands to the video projected on the rear of the stage—the disturbing, not-fit-for-MTV video of an alien straining at his shackles and driving a needle into his head. *Boston Globe* music writer Steve Morse considered Tool, with its Led Zeppelin echoes, illusory tempos, and enigmatic lyrics, the highlight of the main stage. "I thought they stole the show from Korn and Snoop Dogg," he said in a 2014 interview. "They were fresh and innovative and intriguingly mysterious."

Maynard wasn't in the least confident that the audience had deciphered those mysteries. He watched as they flailed in the mosh pit, enraged as ever, and in more than a few shows that summer, he stepped forward and addressed the crowd. "There's a lot of misconceptions about this band," he said softly. "It's not about hate and violence, but about opening your heart."

His lyrics spoke of picking at scabs and the coming Armageddon, but between the lines was a call to resist easy dogma, to see beyond the obvious, to choose compassion over fear and help usher in a new age of cosmic consciousness. "Maynard has always had an undercurrent of something very positive," Morse said. "He doesn't say much onstage, but he comes up with these guru-like aphorisms that are quite striking."

Maynard had paid attention when Paul Grout had cautioned against confusing metaphor with the truth it illuminated. He'd looked old hurts squarely in the eye, examined destructive patterns, recognized self-doubt as a delusion born of taking to heart the opinions of others. He'd translated his quest into songs, but some listeners could not separate the singer from the search.

> I was just interested in figuring out how math applies to human behavior, the geometry of emotions and all those things. Then, people started looking to me like I had something to offer, like they thought I could solve their puzzle. They seemed to think I was the answer. Dude, I am definitely not the answer. I've got ideas. I can put Band-Aids on stuff, but I don't have the fuckin' answers.
>
> Writing those songs and performing them was like scream therapy. It felt good to have a good cry in my Häagen-Dazs. It helped me work through my own issues. You can do that, too. Go get some ice cream and cry in a corner. If you make me responsible for moving that piece in you, then I'm responsible for it all the time. But you can do it yourself—that's the whole message.

For every fan who mistook the pointing finger for the path, countless others understood that Maynard was no run-of-the-mill lyricist. He'd provided a map, but it was for them to determine the destination. They recognized in Tool more than an excuse to slam in the mosh pit. *Ænima* was a mirror held up to fear and unresolved sorrow, an invitation to listen and listen again, to trust their own pure inner voice and step beyond the shadow self to a place of possibility, an album Cleveland music journalist Chris Akin called "a hard rock record for the thinking man."[2]

---

[2] Chris Akin, "Tool: *Ænima*," *The Scene* (Cleveland), December 1996.

11

The medicine drew Maynard deeper into the fire's rhythm, the stories it kept, the spirits of the grandfathers and their grandfathers and theirs that danced in its flicker. He breathed the essence of sage and cedar and his heart beat in time with the water drum and the flames died down then leapt again through the night and the moon made its way across the desert sky.

Lou Maglia had remained in touch with Robby Romero since signing him at Island Records in 1989. Robby was no stranger to the Native American Church. He'd grown up participating in its ceremonies with his mother and had been reintroduced to them through Reuben A. Snake, church spokesperson and national chairman of the American Indian Movement. A sun dancer and pipe carrier, Robby was plenty familiar with the sundown-to-sunrise journey of healing and spiritual transformation.

Robby was not, though, familiar with Tool, but that didn't lessen his sense of obligation when Maglia inquired about his bringing Maynard to the reservation. "I wanted to do it for Lou and for Maynard," Robby would recall. "I remembered what Reuben had told me, that if someone reaches out and it's appropriate, you should always help them."

And on a day in midsummer, Robby's assistant met Maynard at the airport in Albuquerque and drove him across the desert, past sagebrush and cactus and mesas orange at the horizon, ever deeper into the Indian territories and the Dené reservation.

TAKING PART IN A PEYOTE CEREMONY, Maynard quickly discovered, wasn't quite as simple as booking a seat in the teepee. Before the ceremony proper, he must ready himself through the purification ritual that would detoxify his body of impurities and cleanse his spirit, too, of anger and fear, greed and negativity.

The sweat lodge sat at the edge of the reservation, a squat, rounded structure no bigger than an animal's lair or a child's snow fort, far too small, Maynard could tell, for a man to move about inside without stooping. The dome was formed of bent saplings and covered with tarps, and represented, he learned, the womb of the Great Mother, a dark cocoon he'd enter and from which he'd emerge—or so the legends had it—reborn.

Late in the afternoon, Maynard and Robby and the road men who would guide them along the Peyote Road crawled inside on hands and knees and took their places in a circle. The entrance was closed off, and the only light was the red glow of the heated rocks stacked in the circle's center.

It didn't take long for the lodge to grow as hot and steamy as any sauna. Darkness and drumbeats and prayers and the tickle of sweat down his back were the whole world, and time became a concept Maynard could barely remember. Hours later—or minutes—the closeness and the heat and the glowing rocks and the rhythmic drumming became at last overwhelming, and he crawled out into the desert and knelt there, and the scorpion tattoo across his back glistened with sweat. In time, he scuttled across the sand and back inside, determined to remain on this path and discover where it might lead, however strange its course.

He knew that to change his mind now was out of the question. Already, he recognized that his presence was as crucial a part of the ceremony as the words of the blessings, as the precise placement of rocks in the fire pit. "You're not a passenger and you're not a voyeur," he would explain. "From the time you show up, it's all-encompassing. It's not like you buy a ticket and come for the show. You participate in this event and help to create it."

The next day, the group moved farther into the desert to a secluded spot at some remove from the village. Maynard lay long wooden poles on the ground, helped bind them with thick rope, hoisted them until they leaned in perfect balance one against the other, and wrapped thick canvas over the framework.

He stepped back. The teepee stood strong and tall against the evening sky. The desert was empty but for figures he watched approach from all directions: chiefs and elders, road men, a medicine woman and a grandmother, a drummer, people of the Dené and Apache and Pueblo nations, Robby's children. Each came for reasons of their own, and came, too, to walk beside the others in the communal journey.

Now they sat in a circle upon the ground, a family gathered to share green chili, bread baked that afternoon by the women of the reservation, corn grown in the nearby fields, mutton from the tribe's Navajo-Churro flock.

> The whole thing was a sobering experience after going through what I had for the past few years. People kiss your ass because you're in a band and they think they can get something from you. You get all this attention. But the elders and the sacred dancer and the kids don't give a fuck about your rock star status.
>
> And that was very liberating. You're back to being where you can see the struggle on the struggle's level, where you have to prove yourself—or not. Some of these people might not even like you, but you have to be OK with that. You can't expect to be treated differently from anybody else.

Stars appeared one by one in the darkening sky. Bowls and cups and thermoses were packed away in baskets and backpacks, and the teepee glowed, backlit by the setting sun. Maynard took his place in the queue and filed inside with the others. They circled the fire, replicating the movement of the planets around Father Sun. The road man welcomed them and welcomed the spirits of the ancestors, too, that would sit beside them in the circle until morning.

THE ROAD MAN BLESSED THE MEDICINE WITH CEDAR SMOKE and passed it around the circle, fresh peyote buttons and dried, and amber peyote tea. The medicine might bring deep introspection or unexpected insight, heightened perception or strange visions, but Maynard's hours in the dark sweat lodge had left him trusting of the will of the peyote spirit, and whatever it might bring, he accepted the sacrament when it was offered.

> I wasn't a stranger to that sort of thing. But over the years, when I did partake, I respected as much as I could that altered state. You have to honor it. You're there for a reason. It's not about getting fucked up. You're signing off on this thing as a spiritual journey.
>
> You're not going to do peyote and all of a sudden come up with a new

> theory of relativity. Well, maybe you will, but if you do, I think it's in you already.
> The reason you do this is to take a lateral step to the right or the left to look at
> things from a different perspective. You do it to become aware of something
> you should already know but might have missed because you were looking at
> it from the wrong angle.

Each element of the ceremony—every gesture, every object handed from one to the other around the circle—held its story. Its form, its choreography, was determined by nothing less than the laws of geometry: the teepee poles angled to form its conical shape, the entrance situated to face due east, the peyote blessed and the sacred songs sung one, two, three, four times—once for each of the four directions, the four elements. The circles echoed the unbroken connection of all things. The balance of body, mind, and spirit, of fire, water, and medicine were triads sturdy in their grace. And when the flames burned low, the fire keeper brought branches to feed the fire and meticulously arranged them to form a V, its apex pointing toward the center of the crescent-moon altar.

"Maynard knows that we become what we think," Robby would explain. "He understands it's not what we do, it's the way we do it."

The rituals created a pattern, a rhythmic clockwise repetition through the night of songs and prayers and drumming, each step pitching Maynard from the familiar and shepherding him further into the new way of seeing and an awareness of his part in the equation. When it was his turn, he smoked from the sacred smoke. He accepted the gourd rattle from Robby, took midnight water from the drinking cup, then passed it to the grandmother beside him.

The road men spoke their healing prayers, the people shared their stories, their own and those of the ancestors, and each telling created another dimension of the eternal tale. The flames flickered in counterpoint to the jangling rattles, the pulse of the water drums, and the songs. They cast shadows against the walls of the teepee and told the fire's story all night long.

THE WOMEN AND CHILDREN drew back the flap from the entrance and brought dried meat and wild berries and fresh water from the river. And Maynard stepped into morning. The desert was still. The desert crackled with life. Across the lightening sky winged seven black birds as if placed there by design. In the distance, mountains rose against the horizon, sharp and distinct as his own attentiveness. He stood in just that place, the sand cold under his bare feet. From somewhere quite nearby or far, a cactus wren rasped its daybreak song. Beneath a cluster of prickly pear, a horned toad stirred, and the morning star shone in the east.

"I think the ceremony had a profound impact on him," Robby would recall. "After a ceremony, a different spiritual life begins. We respect and maintain that life. What Maynard experienced allowed his spirit to touch the beauty and power of our people. He got to experience medicine in a respectful way, in a good way, in the way the Creator intended."

Maynard's night in the teepee had brought no revelations, or none that he would afterward recall. He'd seen no visions, received no otherworldly advice, and there was no telling what prayer, which word, which blessing would be the one he'd remember always. The journey had been an extended, concentrated moment, a path that opened to the mirror image of discord and anger, opened to a rhythm, a harmony. That was all. At the end of the path was morning, a morning not so different from those when he'd looked up from his notebook at the surprise of gray dawn and discovered he'd created in the night a song where once there had been silence.

"What you see is a validation," he would explain. "But it's not a coupon you can go cash in. It's not a sign. It's just a nod. It's the universe nodding. And you're part of that.

"There's no possible way to explain it to somebody who wasn't there. And you know what? It's OK. You don't have to. You see it. You nod back. And you move on."

Ænima had been certified gold ten weeks after its release and by the time the tour ended was well on its way to reaching double platinum. The album had been a 1998 Grammy nominee for Best Recording Package and had come away with the award for its title track.

Royalties had at last offset the Zoo advance, and nearly seven years after releasing its first album, Tool had begun to see a financial return. Steady paychecks, Maynard realized, meant his days of roommates and substandard apartments could be a thing of the past. "The goal is not the money," he would explain. "Money is just gas in the tank to be able to do the things you love."

During a break in the tour schedule, he'd discovered a rent-to-own house on the outskirts of Jerome, a modest one-and-a-half bedroom on a southwest-facing slope overlooking the valley and Mingus Mountain. Here, just outside the city limits, he could trade the evening gown and high-heeled slippers for bib overalls and work boots and transform his acre into terraced gardens.

It would take some research to determine which plants would actually thrive on the rugged hillside. This was not the black loam of Mike's peony and day lily plots, but a gravely, sandy caliche, commixed with lime and calcium. And the climate might present an agricultural challenge or two as well. He'd experienced the heat of a Jerome summer, and locals had told him of frost on the mountain as early as October and in some years, as late as May Day.

But the little house would be the quiet retreat he needed, the home where he could build Lego cities with Devo and at Christmastime stack books about Native American history under the tree for him. And not far away were Main Street and the Flatiron café, where already Maynard was a welcome regular, and an hour distant, Prescott, the progressive college town offering, he was pleased to learn, periodic sessions of Melchizedek's Flower of Life seminar.

Eager as he was to settle into life on the mountain, he must—for the time being, at least—divide his time between Jerome and his Tool responsibilities in L.A., and he took up temporary residence at the La Maida house, where Billy was busy at work on music of his own. And the arrangement worked out fortuitously for Mike. He and Jan had parted ways, and now he would live in the orchard house across the road and watch over the Jerome house while he enjoyed his retirement years on the hiking and skiing trails of Arizona.

> For the first couple of years after I moved, I spent more time in airports and the tour bus than I did in Jerome. And after the *Ænima* tour, I still had to rehearse and record with the band. Nowadays, you can open your laptop and record an album in your living room wherever you are. But back then, all the equipment and studios were in L.A. You'd have to rent mics and cables and end up spend-ing twice as much if you tried to record an album in the middle of Arizona.

BEFORE WORK ON A FOURTH ALBUM COMMENCED in earnest, Maynard took advantage of his time in L.A. He joined Laura on the Tantrum stage in their "Country Boner" act and with a renewed enthusiasm, revisited the acting lessons he'd begun when he'd first come to the city. It was par for the course, he'd learned, for sitcom stars and singers and sports figures to branch into films, their success in one discipline paving their way to another. If ever he were to follow that path, he'd need to up his performance level.

By now a master of disguise, he enrolled at the Ivana Chubbuck Studio on Melrose as only "James" and came to class in worn leather jacket and jeans, ostensibly just one more unknown with no expectation of special treatment or intention of riding his own coattails to cinematic success. "I busted my ass in that class," he would recall.

He struggled with breathing exercises and cold readings, confronted his weaknesses, and tried his best to play to what he imagined his strengths should be. In his attempt to master Chubbuck's 12 steps to character development as actors Eddie McClintock and David Spade had done before him, he all but ignored his natural comedic talents. And when class was dismissed, he returned to the La Maida house discouraged, frustrated by the challenge that seemed only a chore.

A month into the course, Maynard's concerned coach took him aside. "He said he thought he knew what my problem was," Maynard remembered. "He felt that I was absolutely terrified that I was average."

He knew at once that his coach was on to something. Despite *Undertow*'s platinum status, despite the awards and reviews and sold-out arenas, Maynard still harbored the suspicion that one day, his past would surely catch up with him. The spotlights and applause would be revealed as the illusion they were, and he'd come face-to-face with his true destiny: that of a complacent factory worker nursing forgotten dreams and Bud Light in a gray Ohio living room. "I felt I had to always be one step ahead so I could say I did *something* before that happened," he would recall.

His greatest challenge at the Chubbuck studio wouldn't be earning an A, but outdistancing the echo of dismissal and underestimation, the irrational and persistent belief in his mediocrity. And the course did little to encourage the pace he'd need to maintain if he were to reach either goal.

Every week, we were assigned a partner. We were supposed to meet with them during the week and develop a scene and present it in the next class. I kept

> getting stuck with these actresses or models who just couldn't be bothered to study with me. I was there for like two, maybe three months, and I only did three scenes because these people kept cutting class to go to auditions or photo shoots. It was a waste of my time to be there and not be able to exercise whatever the fuck I had to exercise.

BUT AT THE GRACIE STUDIO, he had only to rely on himself. Jiu-jitsu wasn't a tandem effort; he needn't depend on a partner to earn an above-average score. "It's up to you to work hard," he would explain. "If you're getting your ass kicked every time, you're not getting any better. There's no coasting in jiu-jitsu."

Success was a matter of avoiding the head-on attack, of stepping to a more advantageous position to alter the very dynamic of the game, of diverting his opponent's energy—and redirecting his own.

"If your opponent is driving all his weight on you, you move to the side and let it go into the ground or into the wall," he said. "Instead of trying to push back, I learned to step outside the situation."

In hotel rooms and airline terminals from Fresno to Newcastle, Maynard had used his downtime during the *Ænima* tour to work on new songs, songs more complex, more metaphoric than ever. But a contract dispute with Zoo's successor, Volcano Entertainment, had stalled progress on the next album, and by early 1999, the legal disputes had left the band's creativity blocked and Maynard feeling restless.

"Things weren't moving as fast as I'd like," he would recall. "What was I supposed to do now, sit around the house rereading all these depositions? That's boring. I felt like I wasn't doing enough."

> I knew I had more to offer than the timing of Tool would allow—more songs, more music, more art. I come from a background of people who couldn't do any of those things. They couldn't be in one band let alone three. They couldn't add up the monthly bills or even dress themselves.
>
> If you have the means, the knowledge to create something and you don't,

> shame on you. If you're able to be good at your job, to raise a child, to plant
> a garden, whatever, it's your responsibility to do it—not only for yourself but
> for the world.

Billy Howerdel had his own portfolio of partially completed music—a sort of post-punk, darkwave hybrid he'd spent years tweaking and editing and polishing. He'd never considered the possibility of his songs one day making the *Billboard* charts—or being produced, for that matter. His art was a solitary exercise in craft and composition, a challenge to create with his portable four-track recorder a sonic layering of orchestral movement and heavy metal.

"It happened one day that Maynard walked in while I was working," he recalled in a 2015 interview. "I played him one of my songs, and he said, 'I could hear myself singing that.'" Flattered by his response, Billy nevertheless dismissed Maynard's words as a fraternal pat on the back and returned to his headphones, equalizers, and VU meters.

But Maynard was persistent. Not only did he recognize potential in Billy's work, he saw a chance to sidestep the Tool impasse and broaden his own artistic range. "Billy had these great songs, and I asked him for a tape I could work with," he would recall. "I thought I might be able to punch them up."

Maynard heard in Billy's unique sound subtle echoes of Randy Rhoads, the Cure, Siouxie and the Banshees, an intriguing framework for a new direction his lyrics might take. By the time he'd added vocal melodies and words, Billy's blueprint had telescoped to a three-dimensional structure of harmony and rhythm and story. Even the song Billy had believed was fully realized, an homage to a childhood mentor, Maynard recast to an impassioned screed against blind adherence to dogma. "When I heard what he did, I was just blown away," Billy would recall. "He's the master of figuring out odd puzzles."

It seemed to both a foregone conclusion that they should continue their collaboration, bring in a few musicians, and see just how far their project might go. Perhaps, Maynard thought, forming a band with Billy would give him fresh perspective on the Tool standstill. "When you're in a relationship, you can't see it clearly," he would explain. "I had to look from the outside in, have another relationship to give some contrast."

The two knew enough professionals to avoid the frustration of open auditions. They called in their A-list, members of bands that had opened for Tool and musicians Billy had worked with as a guitar tech. For the cost of lunch and an afternoon in a rehearsal studio, they realized a satisfying return on their investment: players not only competent and personable but who understood their vision for the band. Failure guitarist Troy Van Leeuwen made the cut, and Paz Lenchantin, the classically trained bassist Billy had long admired. He and Maynard gave the nod to both Josh Freese of Devo and Guns N' Roses and to Tim Alexander, who would alternate on drums until one or the other became a permanent member of the group.

With a handful of songs more or less completed and the fledgling band fully staffed, Maynard and Billy took the next logical if somewhat ambitious step. Booking shows a few months out would give them a deadline to work toward, the motivation to fine-tune their material and create a thematic, album-length body of work.

Years of sharing tour buses and the La Maida house had accustomed them to each other's quirks and working style, and they tackled their job with an inspired and coordinated ferocity. Maynard reviewed Billy's music and developed melodies and lyrics, careful to retain the essence of the originals. Each iteration raised the bar for Billy, who then took the pieces to even higher levels of complexity. "I trust him," Billy said of Maynard's input. "Even when he does something and my first reaction is, huh?, I let it go. I don't question it. And not because I don't want to piss him off. It's just literally that I completely trust him."

Maynard's writing for Tool had been a cerebral exercise, a masculine approach of anger and attack. The night in the teepee had freed him to face his vulnerabilities head-on, to face the roots of that anger and move from the abstract to grounded, sensual lyrics—"Pull me into your perfect circle / One womb / One shame / One resolve"—lyrics that defined the music's leitmotif and gave the new band its name. A Perfect Circle would bring to the forefront Maynard's emotions, his experience—his voice.

Billy had for a long time imagined the vocalist who might do justice to his music, the strong woman who would take his songs in a more feminine direction than most mainstream rock and shatter the stereotype of the fragile girl singer. But when he heard Maynard's vocal treatment of their material, he thought again. "Maynard and I were on the same page," Billy would explain. "There was an unspoken understanding that a powerful sentiment could be conveyed from a feminine perspective—sung by a male." Maynard's was the voice that could best tell the APC stories, the voice that ranged effortlessly from anguished scream to tender whisper, from growling aggression to the gentle nuance often lost in Tool's wall of sound.

> The argument that many people had about Tool's music is that they couldn't hear the vocals. I had to scream to be heard, and that's not necessarily a pleasant sound. It works for the rage, but it doesn't work for the art if you have to scream your head off to be heard over the amps.
>
> In a way, besides being its own band, I always thought of A Perfect Circle as a way to serve Tool. I thought if my voice was more audible and people learned how to recognize it, they'd have more respect for Tool if they could hear that fourth instrument.

By the summer of 1999, concertgoers and online reviewers were already referring to APC as Maynard's side project, though he considered the new group anything but a diversion. His bands would be given the time and space each required and deserved—and that included the undertakings of his Puscifer project.

IN MID-AUGUST, L.A.'S ROCK COMMUNITY turned out in force to support one of its own. Former Circle Jerks and Black Flag vocalist Keith Morris faced that summer staggering medical bills following his recent diagnosis of type 2 diabetes and a series of surgeries, and the two-show benefit was one more fundraiser Maynard could get behind. The varied lineup included Pennywise and Fishbone, Gibby Haynes of Butthole Surfers, Thelonious Monster, and actor Johnny Depp—and in the afternoon show at Whisky a Go Go, Recreational Racism.

Maynard opened with countrified versions of Circle Jerks's "Group Sex" and "Back Against the Wall," and then, in platinum pompadour, bushy blond mustache, and beige leisure suit, joined Laura Milligan in "Country Boner," the Libertyville campfire sing-along that had become a Recreational Racism staple.

And that evening at the Viper Room, A Perfect Circle made its public debut. Maynard warned the curious audience that the sound they'd hear that night would not inspire head-banging. A Perfect Circle was AM radio music, he joked, the kind of music Billy liked. "Perfect Circle allowed Maynard to be a little bit looser," Billy would explain. "We bonded over humor even more than music, a dry, love-of-Monty-Python, British, slipped-under-the-table humor."

The six songs they performed that night weren't exactly easy listening but were a delicate balance of heavy rhythms and crunching guitar riffs, atmospheric rock and melodic intervals. New as the band was, its performance was tight, its members attuned to the others' nuances as if they'd played together for years. Percussion and bass interwove with guitar and words of release and remorse, forgiveness and fidelity in songs so new that Maynard from time to time consulted his lyric sheet as he sang.

A few days after its debut, the band played an afternoon show at the Opium Den, the new incarnation of the Gaslight as cave-dark as ever and where water still seeped onto the stage from the men's room upstairs. The performance included the same half-dozen songs they'd done at the Viper Room—and a promise of brand-new material at the Troubadour that night.

Between shows, the band stopped by the backyard of Nine Inch Nails bassist Danny Lohner to join in another of Hollywood's ubiquitous cookouts. While the others passed the potato salad and sipped their Sam Adams, Maynard sat at the edge of the yard, straining to see in the fading light the lyrics he scribbled in his yellow notepad.

A PERFECT CIRCLE MADE ITS WAY UP THE COAST, opening for Fishbone or Oxbow or Dolores Haze in tiny clubs from St. Luis Obispo to San Jose to San Francisco. At each stop, the lyrics were more polished, the presentation more professional, and the gate more satisfying as word spread of this surprising alt-metal, art rock, operatic band.

The mini tour was interrupted by APC's most well-attended performance to date. Maynard fans had looked forward for months to Tool's October 10 appearance at the inaugural Coachella Art and Music Festival in Indio, California, its first show in more than a year. But they changed their plans when they learned his new band would open the festival on the ninth. The 100-degree temperatures couldn't keep them from the Empire Polo Grounds that day, and they carried their water bottles to the mosh pit at the main stage, where they swayed in time to Billy's Les Paul and Tim's percussion and Maynard's songs of emptiness and loneliness and the healing a perfect circle of connection might bring.

If audiences expected the intense, screaming frontman they'd come to know, they discovered instead a more subdued Maynard who uncharacteristically held his spot on the stage and made little eye contact with the crowd. And if they shouted his name when the band made its entrance, he shook his head and held a finger to his lips. No member of APC was more important than any other, the gesture seemed to say. The music was, after all, Billy's dream, a dream Maynard was not about to co-opt. "Maynard was beyond gracious, beyond inspiring, and elevating," Billy would recall of his largesse. "He can really love the underdog. He basically said, 'I'm going to let you steer this ship.'"

A Perfect Circle was an ensemble, a team, and Maynard refused to take the role of frontman or spotlit rock star—despite the message written in glitter across his T-shirt front: FUCK ME, I'M FAMOUS.

The days of rummaging beneath cushions for loose change were over. Maynard's long-overdue financial security meant wining and dining in style the ingénues and fangirls eager to appear at his side—and indulging a bit in the rock star lifestyle that seemed expected of him. But he didn't put his royalties entirely toward vintage Cabernets and top-of-the-line mobile phones, gourmet cat food for his Siamese, Puppy Cat, or Prada skunk-skin blankets.

He and Billy knew that maintaining artistic control of their project must come at a price. Investing their savings and their skills in the production of a demo would ensure the integrity of the singular sound that reflected their shared musical language. "Billy was influenced by things that I felt Tool would never be influenced by," Maynard would explain. "I liked the idea of bringing in some Byrds melodies, some Love and Rockets. The harmonies were all Joni Mitchell." And if they recorded the demo on their own, they could be sure of its timely completion.

> I work best when you give me a puzzle and a set of parameters. Billy had been
> kicking around this music for a long time, and I think it motivated him for me

> to go, "OK, we have exactly five minutes to do this." Eventually, I was going
> to have to get back to Tool and I wouldn't have time to work on anything
> else. So if we were going to do this, we needed to do it *now*. And because we
> just absolutely had no time, we were able to create something pure without
> overthinking it.

That winter, while the rest of the world prepared for the impending Y2K digital shutdown, Maynard placed his trust in Billy's Mac 9600 and his Pro Tools expertise. Renting studio space and recording to tape didn't come cheap, and going digital, they discovered, was economical and efficient. "It's the total norm nowadays," Billy explained in a 2015 interview. "But in 1999, it was extremely rare to record an album yourself." Except for an afternoon at Sound City and two days of percussion work at the home studio of Billy's friend Scott Humphrey, the recording and overdubbing and editing was completed in their own backyard—a room off the garage that Billy had converted to a vocal booth and recording studio.

By the end of January, *Mer de Noms* was a reality, a collection of tales of failure and redemption, of pain born of truth dismissed or overlooked, a chronicle of those who'd shaped Maynard's life for good or ill, their names cascading through the song titles like a log of biblical begats.

The two brought onboard attorney Peter Paterno to guide the demo toward recording companies likely to show interest. The eye-catching cover art couldn't help but make a positive first impression, Billy's ambiguous Perfect Circle logo embodying the album's theme. At first glance, the mismatched arcs weren't a perfect circle at all. But with a shift in perspective, a peek behind the obvious, the image emerged of a layered symmetry, figures eclipsed in shadow, but visible all the same if one were only to look.

It was Nancy Berry's job as vice chair of EMI's Virgin Music Group Worldwide and Virgin Records America to review the demos sent her way by hopeful musicians and their reps. The rock genre was still strong in that winter of 2000, and *Mer de Noms* was just one more in the ever-growing stack of CDs in her inbox. But Berry's friend, Curve vocalist Toni Halliday, had inside information. Maynard and Billy had recruited Halliday's husband, producer and engineer Alan Moulder, to mix the demo, and she knew firsthand that A Perfect Circle was a cut above the average fledgling band. And on that rainy Sunday night in February, determined to clear her to-do list before a new workweek began, Berry took her friend's advice and placed their demo in her player.

"I listened to 'Judith' and absolutely fell in love with it," Berry recalled in a 2014 interview. "I said, 'OK, now I've got to go listen to it in the car,' because that was always the test for me in signing bands." Up and down the glistening streets of Bel Air she drove, aware only of the anguished ache in Maynard's voice, of Billy's atmospheric riffs, of Paz's driving bass. Then she played the CD from start to finish, lost in the haunting Eastern rhythms and dark waves of percussion, the daring segues from orchestral to goth, Maynard's plea for healing, for recognition, for peace. She pressed replay and listened again.

In her years with Virgin, Berry had worked with such talents as Smashing Pumpkins and David Bowie and Janet Jackson, and her standards were high. The final mixing and mastering would come later, but already *Mer de Noms* was a clean, professional production. She recognized that for all its hints of the Cocteau Twins and Swans and the Cure, for all its shifts in tempo and genre, the APC sound was in a category all its own, distinct, cohesive, and radio-friendly. First thing Monday morning, she telephoned Paterno with an offer.

Berry wasn't alone in her enthusiasm. Top labels had already begun their courtship rituals, wooing Maynard and Billy with the usual lobster dinners and overpriced wines and too-good-to-be-true promises. Once more, Maynard had listened over steak and sashimi to chatter of royalty structures and distribution schemes and the band's glittering future. Accustomed by now to the seductive rhetoric, he sipped his Gewürztraminer, imagined floppy rabbit ears, and paid attention only to the practical commitments the labels might bring to the table.

"Virgin seemed to be a more focused company," he would recall. "And 90 percent of the company was women, all hell-bent on proving themselves in a man's industry." And after consulting with her husband, EMI president Ken Berry, Nancy sweetened her offer with terms that tipped the scales toward Virgin even more. "She got us a joint venture deal, which most labels weren't willing to do," Maynard would explain. "We'd be business partners. The band would invest in promotions and marketing and we'd split the profits 50/50 with the label."

A Perfect Union of Contrary Things

With only two months to prepare before APC was to go on the road, Berry made the band a Virgin priority. "I've never in my career done anything as fast and intense as we did for Perfect Circle," she would recall. The final mastering of *Mer de Noms* must be completed, and a music video, the marketing campaign, and the design of elaborate sets in time for the band to open for Nine Inch Nails in its Fragility v2.0 tour that would begin in April.

> Nancy Berry managed to wrangle David Fincher to direct the "Judith" video, which is a gorgeous piece and really did a lot for us. I'm sure dealing with someone like me wasn't anything out of the ordinary for him, but of course, we butted heads a little bit. We had to negotiate a compromise between him wanting to see my face and me wanting to be Cousin Itt behind a wig.
>
> We managed to find a happy medium, and in the course of filming, he expressed interest in having me possibly read for his next film. Legend has it that I was booked for it and turned it down. But no, I had to get to work and go on the road. Dwight Yoakam ended up getting that role. There's no possible way I would have pulled off what he did in *The Panic Room*, so that was probably the best decision Fincher ever made, to not pursue having me read for the part.

SEARCHLIGHTS AND STROBES ILLUMINATED the twin arcs and the rune-like renderings of *Mer de Noms* song titles suspended over the darkened stage. Louder and louder against the crowd's expectant cheers rose Josh's staccato percussion, Billy's wailing guitar, Paz's crashing bass, Troy's insistent rhythms. The music slowed, then expanded, then erupted in sonic chaos.

Through the Midwest, across Canada, up the East Coast, mosh pits exploded in a blur of slamming and crowd surfing. APC, audiences discovered, was a symphonic pop-metal fusion, a balance of grunge and rock, a celebration of the unexpected: an erotic strip-poker intro, a ten-minute mash-up of Ozzy Osbourne's "Diary of a Madman" sung over the Cure's "Love Song," Maynard's frenzied burlesque of self-stimulation.

He and his bandmates communicated cues with no more than a glance, their sensitivity belying their brief partnership. The APC members were mysterious characters in black, their costumes a shadowy camouflage that allowed their stories to take center stage, the tales of dismissal and heartbreak, of rage and introspection and forgiveness. Maynard growled and crooned and raged

Billy's lyrics and his own, lyrics of how much was lost in the blind surrender to love, how much gained in authentic connection, how much destroyed in unquestioned faith in a specious savior. He hunched and crouched and convulsed across the stage, twisted his bare torso and jerked his head, and the long hair of his wig fell across his eyes.

Berry wasn't unnerved by Maynard's insistence on the wig. He'd explained to her the importance of differentiating his APC persona and of walking about unrecognized with his son. "Whenever something was deeply personal to an artist, I tried to understand it and appreciate it," she would explain. "And he really wanted APC to be seen as a unit, not just as Maynard. He's a reluctant rock star."

ADAMANT AS MAYNARD WAS ABOUT STEPPING FROM THE FRONTMAN ROLE, his name undeniably drew the curious public to APC. But they paid attention because of the music. Released on May 23, 2000, *Mer de Noms* entered the *Billboard* 200 at Number 4, higher than any previous ranking of a rock band's debut album. The record sold more than 188,000 copies in its first week and would remain on the charts for just short of a year.

"*Mer de Noms* was a group of people coming together at the right time," Berry would explain. "It was the perfect combination of the talent, the look, the personalities. And Maynard brought something else with his theatricality, the sensitivity of his voice, something intellectual and dreamy with the lyrics."

Even so, fans who didn't know the backstory of the Volcano impasse perceived APC as Maynard's abandonment of Tool. They posted on message boards and online forums their disappointment in his desertion and their demand that he return to the only band that really mattered. But reviewers and critics recognized in *Mer de Noms* more than a flash-in-the-pan side project. Steve Morse, in his coverage of the May 2 show at the Worcester Centrum in Massachusetts, reported that while the jury was still out on some of its songs, A Perfect Circle appeared to have "a can't-miss future in the marketplace."[1]

And far from a trivial pastime, APC was Maynard's opportunity to exercise his marketing savvy and meet the challenge of a music industry in flux. In the wake of a changing business model, mega record stores had begun to give

---

[1] Steve Morse, "NIN's Hammerings as Hard as Ever," *Boston Globe*, May 3, 2000.

way to online retailers and music-sharing sites like Napster—sites that might or might not compensate artists for downloads of their work.

Touring was where the money was, and the joint venture meant that in exchange for bankrolling the cross country road trip, the band would reap 100 percent of tour profits and drive CD sales along the way.

> Billboards and magazine articles and radio play would never generate enough sales. We had to get in front of people and stay on the road long enough to build awareness. I'd learned that the best way to do that was to play a city and circle back a couple more times. That creates three points of reference for people to remember. And that costs money.
>
> Whenever you can figure out some way to cross-promote things, it helps. If you can partner with friends with successful businesses, at least it doesn't feel like you're selling out. You feel good because you believe in what they're doing. Everybody wins.

Maynard had worn the Oakley sunglasses marketed by Tim Cadiente since 1995 and was well aware that his celebrity had boosted sales. Involving Cadiente in promoting APC would create a mobile chew-bone pickup, increasing sales of one product via awareness of another.

"Maynard came to me," Cadiente would recall. "He said, 'Hey, I've got this new band and we need tour support. What can you do for us?' It was simple. I'd get companies to wrap the tour bus." Cadiente would enshroud the APC bus in oversized vinyl sheets printed with colorful advertisements for Oakley sunglasses and goggles and Paul Frank tees and tote bags. The band's share of the revenue would enable APC to extend its tour, compensate the crew, obtain even more spotlights and gels.

Bus wraps were virtually unheard of in the States despite their popularity in Europe, but Maynard understood the potential impact of such a blend of the artistic and practical. "Maynard's always had that ability to separate himself from what other people are doing," Cadiente would explain. "Everything he does, he's a step ahead of everybody else."

The two-month NIN tour was followed by appearances at the Fuji Festival and Canada's Summersault Festival, and with few breaks, eight months of headlining sold-out shows in Australia, Europe, and the U.S. And at every stop, from Sydney to Stuttgart, from Saskatoon to Sacramento to the Grand Rapids Deltaplex, Maynard paused between songs and reminded the crowd that the force behind the music, the mastermind of A Perfect Circle, was Billy.

"It says a lot about Maynard that he didn't just insert himself," Billy would explain. "In every photo shoot, he said, 'No, put Billy up front. It's his band.' He was very clear about the fact that I had done the work ahead of time. He appreciates and demands hard work. The last thing he wants is a lottery winner who got there by happenstance."

Nor would Maynard allow himself to coast, to amble when a concerted sprint was required. If anything, the breakneck recording pace and nonstop tour fueled his imperative to take advantage of every spare moment to imagine, to write, to compose.

And when Devo expressed an interest in making music of his own, Maynard wasn't one to discourage him. "I'd heard Paz's sister Ana practicing her cello, and I was absolutely enamored," Devo would recall in a 2015 interview. "A few years later, Dad gave me my cello. He's always been encouraging and excited about my playing."

From Portland to Pensacola to Pittsburgh, while his bandmates read or rested or reviewed the next night's set list, Maynard curled in a quiet spot at the back of the bus and worked on the songs Tool fans had impatiently awaited for nearly four years.

Entr'acte

A half-open suitcase stood always at the ready in a corner of Maynard's bedroom, and beside it, a satchel bulging with Rube Goldberg–style lash-ups of cables and U.K. and German adaptors. A month and a half after the final *Mer de Noms* show, he was off again, this time to Europe and the first leg of Tool's *Lateralus* tour. The band's legal battles had been resolved, and on May 15, 2001, the first in its new three-album deal with Volcano Entertainment debuted at Number 1 on the *Billboard* 200 chart.

Recorded during breaks in the Perfect Circle tour, the 12-song collection took the band beyond alternative metal to art rock—to, in fact, math rock. The notational structures and syllabic arrangements spiraled in a 79-minute suite of Fibonacci precision, inspired even more than *Ænima* by the concepts of sacred geometry.

As always, Maynard's lyrics urged critical thinking and transcendence of stasis. *Lateralus* was, he admitted, "a soundtrack for healing," a blueprint for enlightenment that might come from tapping into the energies that lay in mathematical symmetry—and the position of the planet Saturn. Every 28 years or so, astrologers claimed, Saturn returned to the place in the sky it had been at the moment of one's birth, marking the beginning of a new life stage—adulthood, maturity, old age—each an opportunity to reassess one's purpose. "You either let go of past delusions and ascend to the next level, or you sink like a stone," Maynard would explain. "If you can't make it past your Saturn return, you remain stagnant."

The kaleidoscopic gestalt of image and sound that was *Lateralus* more than made up for the long wait between Tool releases. The circle of stylistic eyes that illustrated the disc was visionary artist Alex Grey's invitation to look closely, to see beyond the obvious. The transparent pages of the layered insert in the jewel case were a reminder of multiple meanings, of the union of the physical and the spiritual. Curious audio effects were as well an invitation to listen—and marked the recording debut of Puppy Cat.

The concert set was an elaborate palimpsest of videos, oversized banners depicting Grey's anatomical paintings, a glittering backdrop of prismatic human eyes—a collage of sound and light choreographed in what Steve Morse called "the best multimedia rock event so far this year."[1]

A backlit Maynard in Speedo and blue neon body paint performed from the rear of the stage, and above him, awash in pulsating light, was suspended the design of seven points and seven intersected lines—geometric perfection in the shape of a star.

THE BAND WOULD CRISSCROSS EUROPE, Asia, Canada, and North America, enjoying little downtime until December of the next year. The September 11 show at Van Andel Arena in Grand Rapids was by necessity postponed until the 13th. The nation's response to the attack on the Twin Towers had already begun to morph from a healthy patriotism to dogmatic nationalism, and though never one to broadcast his political views, Maynard broke character and reacted to the crowd's insistent shouts. "The audience was chanting 'USA! USA!' between songs," he would explain. "I lost it and said something like, 'Maybe instead of chanting like sheep, we should take a minute to figure out what we did to provoke this.' Sometimes my mouth opens and stuff comes out."

Lest the crowd believe he'd bought into the already-emerging conspiracy theories, he dialed down a notch and led them in swearing what he called the Nonconformist Oath, a pledge that borrowed from a Steve Martin comedy routine, a vow to question authority and never repeat what others said. His audience obediently echoed the mantra word for word.

In light of the tragedy, the themes of *Lateralus* seemed curiously prophetic. The world was indeed in need of healing, and if the lyrics encouraged anything,

---

[1] Steve Morse, "Tool Hammers Out a Multimedia Triumph," *Boston Globe*, August 17, 2002.

it was a breaking down of barriers between individuals and thinking for oneself, and Maynard closed the show with a heartfelt entreaty. "Take the feelings you've experienced in the last few days and hang on to them, good or bad," he urged the Grand Rapids audience. "And please create something positive with them."

Maynard had never trashed a hotel room, never stalked from the stage in a petulant snit and refused to finish a show. But the lessons of the peyote ceremony and yet another reading of Joseph Campbell hadn't been enough to stem his becoming a celebrity cliché. The lights and applause were seductive, and Maynard's success guaranteed that at every tour stop would be willing women, clichés themselves seeking a one-night dalliance with a Grammy-winning rock star.

> It happens to almost everybody who suddenly becomes famous. We're not wired to handle that much attention, but it just seems like the path you're on, so you go down it. You want intimacy, but you're in motion. You're not ready to settle down, so you just follow the sexual thing.
>
> Most people fall into chemical addiction, which is harder to get out of. I was lucky enough to fall into a kind of ego addiction. She likes me! She likes the name of the band! She likes what I sing about!
>
> And the more you dabble in that, the less chance there is of a relationship. She has no idea who I am. I knew the difference between attention and real connection, but I forgot it for a minute. I didn't even think about what I was doing. I was just having fun.

He might prearrange a tryst with the woman in Berlin he'd met the last time he'd passed through, never doubting her interest. And he cavalierly skipped after-show drinks with old friends to prolong a rendezvous with an attractive stranger selected from the Seattle audience the night before.

The assignations were consensual, no-strings-attached, seemingly perfect. But the validation was short-lived. "You're left wanting to be wanted for *you*, and you're not going to get that with these people," he would explain years later. "They're looking for something else, that larger-than-life thing. But you

lose track of that and fall victim to your own behavior." And in Düsseldorf and
Providence, he knew, some exciting someone would be waiting.

Since Tool's first tour, Maynard had made sure the Midwest schedule included
a free day or two in Ohio. His mother had treasured the rare visit with her son
and ignored his Mulhawk and leather jacket, the shaved head and tattoos. And
no matter his deadlines or recording commitments, he'd called her often with
news of Devo's progress at the Waldorf School, his finches, a surprise frost on
the mountain. He'd wired her favorite flowers on her birthday, sent gifts and
money orders when he could, and when the *Lateralus* tour made its way to
Cleveland, he brought her to the show.

Judith sat in her protected spot in the sound booth, oblivious to the fans who
screamed Maynard's name, to the tongue studs and nose rings, to the security
crew patrolling the arena. She saw only her Jimmy. He stood on a raised platform on the stage, mic in hand, and gyrated his way through "Stinkfist" and
"Pushit," a circle of light swirling at his feet. She watched colored spotlights
wash over her surprising son, her son whose sure voice rose over the crowd—
and did her best to ignore his lyrics. "She wasn't fond of his music," Maynard's
aunt Pam recalled in a 2013 interview. "The song that said 'Fuck your God'
was hard for her. But any attention he gave her was the world."

IN THE 27 YEARS SINCE HER STROKE, Judith's condition had steadily worsened
until she could no longer balance against the kitchen counter while she made
dinner. Placing one foot in front of the other and walking from the couch to the
bathroom was a struggle, and in time, even moving about in a wheelchair had
become impossible. Her speech was halting, and more often now, the precise
word eluded her. Her marriage had ended some years before, and her meager
Social Security checks were barely enough to cover her care in a third-rate
nursing home. A six-month break from touring in 2003 would give Maynard
time in Jerome to devise some under-the-radar way to improve her situation
without jeopardizing her benefits. "My intention was to get her into a better
place," he would explain. But the family's streak of Midwestern self-reliance
sabotaged his efforts.

"Jimmy would call and ask what Judy needed," Aunt Pam would explain. "But the family was too proud to ask for anything. Our mother went every day and took care of her, but Mom acted like everything was OK, so what was he supposed to do? Judy could have been better off, but they never asked for help."

And one bright June morning, as Maynard looked out on his garden and contemplated what he might plant there, the call, as he'd known it one day would, came at last.

His mother could no longer breathe on her own, Aunt Pam told him, or swallow, or speak. "Judy kept pulling off the oxygen mask," she would remember. "She wrote me a note that said 'Help me.' I called him, hysterical, and told him, 'She's dying, Jimmy.'"

He took up the suitcase and made straightway for the airport.

Through the day and the night, Maynard sat beside his mother. She lay pale and small under the thin sheet, her hand motionless in his. "I stayed with her for hours and explained to her that it was OK to go," he would remember. "I could see in her eyes that she understood. I told her I would be all right. I'd be fine. She could go."

Judith nodded. She looked up at her son, her eyes bright with tears. She nodded again.

MINGUS MOUNTAIN ROSE IN A NIMBUS OF CLOUD. Jan was there, Devo and his mother, Maynard and his girlfriend of the hour, Mike and his partner Lisa, and the minister brought up from Jerome to perform the ceremony. They stood close beneath the wide blue sky, this cluster of people who had loved and sparred, known each other well and not at all, gone their ways or never truly met and now had gathered in joy.

The day would be one of celebration for Mike and his new bride, and no one spoke of Maynard's loss. "It took the sting out of the whole thing because I could watch my father follow his bliss," Maynard would remember. "Nobody knew what I was going through, and it wasn't really the appropriate time to talk about it." The silence was not precisely denial, but a stoic determination to look only forward.

MAYNARD GLANCED INTO THE REARVIEW MIRROR until his house disappeared from sight. The wedding festivities over, he drove the next morning out Interstate 17, past black outcroppings and stands of pin oak.

He thought of the Ohio parishioners who'd convinced his mother that her paralysis had been God's punishment for her sins—members of the church she'd attended four times a week for as long as she'd been able, the church where she'd organized events for children and ministered to the sick. His mother, who'd testified of God's grace in seeing her through her long illness and for teaching her the meaning of faith.

> I thought about this incapacitated older man she'd met. They'd moved in together to help each other and because they were lonesome. Then the church took her off their roster for living in sin. This was a couple who couldn't even make love.
>
> I thought about the groupies who wanted to get close to me but never bothered to find out who I was. I thought about people who can move and walk and see, who have every advantage, but who just bury their talents. I thought about people who aren't conscious of the most fucking important things around them.
>
> I'd left L.A. to get away from this disconnected horseshit.

He drove.

AT THE HORIZON, the Chiricahuas, the Dragoons, the Dos Cabezas glowed red in the dawn. Farther still, he knew, was Skeleton Canyon, where Chief Geronimo had surrendered to authorities more than a century before. Through this very desert, he and the Apaches had run one step ahead of the cavalry and the Mexican army, across canyon and creek bed, past saguaro and prickly pear, intent on defending their land and their tradition. At least, that's what Maynard remembered from his reading of *Cry Geronimo!*, the story he'd long ago made his own.

> What a nice little irony that now I owned a piece of the land Geronimo ran across, right there in Cochise County in that elevated playa between the mountain ranges. "Wait a minute," I thought. "This is that place I read about!"
>
> At some point, if you're lucky, you realize you're not *the* story. You're *part* of the story. The story is much bigger than you.

He'd come to this place to remember the seasons' cycles, to learn again the rhythm of the sunrise, the work that could be done before it set. In this place, spring water flowed down the mountainside behind his house and meteor showers spangled the August sky. The earth spirits Geronimo had called upon for protection surely whispered here still. In this place, he might find again the unobstructed path that led toward his deepest desires.

And the story, like the very best stories, need not have one outcome only. Its narrative, he thought, was like a spread of tarot cards upon a table draped in a bright red cloth. It was within his power to read in it one or another destiny, or many, and none an exile from the magic. With the slightest shift in perspective, the stories would branch like the stream in the valley in turnings at once parallel and divergent, and one story all the same.

AT THE HEIGHT OF MIDSUMMER, Maynard received in the mail a compact package weightless as light and bearing an Ohio postmark. He filled two five-gallon buckets with caliche and limestone soil and blended with it the gritty powder packed inside.

On the hillside beside his house, workmen bent over their shovels, digging holes in tidy rows, and into each, Maynard placed a quantity of the mix. He scooped from one of the buckets a handful of earth and ashes, opened his palm, and let the small breeze carry it over the land, over the terraced garden where Cabernet and Nebbiolo and Malvasia vines would grow.

12

Maynard hadn't moved to Arizona to start a vineyard. A decade into his music career, there was no logical reason to change course now.

> Tool and Perfect Circle were creative outlets, and I wasn't about to abandon them, but I felt unbalanced. No, I didn't move to Arizona to start a vineyard, but when I got there, I wanted to express my ideas in a three-dimensional form— which becomes a four-dimensional form if you do it right.

Rehearsals and recording kept him in L.A. much of the time, and to maintain his center as best he could, he installed mats in the Tool loft and scheduled private jiu-jitsu lessons with Gracie studio instructor Henry Akins.

Akins arrived one afternoon with his friend and fellow martial arts enthusiast Todd Fox. "Tool had just wrapped a rehearsal and Henry was going to give Maynard a lesson," Todd explained in a 2014 interview. "He asked if I'd mind helping him do a little training."

In his years working security for celebrities from Janet Jackson to Madonna to Mötley Crüe, Todd had crossed paths with plenty of entertainers, and after an afternoon of wrestling and leverage training, he knew that Maynard was unique to the industry. "He was quiet and down to earth, and there was no pretentious vibe," Todd would recall. "Maynard can get work done and he can joke around, too. He can transition between worlds, which not a lot of people can do."

It wasn't long before the two had found a comfortable camaraderie. They met often to discuss their shared military backgrounds and their careers, their common interests in travel and music and fine wine. And just before the *Lateralus* tour began, Maynard suggested Todd come onboard to not only provide security, but to serve as Maynard's on-the-road jiu-jitsu instructor.

FROM THE DAYS OF TOOL'S FIRST EUROPEAN TOUR, Maynard had seen from the bus windows the terraced hillsides of Tuscany, vines trained up over trellises, and plump clusters of grapes among the leaves. His cellar and his palate had expanded since Tori's gift of the Silver Oak, and he'd grown more and more curious about the process that could transform fruit and rain and sunshine to Barolo and Shiraz and bold California Cabernet.

A free afternoon in Italy during the 2000 *Mer de Noms* tour had left time for a stopover at Ken Berry's vineyard just outside Siena. The head of Virgin Entertainment managed every facet of his small winery on-site, and the visit would be Maynard's chance to conduct a bit of firsthand research. "He wanted to know everything," Nancy Berry would recall. Ken pointed out his vats and barrels, explained the quality-control lab and the bottling area and the corking apparatus. Maynard looked out over the lush rows of vines as Ken described the soil composition and climate that made Siena an ideal spot for a vineyard. "I had no frame of reference to understand what he was talking about," Maynard would recall. "I just knew this is what it felt like when I stood outside my house. It didn't look much different from where I lived."

And not long after, a break in the *Lateralus* tour allowed him to accept an invitation from concert merchandising exec and oenophile Bruce Fingeret. The dinner would include a double-blind wine tasting, and Maynard thought it might be his next step in understanding.

Never one to blindly follow standard operating procedure, Maynard insisted Todd join him at the table. Bodyguard protocol required that security station themselves apart from the main event and keep the curious and the questionable a safe distance from their charge. But, Maynard reasoned, Todd was a part of the team, and he would share in the experience. And Todd was no stranger to fine wines. "I'd sometimes run errands for the artists I'd worked for," he would explain. "I'd bring back Gaja or Lafite or Latour to them and attended samplings on my nights off." He'd surely enjoy the evening as much as Maynard.

Appetizers and entrées and desserts appeared in their turn—dishes chosen to complement and contrast with the wines and create pairings that enhanced the subtle characteristics of both. Sommeliers circled the table with Burgundies and Bordeaux, their labels disguised in brown paper wrappers, and the guests accepted the task of identifying just what they were drinking. Maynard and Todd—spittoon at his side—sipped Lafite Rothschild and Ponsot Griotte and Montiano and tried their best to appreciate balance and texture, hints of fruits and flowers and spice. They left it to the others to discern varietals and vintages and even—based on subtle terroir—particular vineyards, to peg the 1997 Flaccianello, the 1998 Cheval Blanc, the 1982 Trotanoy. "I'd never seen anything like it," Todd would remember. "If you'd told me somebody could do that, I would have called bullshit immediately. But several of them were around 80 percent accurate, which is pretty phenomenal."

Maynard and Todd didn't have quite the refined palates of their companions, but they'd uncorked their share of Merlots and Rieslings and were experienced enough to realize that the 1990 Gianfranco Soldera Riserva far outranked the other wines in the flight. "It was just off the charts," Todd would recall. "It was as velvety as you can get and really round with a long finish. No bitterness or bite whatsoever. It was like experiencing four or five or six different things off one sip. It was like cherries on steroids."

> Everybody has that moment when they suddenly see the light about wines. I had that moment with the Silver Oak from Tori. Then this dinner flipped the other switch. Not only was I into wine, I now wanted to plant vines and see where I could take this.

MAYNARD REALIZED HE WASN'T FAR from the makings of fine wines. The hills surrounding the Jerome house were the same southeast-facing slopes he'd seen in Spain and Piemonte, the Arizona soil similar to that in Bordeaux and Champagne.

But constructing a vineyard would take work, more work certainly than pulling together a band. It would mean dirt under his fingernails and learning about zoning regulations and water rights and root systems and powdery mildew. But he approached his mission with the same methodical passion he'd brought to Tool's formation. "Maynard's projects are not just businesses to him," Nancy Berry would explain. "He has a very deep personal commitment to everything he does, and he's very hands-on."

One step at a time, he would put the pieces in place. He drew sketches of vineyard design and read about pH levels and soil preparation. He bought up suitable properties and hired contractors to grade the earth. And by 2003, the garden near his house had been planted with Cabernet Sauvignon and named the Judith block.

By necessity, much of the initial development was done remotely, with help from Mike, who'd stayed in Jerome when Maynard set off on a 19-city Lollapalooza tour to promote APC's second album. Recorded in Billy's basement studio with assistance from guitar tech Mat Mitchell, *Thirteenth Step* was a 12-song collection that moved from hard-driving rock to symphonic instrumentals to Joni Mitchell–inspired guitar, reflecting its theme of multiple paths to self-discovery. The album's release on September 16, 2003, kicked off the tour in earnest, a tour that would keep APC on the road for nearly a year.

When Maynard at last unpacked his suitcase the next summer, it was time to begin work on the next Tool album. If the vineyard was ever to be a reality, he'd need help keeping his plates spinning and the pieces of his life in order.

Lei Li had never intended to work for a rock musician, particularly one she'd read could be difficult and distant. When a mutual friend introduced her to Maynard, she was far from starstruck. "I knew of Tool, but I didn't listen to their music," she recalled in a 2015 interview. "I'd heard that they weren't nice to people, so I didn't really want to meet him because I was afraid. What do you say to somebody like that?"

To her surprise, she found Maynard soft-spoken and approachable—and not a little attractive. They eased effortlessly into a comfortable friendship, and when he asked if she'd become his personal assistant, she realized it might be her ticket out of her small Midwestern town and a step closer to applying her art degree.

For the next two years, she maintained Maynard's schedule and ran his errands and kept the L.A. house functioning smoothly, a plum assignment while she searched for the perfect job with one of the city's galleries or museums. And when plans for the vineyard were well under way, he suggested she come to Jerome and oversee operations there. "I was like, yeah, right," she would recall. "I'd always wanted to move to the city, and now he was asking me to come to this town that's smaller than my high school class."

But the two worked well together, laughed and conversed and enjoyed each other's company, and joining him in Arizona wouldn't be the worst move she could make—so long as she kept an eye out for other opportunities and maintained her professional distance. Over the years, she'd had a front-row view of his romantic indiscretions, the dramas and deceptions, and she knew he wasn't exactly prime relationship material. She'd seen too *All We Are Saying*, Rosanna Arquette's 2005 documentary of entertainers from Burt Bacharach to Yoko Ono to Steven Tyler, who spoke of their inspirations, their struggles to balance family and fame, and their takes on the changing music industry. She'd listened to her boss explain in his two-minute monologue that, at 40, he was too old to change, that his destiny would never include monogamy.

"I thought I was doomed to a series of failed relationships and sexual recklessness," Maynard would explain. "Ending that took getting a dog."

The family dog, a white picket fence, Saturdays spent planting peas and lettuce with his children: Despite his doubt, the dream was still attractive. Just maybe his girlfriend of the moment was the one he'd been waiting for—he'd moved her some time before into the L.A. house. But one afternoon, Maynard and his little Yorkie, Miho, discovered she hadn't taken her vow of fidelity quite as seriously as he.

> I came home and found that my home and my trust had been violated. I was enraged. Then my dog looked up at me. She looked down at the truck keys I'd thrown down and then up at me. Here was the physical manifestation of my inner voice in the form of Miho. It's like she was saying, "Let's just pick up the keys and drive to the vineyard and walk away from this chaos."
>
> Things had to change. I picked up the keys. I picked up the dog. I got in the truck and headed to Jerome. The dog saved my life.

Maynard's friends had for years cleared their social calendars when Tool or APC came through town. When he'd begun to cut breakfasts short and bring glamorous strangers to dinner, when his phone calls stopped altogether, they joked among themselves that he'd gone hopelessly rock star. But they'd been patient. They knew that no matter how circuitous his detour, the Maynard they remembered would be back. "Maynard always opts to reconnect," Todd would explain. "Comfort and familiarity are fuel for him. He needs that foundation to continue moving forward. And once he establishes a sense of connection, he rarely lets it go."

It remained in city after impersonal city, that connection forged over seafood omelets and turkey dinners, the family created from strangers on sunny roof decks and fifth-floor walkups where candles burned and where, regardless of miles and time, no one needed be alone.

"There were a couple patches of years when I didn't even talk to him," Laura Milligan would recall. "But Maynard is loyal. When he's your friend, he's your friend forever." When he returned to Tantrum, she'd be in the wings ready to pull on her cowgirl boots. Sheila would welcome him at the Neighborhood and refill his coffee cup before he asked. Steele would retell stories of fish food hors d'oeuvres, and Ramiro would be waiting to puzzle out with him synchronicity and convergence. Kjiirt would turn, catch his glance, and understand the unspoken joke.

"I didn't have a trail of bread crumbs to get me back," Maynard would explain. "I had 30-pound-test fishing line. The tether was strong. These weren't bread crumbs. They were shining rubies."

HE TURNED FROM THE DUSTY ROAD and parked the truck in the driveway. In the backyard, Lei Li was hard at work, surrounded by hammers and drills, repairing the dog house. She'd filled the irrigation pool, coiled the garden hose neatly around the hook at the side of the house, and shut off the sprinklers in the vineyard.

Plenty of naysayers had told Maynard his venture was a fool's errand, that grapes could never grow in the Arizona desert. But Maynard had done his research and accepted the job not as a chore but a perfectly doable challenge.

Miho bounded across the yard to greet Lei Li, and Maynard stood for a moment and looked out over the Judith block, where green shoots trembled in the evening breeze.

> At the end of the movie *Bliss*, when the father plants trees, it's really a love letter that took seven years to deliver. I understood that planting those vines on some level was my love letter to my family, to my community, to my younger self, to my future self. I'd already started writing that love letter, but I'd been sending it in the wrong direction.

> If you're going to do something, you do it. You don't worry about who your
> audience is. You do it for you. You do it for the music. You do it for the art. You
> do it for the vineyard.

The vineyard was an oasis of greening vines, of hummingbirds and hawks overhead and praying mantises in the grass and the resident roadrunner just down the hill. Maynard rose with the sun and knelt in his gardens, his senses tuned to breezes and honeybees, to rain clouds that gathered each afternoon in the east. He helped his crew remove weeds and clear debris from the paths between Sangiovese and Cabernet and lined the steep terraces with white limestone boulders the way he'd seen done in Tuscany and Siena.

Creating a vineyard was a test of himself as much as of the land, a chance to allow the synchronistic accidents of weather and will that might alter his story. And in a few years, he imagined, his harvest might produce a palatable bottle or two.

His dream wasn't so far-fetched. "Grapes actually started in the desert," he would explain. "They were originally drought-tolerant plants, bred for exactly this kind of environment. Read your Bible."

The Arizona soil was ideal for grape growing: the layers of volcanic ash deposited long ago and the rich caliche, the remnant of the vast inland sea that had once covered the state. Spanish missionaries had arrived there in the sixteenth century and found the valley purple with wild grapes, and they'd made of them their sacramental wine. Later, Prescott hotelier Henry Schuerman had established the area's first winery and provided libations for loggers and cattle drivers and miners—until the vines were destroyed with the advent of Prohibition in 1915.

By the late 1980s, a hopeful few had begun to resurrect the state's vineyards and try their hand at wine making, and Maynard saw no reason he shouldn't join them.

STEPPING FROM THE SPOTLIGHT never crossed his mind—not while his career continued its upswing. Just before his first vines went in the ground, *Ænima* was certified triple platinum, and *Lateralus* reached double platinum by that August.

The next November, just in time for Election Day 2004, when foreign relations and the War on Terrorism were top of mind, A Perfect Circle released its third album. Certified gold only a month after its release, *eMOTIVe* included originals and covers of antiwar anthems from Joni Mitchell's "Fiddle and the Drum" to John Lennon's "Imagine," the fresh interpretations a portal to hearing the familiar lyrics as if for the first time.

And the next year, Maynard's acting chops were at last showcased. He'd appeared a few years before in the low-budget *Bikini Bandits* action film parodies, but it took his role opposite Ed Asner and RATM's Brad Wilk in the indie murder mystery *Sleeping Dogs Lie* to bring accolades from reviewers and recognition of his comic skill from fans. "Maynard brought such a depth to the character," coproducer Ford Englerth said of his deadpan portrayal of bumbling Deputy Sheriff Lance. "He took a character that was a very kind of quirky, not so bright kind of deputy and he spent a lot of time developing particular nuances about how the character thinks and his motivation."[1]

Limelight aside, what mattered now was determining which vines might be best suited to conditions on the mountain. Keenan family lore included the tale of Great-Grandfather Marzo, who, in some time out of mind, had lived on the Italian-French border and made wines from grapes that grew in his arbor. Maynard knew little more of his paternal heritage, and in a nod to this Marzo—whatever his full name, whatever his story—he planted on the Judith block alongside Aglianico and Tempranillo a Nebbiolo clone of a grape native to his ancestors' homeland.

He planted too descendants of the Luglienga, the strain that had been all but lost in 1915. "A neighbor found a vine nearby that had been kept alive by two sisters we call the Tamale Ladies," he would explain. "One of them was Auralia, and her husband was a Spanish gentleman the miners had brought over to make their wine. When Prohibition hit, they had to pull out their vineyard." But the sisters had rooted cuttings in glass jars on their windowsill and transplanted them in their garden, and Luglienga had survived to begin its new history in Merkin Vineyards.

Maynard's travels had prepared him well for the challenges ahead. During APC's 2000 Adelaide stop, he'd walked the Penfolds acreage, toured its cellars,

[1] Sarah Jensen, "What's Maynard Been Up to Lately?" *Ludington Daily News* (Michigan), February 15, 2005, 4.

242

and listened to master winemakers John Duval and Peter Gago. "He wanted to know about anything and everything," Gago recalled in a 2016 interview. "He was interested in canopy management, the wine-making process, barrel maturation—and tasting."

> Peter told me how back in the '50s, a young Penfolds winemaker, Max Schubert, coming from a background of sweet fortified wines, was sent to France to study sherry making. He discovered over there the dry, intense, delicate reds.
>
> He came back with a glow in his eye and tried to explain to his bosses that this was something they should embark on. They reluctantly gave him a small budget, and he figured out through trial and error that the best fruit they had in the area was the Shiraz grape. When they finally released the wine, people were so used to sweet sherries, ports, and brandies that they didn't understand this dry red with aging potential. So they laughed in his face and shut him down.
>
> But he knew the truth. He knew he must continue this for their sake, so he continued in secret. Then in 1962, he entered his Penfolds 1955 Grange Hermitage in wine competitions and blew everybody else away.
>
> The reasons you're even aware of Australian wine is because Schubert and like-minded people made the right choices and pushed through. He was the kind of pioneer who said, "I have a vision. You're wrong now, but you'll be right and you'll all benefit." He stuck to his guns and he didn't give up.

If Schubert had surmounted his obstacles, Maynard would have an even easier time of it, with Google at his fingertips and reference books delivered overnight to his doorstep. A successful vineyard, he learned, was an exercise in balance. If he pruned too much, the fruit would shrivel in the sunlight and become useless. A light hand on the pruning shears would bring on voracious foliage that trapped rain and dew, and then he'd have to deal with bunch rot. There would be monsoons and winter frosts, pesticides that might do more harm than good, and the red-tape nightmares of applications and regulations of a bewildering bureaucracy. "When we started planting, I installed a tank to collect spring water that flowed down the hill to irrigate the vineyard," he would recall. "The town couldn't wrap their head around that. The word *tank* wasn't in their ordinance code."

It would take time to outfit a winery of his own and years before his fruit would be ready for harvest. But if he had to put one goal on the back burner, he'd take advantage of the delay and reach another. Working as a custom-crush client at a brand-new winery in nearby Cornville would give him access to its facility, and sourcing fruit from California growers and turning their grapes to wine would be a hands-on PhD program in fermentation and filtration and temperature control. He might not know from one year to the next which grape he'd receive, but the annual surprise would force him to learn the qualities and potential of Malvasia and Syrah.

Smoky and citrusy with a curious black tea finish, his debut, the Caduceus 2004 Primer Paso—literally his first step—caught the attention of music fans and oenophiles curious to sample the latest celebrity release. The limited-edition Syrah and Malvasia blend sold out in no time and paved the way for the earthy Nagual de la Naga, the oaky, plummy Nagual del Sensei, and the Merkin Vineyards smoky-smooth Chupacabra.

Encouraged by the success of his custom-crush creations, Maynard began to imagine what might come of his vines growing now on just under seven acres—Sangiovese and Tempranillo thriving in the Arizona sunshine, the Cabernet in the Judith block the most vigorous and hardy of all.

Nearly a year and a half on the road would take him from pruning and pressing and blending, but Tool's *10,000 Days* tour that began in 2007 wouldn't interrupt his studies. Stops across Europe were scheduled to coincide with the release of Italian and Bordeaux vintages, and wine aficionados were introduced to a new side of Maynard via his *Wine Spectator* blog, *On Tour with Maynard James Keenan*—his chronicle not of performances but of vineyard visits and the wines he sampled in fine restaurants across the continent: a 40-year tawny port in Lisbon, a Vieux Télégraphe Châteauneuf-du-Pape in Paris.

By 2009, Caduceus Cellars was licensed and outfitted and operational. The compact bunker attached to the Jerome house was an assembly line of de-stemmers and vats and testing lab and oak barrels modeled after the wineries he'd explored. "I'd watched the basic process," he said. "The fruit comes in, you either de-stem it or you don't, you either press it or you don't, it ends up in a bin or a tank. Then you ferment it. Every facility is going to be a version of that."

The setup was simple, yes, but mastering the more esoteric tricks of this new trade—the tricks that would transform grape juice to tannic reds and dry whites and oaky blends—would take more than observation. He must incessantly taste and test and tweak, make on-the-fly decisions about too-high sugar levels or too-unripe grapes. Most important, he must keep always in mind Peter Gago's advice and step out of his own way and let the grapes guide the process.

> People come in and taste wine that's fermenting. They make an ugly face and say it's awful. Of course it is. It's not done. Same as if I play a rough track. You can tell they want to say it's terrible. Then I play the song when it's completed or pour the finished wine, and they think it's great. It's the same with anything you do. Getting to the finished product is about patience, understanding—and a faith in the process.

It wasn't a process he would tackle solo. The vineyard would require a harvest crew and a vineyard crew, drivers and accountants and sales reps, and to oversee them all, a manager in Chris Turner, trained in his family's California vineyards and who now made it his mission to understand the challenges and advantages of growing grapes in Arizona.

It would take too someone to test pH and sulfur dioxide levels and conduct assessments to gauge the fermentation process. "I had avoided chemistry when I was in college," Lei Li would admit. But she'd worked side by side with the pros at the custom-crush facility and had studied wine making nearly as diligently as Maynard had, and her respect and admiration for him had risen over the years until she believed as strongly in his dream as he. "We worked really well together," she explained. "I knew even then that I always wanted to be a part of whatever he did."

And despite her early reservations about such things, she found herself promoted from personal assistant to lab manager, a part of the team that would hold one another accountable and recognize the importance of their individual excellence to the success of Caduceus Cellars.

"In the beginning, anyone would think, 'You're going to start a vineyard in Arizona?'" Nancy Berry would reflect. "But Maynard did it. And not only did he do it, he takes so much pleasure in it and he puts so much physical hard work into it."

This was no prima donna celebrity cavalierly adding wine making to his résumé. From the beginning, Maynard was the one slipping Led Zeppelin and Joni Mitchell CDs into the player in the bunker and bending over the vat punching down with his fist the thick stew of grape skins and purple liquid. He was the one who monitored the juice as it aged, sampled the blends at every stage, and moved tons of Sangiovese Grosso and Tempranillo during the long, hot weeks of the harvest season.

> Once the grapes are picked, I'll be at the bunker waiting on the forklift. Chris backs the truck up and I unload the fruit, weigh it, and put it in the de-stemmer. From there, it goes into bins, where Lei Li does all the testing. Then I either inoculate it or allow it to naturally ferment, then press it and put it into bins to settle. Eventually it goes into barrels, and I stack them.
>
> Or I'm cleaning up. I power wash the press and the de-stemmer, because that's what has to be done. I'm not going to go find some manservant to do any of that for me.

"There have always been surprises," Tom Morello would say of Maynard's new role. "When we lived in L.A., we were driving around and he told me he had a West Point background. He went from whatever he was before that to being a West Point guy to being a pet store guy. Maynard's not afraid of a sharp left turn."

But wine making was not so much a change in direction as a shift in perspective—a seamless opening to another aspect of Maynard's art.

Maynard and Chris had nurtured the vineyard through 100-degree August afternoons, hail and monsoons and drought, Pierce's disease and too-high potassium levels and the weedy jungle that overwhelmed the plots with the first drops of rain. They'd placed frost fans and covered with tarps the tender vines against icy winds and followed the advice of Kjiirt—who'd experimented with grape growing on his Vermont hilltop—and laid a crushed-rock ground cover to insulate against the night air that settled over the valley.

They learned that the stressors only produced grapes more hardy and resilient, and learned too to avoid tarantulas and scorpions hiding among the leaves, and that warding off angry javelinas was a snap. "You scare the boss off with an air rifle and they don't come back," Maynard would explain.

THE ALCHEMY OF RAIN AND SUN AND SOIL—and six years of backbreaking work—had transformed the dream to reality. In 2009 Maynard released the first wine made entirely from Caduceus Cellars grapes, the 2007 Nagual del Judith, named in memory of his mother. The tannic Cabernet echoed with cassis and black olive, and Judith's dream was printed on the back of the dark bottle.

> *As a child I used to dream that I could fly. I would stand on one leg, look up towards the sky, and with my arms lifted out and up, my fingers stretched towards the sun, the wind would come and swirl all around me and then gently lift me up into the air.*

On that mild April day, a soft breeze rustled the Cabernet leaves, and Maynard stood on the eastern slope of the Judith block. "These vines and wines are her resurrection and her wings," Maynard said. He uncorked the first bottle, tipped it, and returned the wine to the earth, a ritual of new beginnings.

WITH ONE CADUCEUS SUCCESS UNDER HIS BELT, he set his sights on the next challenge. "Maynard always asks, 'How do we make this more interesting?'" Todd would explain. "'How do we make it more fun and better than what it is?'"

The barreled Sangiovese and Cabernets in the bunker were redolent of Old World blends, and given another few months of aging, Maynard imagined them an Arizona interpretation of the Super Tuscans he'd sampled in Italy, a confluence of his heritage and his future.

> I had a free afternoon during the *10,000 Days* tour, and we had a family reunion of sorts at Bern's Steak House in Tampa. My dad had flown down from Michigan to visit my uncle Herb, whom I hadn't seen in about 30 years, and we toasted each another in vintage Lafite.
>
> I told Uncle Herb all about the vineyards, and I told him I was doing a new blend in honor of his grandfather that I was going to call Nagual del Marzo. I explained that I knew next to nothing about this guy.

> But Herb knew something. "His name was John Marzo," he told me. "His nickname was Spirit." I looked around the table to see if Todd or my dad were playing some kind of prank. They do that kind of thing.
>
> But they weren't messing with me this time. My great-grandfather's nickname really was Spirit. And I'd already named my wine. It would be called Nagual del Marzo—which means "The Spiritual Essence of Marzo."

With an eye for beauty and balance and style, Maynard oversaw the design of all things Caduceus. He'd discovered that marketing was far from a soulless chore. "Maynard is very sensitive to the imagery involved in marketing and publicity," Kendall instructor Deb Rockman would explain. "He wants art to be a significant part of everything he does."

He led the creation of the Caduceus Cellars website, a virtual diary with deckle-edge pages rich with photographs and maps and pen-and-ink illustrations. He imported from Canada sleek, weighty bottles and made of each an objet d'art. Name and vintage and alcohol content were printed in bold inks directly on the glass, and lyrical tales of fantastic beasts and magical guardians and shape-shifters, and the Merkin logo a swirling interpretation of classical artworks and geometric symbols, their meanings as multilayered as the wines' finishes. Ramiro's paintings and woodcuts had been adapted for use in Tool promotional materials since 1994, and now his image *Touch Down* appeared on a Caduceus T-shirt.

When space became available in Jerome's historic Connor Hotel, Maynard realized that its footprint matched plans he'd sketched for an offshoot of the vineyard. He supervised the metamorphosis to the Caduceus Cellars Tasting Room, a welcoming space of wood and brick and sunny window tables. The Flatiron—the Main Street café that had won Maynard over to Jerome—was no more, and its managers, Brian and Alan, took charge and created a destination for locals who gathered for their daily espresso and for visitors eager to sample a flight of Arizona wines.

Maynard planned rehearsals and recording sessions around the harvest and production schedule and—ever the businessman—continued promotions along the tour route. At every stop, he dispatched Todd to call on distributors and retailers and restaurant owners and tell the Caduceus story. "At first, it was very difficult to get people to listen," Todd would recall. "People in the wine community had no time for Maynard. They didn't care about another rock star slapping their name on a label. True wine connoisseurs, like sommeliers and buyers, they were kind of shunning it."

But after sipping the tannic reds, the rich rosés, the Caduceus Naga or Sensei or Sancha, the restaurateurs sat up and took notice. These were intriguing wines, they realized, complex and delicate, wines that would step from center stage and allow the flavors of their entrées to expand and transform. They recognized the win-win wisdom in giving their chefs a free hand in creating pairings to enhance both the wines and their cuisine—fish eyes and fish sperm in Tokyo, pastas and meats and cheeses at Babbo on Waverly Place in Manhattan, guinea hen and creamy polenta at Mark's American Cuisine in Houston.

The all-Arizona wine list at Scottsdale's FnB restaurant soon included Caduceus Dos Ladrones and Oneste and Malvasia blends. "We serve an heirloom tomato salad with golden, crispy, steamy hot polenta croutons," Pavle Milic, FnB co-owner explained in a 2014 interview. "You need a wine that's not going to overpower the sweet tomatoes and red wine vinegar and onions. Maynard's Marzo Sangiovese rosé with that dish is out of this world."

It didn't take much convincing before Mark Tarbell, *Arizona Republic* wine columnist and proprietor of Tarbell's in Phoenix, offered Caduceus wines in both his dining room and in the restaurant's wine shop. "I am my customers' advocate," Tarbell said. "I have to put wine in front of them that has value, and some of Maynard's wines are outstanding. I see honest expression in his bottles and grapes and choice of blendings."

And Maynard began to take part in Tarbell's annual dinner gala to benefit the Arizona Wine Growers Association. "I'm the chef and he's the celebrity," Tarbell explained. "He'll cook, plate, and serve. He's got some good skills and some good moves around the kitchen."

THE KITCHEN IN THE JEROME HOUSE SHIFTED INTO HIGH GEAR. Maynard slipped over his head his white apron and re-created the gnocchi and roast lamb he remembered from the North End, grilled salmon, a Thanksgiving pizza. "I go to Maynard's house, and he'll be waiting on me like I'm in a restaurant," Todd explained. "That love comes from a very specific place."

Maynard's feasts arose too from the need for a bit of bench research.

> People usually drink my wines in restaurants, so I experiment by pairing them with restaurant-style food. I make a ravioli from Arizona wheat dough and local eggs and herbs, and serve it with my wine and a top-notch wine as a comparison. If mine doesn't measure up, I've got to figure out what I did wrong, and if it does, figure out what the heck I did right so I can repeat it.
>
> Thanksgiving pizza was Lei Li's idea. Derek, who works in our vineyards, is an awesome pizza maker, so he did a dough and we lined the deep-dish crust with gravy, turkey, and stuffing and topped it with cranberries. With that, we opened a Tuscan blend and barrel-tasted some Oneste, our Caduceus Merlot-Barbera blend.

Wine making was certainly no longer just a hobby. By 2015, annual production had reached 6,000 cases, Cadeuceus wines were sold in 1,000 retail outlets and shipped to customers in 33 states, and Maynard's vineyards covered 115 acres throughout Arizona.

His collection of silver and gold medals only grew, awards from the Jefferson Cup Invitational, the Texas Sommelier Conference, and the San Francisco International Wine Competition, and the FnB Judgment of Arizona blind tasting that pitted Arizona wines against those of California, Italy, Spain, France, and Australia—and ranked the Caduceus 2008 Nagual del Judith above all other reds.

Doubters had set a lofty bar, but there was no denying it now: The rocker in blue body paint and Mulhawk was a winemaker.

"Things have changed a lot," Todd explained in a 2014 interview. "When Maynard talks about wine making now, people realize he's not some clown off the street."

The job of Merkin Vineyards frontman would involve more than producing a fine bottle of rosé, and Maynard added to his e-mail signature "World Class Multitasker." The hard-won lessons of the vineyard must be shared.

"Maynard really does give a shit about what's happening here," Milic explained. "Let's call him the gateway winemaker."

The picture of professionalism in tailored suit and tie, he quietly articulated at Jerome community meetings the needs and triumphs of area winemakers and took part in winemaker panels and seminars on cultivation and pest control and the latest in submerged cap fermentation. And as part of the 2012 Arizona Centennial celebration, he stressed the importance of sustainable agriculture to the state's future.

> Back in Scottville, I watched my family and neighbors grow much of their own food, so I understood even then what it is to be sustainable. We lived within our means and were creative with what we had. If you have a farm or a vineyard, no matter what else is happening in the world, you can survive.
>
> Throughout history people got by in spite of wars and weather and whoever was in charge—kings, queens, dictators, fascists. They understood how to maintain a connection with their place and how to feed themselves from that place. The cornerstone of that activity was most often vines.

If the effort were properly managed and regulated, Maynard imagined, wine making could become the industry to bring economic stability to Arizona. His vineyards did their small part—provided his crew a living wage and, by extension, strengthened the local tax base—and should the wine making movement go statewide, the effect could be far-reaching.

Maynard—one of ten Arizona thought leaders invited to speak at the 2015 Local First Arizona event—encouraged potential growers to do their part, to commit themselves to possibility, to avoid the easy path and work through the inevitable friction that would yield the greatest rewards. "That's where the art happens," he explained, the sweetest music from strings stretched to their limit, the most moving poem created in the night's darkest despair, the finest wines from vineyards tested by drought and frost and blight.

If new vintners were to succeed, they would need an advocate, and Maynard became a self-appointed spokesperson, appealing to legislators for fair zoning and distribution policies that would move wine making from a cottage industry to a significant economic force. Arizona wine, he insisted, was a unique commodity, a global export that celebrated the local, each bottle the essence of desert herbs and spice, of chalky earth and palo verde in bloom.

> Wine is a product that can't be outsourced to China or Mexico. It expresses our home, our place, our Arizona. The essence of why a wine is interesting and

> what compels people to talk about it is the idea of place, of uniqueness. Within
> that uniqueness that's fairly consistent from year to year, you have the varia-
> tions from year to year based on weather patterns.
>
> But at its core, this place is expressing itself through that bottle, provided
> the stewards of that grape and of that place are getting out of the way to allow
> that to happen.

"Maynard is an Arizona enological pioneer," Gago explained. "He is creative and quality-oriented and brings new perspective and a new audience for
wine."

AFTER EARNING HER AGROECOLOGY DEGREE from Prescott College, Nikki
Bagley had been eager for practical experience. Joining the vineyard crew
to hoe Bermuda grass and help bring in the 2008 harvest fit the bill. "It was
great to see some truly sustainable agriculture going on in Yavapai County,"
she would recall. "I had struggled to imagine how agriculture fit into this arid
county with all its water issues. It was wonderful to get in on the ground level
of this amazing industry." It wasn't long before Maynard promoted Nikki to
vineyard co-manager, and the two joined forces to help bring viniculture to
Arizona.

Winemaker allies who attended the first meeting of the Verde Valley Wine
Consortium in 2008 were unanimous: Yavapai College should be the epicenter
of education and resources for new winemakers. Trowel in hand, Maynard
provided two years later an on-campus experimental site, the Negro Amaro
vineyard he planted where the campus racquetball court had once been. "It
was his investment that really showed the college that they could do this on a
large scale," Nikki—the program's first instructor—explained.

The next summer, Yavapai's Southwest Wine Center in Clarkdale became
home to Arizona's first program to offer degrees in viticulture and enology.
From a first-year enrollment of 30 students, the program had grown by 2016
to more than 90 future winemakers and vineyard owners and tasting room
managers.

Maynard and Nikki supported winemaker Joe Bechard in his instrumental
role in creating 2014 legislation allowing alternating partnerships, the ability
for multiple Arizona wineries to share common production space. Owner of

Clarkdale's Chateau Tumbleweed, Bechard enabled Maynard's transformation of Camp Verde's former meatpacking plant to Four Eight Wineworks, the shared incubator allowing experienced but underfunded vintners to produce their limited releases until they are solvent enough to build bunkers of their own. In a spirit of camaraderie and support, winemakers share de-stemmers and tanks and the bottling line, knowledge and insights and muscle at harvest-time.

And the next year, Maynard joined forces with equally committed professionals to put in place the Arizona Vignerons Alliance, a group dedicated to establishing parameters for grape growing and wine production and holding vintners to recognized international standards.

> In light of the farm-to-table and Local First movements, it's important for us as a wine industry to at least start there. No product from an area will speak as loudly as wine about a specific place and time. The AVA is about aligning ourselves with the idea of the local and increasing understanding of what makes a region unique.

"Of all the people in this industry, Maynard is one of the few that has taken a long-range view," Nikki said. "He's one of the state's most visionary winemakers. He sees the future of Arizona wines, and he's pushing hard to get us there."

As if his e-mail ID needed further justification, he began investigating the development of next-generation subsurface drip irrigation. "This could be a game changer for vineyards in Arizona," he explained in early 2016. Growers and environmentalists would be pleased with the novel belowground method that encouraged stronger root systems, conserved Arizona's precious water, and left no carbon footprint.

"Because of Maynard's generosity, these are significant things that will make a difference in Arizona," Tarbell would explain. "He has the clearest voice about what Arizona wines are and could be. He's providing a very articulate, strong, intelligent role of leadership to the state's budding wine industry."

And at every conference, every meeting, every planning session, Maynard shared stories—stories of September afternoons in an apple orchard on Darr Road, of dreams of flying high above the evening desert, of a view from a rooftop in Somerville. "Things come up that to most people would be irrelevant," Todd would explain. "But they're so relevant and such a part of where things came from, that for Maynard, they're a constant frame of reference. And they *are* relevant if you know the story."

13

The magic of stories, or so Kiss and Melchizedek and Anne Meeks had taught, lay in making them one's own. The infinite settings and plot twists told after all a personal tale, the tale of trial and possibility, of chance encounters with characters who were purveyors of epiphany and keepers of dreams, their influence clear only when remembered across the repeating spiral of time.

During Tool's Seattle stop on the 2002 *Lateralus* tour, Maynard and Steele had spent a long-overdue evening recalling their time on Pearson Street and plotting their next adventures. "He told me he wanted to start a new band," Steele would recall of their talk in the tour bus. "He told me about this Puscifer idea, the fun and different music he wanted to do."

Maynard had released angst and anger, had exorcised through his lyrics his personal demons. It was time to take another direction, a road that paralleled Tool's, but one that would give free rein to his creativity. It was time to honor the story of hope and survival, of the uniquely human ability to cocreate the universe. "I wanted to do something serious, almost as a religion, in reverence to where we've come from," he would explain. And Puscifer—the multifaceted project he'd envisioned more than a decade before, would be his vehicle.

> A long time ago, people understood that the only thing that kept them alive was coordinating in groups and being more creative than the creatures that were threatening them. They were never going to be stronger or faster than those creatures, so they had to be smarter. We're losing touch with that, be-

> cause everything we need is readily available. You can't walk ten feet in any direction without running into food, shelter, or clothing.
>
> I feel like art has taken a backseat. The whole creative process seems kind of odd because we don't think it's relevant to keeping us alive. But we need to use every fiber of our imagination, every spark of our creative energy, to stay ahead of what's happening to our planet, to our relationships, to our ability to think for ourselves.
>
> Life is too short not to create something with every breath we draw.

"I didn't see Maynard that much," Laura Milligan would recall of the years he'd busied himself with Tool and APC and the vineyard. "But every time I did, he would say we had to do this, we had to do that, we needed to put together something like what we'd done at Tantrum. He was always brewing that idea."

Puscifer would be an homage to art, he told her. Puscifer would be sound and color, country and rock and symphony and jazz, costume and story and non sequitur, a friction-driven work in progress, open-ended to leave room for surprise.

The revolving troupe might include actors and comedians, guitarists and vocalists and sound engineers who had become over the years family. He'd reprise his Billy D character, the roué in wig and mustache, and Laura and her cowgirl boots. Puscifer would be the cabaret at the crossroads of Joseph Campbell and *Hee Haw* and Sonny and Cher. Puscifer would be funny.

"I was losing touch with the comedy part," Maynard would explain. "That's why Puscifer had to come back in a big way. "If you want to follow me as an artist, you have to laugh. You have to stop taking yourself so seriously."

Fans had appreciated—or at least tolerated—the humorous elements of his work: the padded bras and Kabuki makeup, his blowing paper towels at guest drummer Coady Willis mid-song during the *10,000 Days* tour, the irreverent Rev. Maynard. Once they were let in on the joke, they'd delighted in the Teutonic chants and the vineyard's suggestive name. But they'd never been forgiving of a comedy routine as part of a live show.

Tool's audience at the Hollywood Palladium in 1998 had been impatient for the show to begin, no matter how entertaining the opening act. They were mildly amused when Bob Odenkirk and David Cross stepped to the stage in surgical garb, examined Maynard, and diagnosed him with the rare disease tittilitis. But by the time Maynard was draped in a hospital johnny and guided to a wheel-chair, they'd had enough and chanted their insistent demand for the main event.

But Maynard had known that silliness should be integral to his act ever since he'd catapulted hot dogs to the English Acid crowd. "At the time, it looked like misspent time, like so many things he did," Jack Olsen would remember. "In retrospect, of course, it all seems to line up beautifully toward what eventually happened."

Mounting such an ambitious effort would take a pro, and Maynard realized that Mat Mitchell was the right man for the job. Mitchell came in with not only the technical skills to produce recordings and videos, but a background with video game developer Electronic Arts, and he understood the importance of schedules and deadlines and practical details. "Mat is the steady, grounded piece of this puzzle," Maynard would explain. "While I'm out there like a kite, he's the one hanging onto it."

AND IN 2007, PUSCIFER WAS LAUNCHED in all its punk-inspired purity, an independent band with no sponsorship and no obligation to recording industry dictates. Maynard and Mat created not only lyrics but arrangements, incorporating rhythm machines and techno programming and digital soundscapes, echoes of the delay pedal effects and Mike Meeng's drum machine at Gaia's decades before.

"It's very refreshing to work with someone who's open to experimenting and allows me to experiment as well," Mat explained in a 2016 interview. "Maynard's always looking for the next thing. He looks at every pebble and asks, 'Where do I leap from here?'"

In spare moments during the last leg of the *10,000 Days* tour, Mat set up his laptop and worked with the cadre of musicians and writers and vocalists to ready Puscifer's first songs for the final mix. APC's self-recording of *Mer de Noms* in 2000 had been big news at the time, but seven years later, it had become commonplace—and economical—for bands to take the independent approach.

> Back in the day, a band would have to sell at least half a million records before they saw a profit. But now, music can be as sustainable as wine making. We can have far fewer sales and still pay the rent because there's no middle man, no bunch of executives in the way, nobody sticking their fingers in the pie.

And in those days of MTV and music magazines and a brick-and-mortar record store in every mall, new recordings had been spoon-fed directly to consumers. "What musicians did then, we could not do now," Maynard would explain. "Without that machine in place, people have to discover music in other ways." The Internet, the go-to information source of the digital generation, had enabled real-time promotion, bringing news far more quickly than print publications could go to press. The public would generate the Puscifer buzz.

The group's first single, "Queen B," was released as a video and a podcast on Puscifer.com, priming fans for the release in late October of its first album, *V Is for Vagina*, and assuring its debut spot at Number 25 on the *Billboard* 200. The Puscifer team broadened its reach with pages on Myspace and Facebook, allowing fans to discuss this new trip-hop phenomenon, and more important, spread word of their discoveries and upcoming releases.

Puscifer followers logged on one morning in early 2009 and discovered a comedic video announcing the group's long-awaited live debut. Maynard, in full military regalia as the stern, pedantic, and quirky Major Douche, took questions from a largely clueless press corps about what they might expect from the show. He promised nothing less than shock and awe.

THE SCREEN ABOVE THE STAGE BRIGHTENED to reveal Major Douche, service cap in one hand, flask in the other. He stood before an oversized American flag, glared at the concertgoers, and barked orders to silence all cell phones and stow all cameras. The sold-out Valentine's Day weekend shows were not the elaborate production Maynard fans had expected. The Pearl Concert Theater at the Palms Casino in Las Vegas was set with Tim Alexander's and Gil Sharone's drum kits and Rani Sharone's bass, floor-stand mics for Maynard and Juliette Commagere, and, suspended over the stage, her eyes staring straight into the crowd, was the image of the Queen B herself, Ms. Puscifer.

And Maynard stepped to the stage.

The crowd was on its feet at once, caught up in the cacophony of opener Uncle Scratch's Gospel Revival, the rockabilly duo of Brother Ant and Brother Ed and their chaos of bullhorns and percussion section of cardboard tubes and cartons. The show segued from sketch comedy to video to song, song that ascended in Eastern ululation, dipped in guttural chants, slowed in sultry R&B rhythms that evoked a summer night in Motown.

Maynard's rich, clear voice rose in rap and blues and pure rock. He was the impassioned tent revivalist urging his flock to transcend dogma and recognize the earthly paradise, then, in a sharp left turn, a lounge singer delivering his paean to the erotic. "Maynard has to be one of the most idiosyncratic frontmen that rock has every had," music writer Steve Morse would explain. "He's a puzzle, but under it all, there's a consistency and a need to communicate. He challenges us to examine our idea of a frontman."

The company came together in layered harmonies, parted for solos and duets, joined again in the trancelike "Indigo Children," and then cleared center stage for Milla Jovovich's solo of the ways of the underside, her scarlet dress shimmering against the monochromatic set.

"It was a vaudeville show for the twenty-first century," Alexander said.

If the vineyard was the quest, the struggle, Puscifer was the dance that followed, the celebration of song and laughter that continued in a wash of colored strobes long into the night.

Puscifer's debut triggered in Maynard a burst of productivity. Only five months after the group's live launch, he was back on the road with Tool for a mini tour that included the Mile High Music Festival in Colorado and Lollapalooza 2009 at Chicago's Grant Park. And following the November release of its EP *"C" Is for (Please Insert Sophomoric Genitalia Reference HERE)*, Puscifer was off again across the U.S. and Canada. For much of the next two years, Maynard took his turn now with Tool, now with APC, again with Puscifer in a round robin of tours across the U.S., Canada, New Zealand, and Australia.

"I remember him coming home from a long tour," Tim Alexander would recall. "I had lunch with him the next day, and he told me he'd been out in the vineyard at 6 a.m. picking grapes. That's why he creates success in his life. He puts in everything he has."

With Chris and Lei Li at the helm, the vineyard was in good hands during his absences, but Maynard used his time on the road to his advantage. Concerts were an opportunity to cross-market his varied brands, he realized, to raise awareness of his Sangioveses and Cabernets. "With Maynard, there's so much complexity. He's not just a musician or a songwriter," Nancy Berry would explain. "He's a very astute businessman with an entrepreneurial spirit."

A ticket upgrade admitted fans early for the preshow VIP wine tasting—a Caduceus 101 course in assessing bouquet and balance and finish. Maynard delegated classroom duty to the best man for the job, the man who'd sat beside him at tastings and pairing dinners from the beginning. "He needed someone to teach fans how to interpret wine," Todd would explain. "So now the security guy teaches the wine course."

PUSCIFER'S SECOND FULL ALBUM, *Conditions of My Parole*, debuted at Number 27 on *Billboard*'s 200 list in October 2011. Recorded among the barrels in the bunker when the tour schedule allowed, the collection was an ode to the Verde Valley in all its contradiction. The album brought together original ensemble members and newcomers including British vocalist Carina Round, drummer Jeff Friedl, bassist Matt McJunkins, keyboard player Josh Eustis—and Devo on cello. The *Conditions* tour kicked off with a Halloween appearance on *Late Night with David Letterman*, the infectious energy inspiring music director Paul Shaffer to break into a spirited keyboard rendition of the title track.

At last, Maynard had solved the dilemma of rock and comedy sharing the stage. Puscifer was, after all, theater, and he wisely booked venues designed for just that. A 15,000-seat auditorium would never provide the intimacy a variety show demanded, but conservatory auditoriums would fit the bill, and historic performance houses that had been stops on the circuits of nineteenth-century lecturers and Shakespeare companies and vaudeville troupes.

> The beauty of Puscifer is going into theaters where there are ushers, not the rock clubs that people are used to. The unfamiliar forum throws audiences off their normal game. They're out of their element, because they have to sit in their own seat and they get chastised for pulling out a camera or invading someone else's space. It's like boot camp for them, breaking them down to build them back up so they can pay attention and appreciate what's happening in front of them.

The spaces were ornate with Corinthian pilasters and gilt-edged balconies and pastoral paintings above the stages, but the mood was anything but reserved. "Puscifer is a many-faceted building with many cornerstones," Maynard would explain. "The first is to remember to have fun. Remember to dance, to follow your bliss." And the fun began before the theater doors opened. As fans queued on the sidewalk, Brother Ed strode among them and, zealous as any street preacher, implored them to turn away from sin, to avoid the show and save their hell-bound souls.

The houselights dimmed, and Maynard pulled an aluminum Airstream from the wings. Carina stepped from the trailer and helped him arrange a charcoal grill and lawn chairs at the edge of the proscenium, and a red-and-white-draped table set with bottles and goblets. While the players awaited their turns in the spotlight, they sat in a circle and sipped wine, the orange paper flames of the barbecue fluttering toward the fly.

Conditions of My Parole was smooth guitar and ominous chant, curious electronic distortion and melodic harmony, lowbrow humor and linguistic play, rock and country and karaoke in a trailer park. "In Maynard's shows, you come off this rush of intensity, and then it's him coming out of an Airstream," Steele would explain. "He's a combination of the spiritual, and then, 'Here, have a dish of fish food.'"

The performance was punctuated by video interludes that told the story of eccentric desert dwellers: the crass and bumbling Billy D, Hildy in crop top and leopard-print kimono, Peter Merkin and his infatuation with conspiracy theories and Debbie Gibson. Concertgoers began to suspect there was more to the skits than tales of make-believe people. The characters seemed some-how familiar, no different really from the dreamers and the downtrodden and the wannabe bass players they'd known, the uncle who every year dominated Thanksgiving dinner with rants about dope sniffers. Maynard's lyrics of echoes and ghosts and omens could have been about the fears and passions of real people just like them, their ambiguity an invitation to make the stories their own and to accept their part in their creation.

"Puscifer works through the whole chakra system," Laura Milligan would say of the shows' format. "You go through the entire gamut of human experience. You have that connection with your belly and your first chakra, you get silly and laugh, and then you move up to that beautiful place at the end when he's just soaring with Carina and the mandolins."

Maynard's intense scream, unrelenting stare, and bold lyrics had gotten the public's attention, and they couldn't stop listening now, when his art had become more complex and multilayered. Steele had recognized Maynard's spiritual depth, but it could never be said that the man who'd sung "Fuck your Christ!" embraced mainstream religious views. He and Ramiro had discovered in their long-ago late-night discussions Joseph Campbell's concept of "religio," a linking back, a reconnection with ancient mythologies, not through blind belief in parroted dogma, but an understanding of their practical purpose.

> Religion helps explain important information so it's easy to understand and doesn't have to be explained every time. People living in the desert thousands of years ago couldn't eat pork because it was full of worms and they'd die if they ate it. In order to keep people from eating it, it became a religious proscription, and then avoiding it just became a part of the daily routine. They didn't think about the survival mechanism attached to the ritual. "Why don't we eat pork again?" "Don't worry about it. Just don't eat pork."
>
> The Japanese tea ceremony started because if there's a tsunami, boiling the water purifies it so it's safe to drink. It became part of their religion to boil the water.
>
> We just casually make these things part of our daily routine so that when a tsunami hits, at least our family might survive, almost accidentally, because our ritual taught us how to boil water and drink that instead of the contaminated water. Honoring that ritual is heaven. The *knowledge* of good and evil is salvation.

The searchers and seekers and mastodon fleers of the old stories, he and Ramiro had learned, were but characters in one story with infinite variations, eternally replicating the human tale of possibility and survival. Carina in her black gown, Maynard in his Italian suit or his cowboy costume, Friedl at his drum kit: The story was repeated once more. The crowd sat as rapt as magi, pitched to a weightlessness beneath projections of swirling stars and the moon that floated fat and full in the desert sky.

THE CONDITIONS TEAM BROUGHT ONBOARD musicians Zac Rae, Josh Morreau, and Claire Acey to record 2013's *Donkey Punch the Night*, an EP of two new songs and their techno remixes, and a Puscifer treatment of Accept's "Balls to the Wall" and Queen's "Bohemian Rhapsody." In the early days of C.A.D., Maynard had vowed he'd never take the easy way out, and tackling Queen's masterpiece reminded him that he'd kept his promise. "Re-tracking 'Bohemian Rhapsody' almost note for note forced me to pay attention to its complex harmonies and multiple movements," he explained. "It reminded me of how I'd always believed music should be approached. I've never stuck to that simple intro-verse-chorus-bridge format."

IF MITCHELL WAS A GROUNDING INFLUENCE, so too was Maynard's time on the mat. He'd begun each winter to join interested high school wrestlers in the MCC gym, assisting coach Jim Allen in teaching them the fundamentals just as Mike had taught them, the pure math and physics of the leverage the sport demanded. And he didn't stop there. He helped fund the team's summer wrestling camp retreat—and let them know the gift came with a price. "I had them write essays," he would explain. "I asked them to tell what wrestling means to them, or why wrestling should be kept in the Olympics."

"Maynard's level of give-back is amazing," Steele said. "I imagine him telling the wrestlers, 'Don't let anyone tell you what you should do. Find the things that make you healthy and happy.' But then he would probably add, 'And if you haven't seen the Will Ferrell movie *Old School*, you're doing yourself a disservice.' He always does some form of comedy."

And in 2015, during a long-overdue vacation, Maynard visited Limão Herédia's Maui Jiu Jitsu academy, the island's premiere Brazilian jiu-jitsu school. It had been a long time since he'd studied under Herédia at the Gracie academy, and their reunion would be a chance to train with him again. "I was honored that after 20 years, Maynard came to see me," Herédia said in a 2015 interview.

On their second afternoon of training, Herédia turned to Maynard. In his hands he held a purple belt, the level in Brazilian jiu-jitsu signifying conscious competence. "He earned the belt because he's tough," Herédia would explain. "He's capable and focused and a good student. But I also wasn't going to pass up the chance to thank him for all he's done for jiu-jitsu. His involvement brought an awareness of the sport. How many musicians and fans are studying jiu-jitsu because of Maynard?"

DEB ROCKMAN HAD LOOKED FORWARD TO PUSCIFER'S CHICAGO PERFORMANCE as much to celebrate her former student's success as to forget for an evening a time of too much illness and death, too much grief. "It had been a difficult, difficult year," she explained in a 2013 interview. "I e-mailed Maynard and poured my heart out to him, and he opened his heart and listened to me."

And that night at the Cadillac Palace, Maynard's voice rose in a hymn of beauty and peace, of surrender to the healing rhythm of the sea, the cleansing waves that gather then break across the sand. He sang of the hope that remains in the wake of sorrow, he sang the song he dedicated that night to Rockman.

Weary traveler, calloused and sore
Time and gravity followed you here
Rest, my sister, and tell me
All about the ocean
Spoils and troubles, the burden you've bore
Pay them no mind, they matter no more
Leave them behind and show me
All about the ocean

Look in your eyes
I've never seen the ocean
Not like this one

"How else could his fan base get exposed to such ideas?" Moon Zappa would reflect. "It's miraculous. And he does it in a relatable way, with sound and lights and artistry. He's an alchemist and a wizard for sure. A merry trickster."

The merry trickster, quite unbeknownst to Lei Li, booked the underground bar of Louisville's Seelbach Hotel for the afternoon of Puscifer's Leap Day show. And after a 30-year gap in communication, he invited his Church of the Brethren pastor Paul Grout to join him for brunch at the Neighborhood before Tool's Boston performance in January. He had important arrangements to discuss.

Puscifer's success was due in great part to Lei Li, who had taken on filling customer orders and managing the Puscifer store in Jerome where fans stocked up on T-shirts and posters, vinyl and CDs, locally roasted coffee beans and squid-ink pasta. At last, she'd put her art degree to good use in designing Puscifer's women's clothing line, and Maynard relied on her to assemble tour merch and to arrange for flights and shuttle buses and meatless meals for the vegetarians in the cast. Lei Li got things done.

She'd never been dazzled by Maynard's celebrity. The respect and admiration she'd felt for him from the beginning had only grown stronger, but happy in her work—and fully aware of his dalliances—she'd kept her professional distance. "I definitely didn't want to jeopardize my job," she would recall. "If he didn't reciprocate my feelings, it could be awkward." But the more evenings she spent with him, the more Thanksgiving pizzas they shared, the more old friends and family she met over Cream of Wheat before a show, the harder it was to deny what her heart was telling her.

Meanwhile, Maynard looked forward to returning from the road or a long day in the bunker and finding her there to share Cabernet and a discussion of the finer points of Carlos Castaneda. Lei Li had become more than an employee, more even than a trusted sister.

And there came the day when he recognized in her the one person who could catch his glance from across the room, smile with him at the inside joke, stand beside him in the face of all possibility. He'd fallen, to his surprise, in love.

> You have to lose your way to find your way back. I reached the point where I needed to stop going down the wrong path, because the only thing I saw was that there's nothing to it. You're never going to find connection or love or commitment in transient relationships. It's like in *Charlotte's Web*. You see "Some pig!" and you forget that actually, the spider pointed it out and the pig is nothing. You're looking for the web and the spider, and you get distracted by the pig. Several pigs.
>
> I don't regret one single step I took down that road. I learned a lot about myself and turned those experiences into something positive, into songs and art.
>
> In the words of Bill Hicks: "In this business, it takes a very special woman— or a lot of average ones." I finally understood what he meant.
>
> Meanwhile, in the distance, you have Lei Li going, "Fuck. Finally."

ABOVE THE BAR AT THE RATHSKELLER in the basement of the Seelbach Hotel, gold-leaf signs of the zodiac glinted in the candlelight. The space was lined floor to vaulted ceiling with hand-painted Rookwood tiles depicting scenes of apple orchards and walled cities, and about the old speakeasy, sturdy pillars were encircled with pottery pelicans, a symbol of good luck.

Maynard hadn't told Lei Li the details of his plan until the stage had been set. He'd left her just enough time to choose a gown and visit the florist and, after a two-year engagement, presented her with a perfectly choreographed afternoon. And while the band performed the sound check before that night's show, they slipped away to the Rathskeller to be married.

The winding path, the switchbacks and wrong turns and detours had inexorably led to this: Maynard's bride in beribboned gown, her bouquet of red roses, her smile as he came near.

Jan was there, and Lei Li's parents, Puscifer's tour manager, Todd, a photographer, and the Rev. Grout. "Our long-ago connection was meaningful to Maynard, and it was meaningful to me, too," he said of his agreement to travel from Vermont to perform the ceremony. "I thought he was pretty amazing back then, and I was struck that he'd carried that uniqueness for so long. The fact that he remembered the things I'd told him was touching."

Maynard and Lei Li listened to Grout's words of the joys and challenges and necessary forgiveness they would share. Then Maynard looked into her eyes and she into his, and they whispered their vows.

"Then we went to the Brown Theatre and threw the garter and bouquet to the band," Lei Li would remember, "and shared cupcakes with everyone."

THE TWO-WEEK STAY IN ITALY was as much a research project as a honeymoon. Maynard and Lei Li had visited Piemonte vineyards, the terraced Barolo and Barbaresco acres near Alba, and next on the itinerary would be a stop at Luca Currado's Vietti winery in Castiglione Falletto. "I'd met Currado at a wine distributor meeting in Denver years before," Maynard would explain. "We hit it off and kept in contact."

Currado led the newlyweds through his cellar, fed them wine and cheese, and Maynard, in a rush of Midwestern gregariousness, told him of their plans for the next day. They'd hire a driver and explore, he explained, and search for details of Spirito Marzo and Clementina Durbiano, his great-grandparents who—according to vague family stories—had been married somewhere in the Val di Susa more than a century before.

If Maynard needed assistance in his sleuthing, Currado and his wife Elena were just the pair to help. Currado knew Susa well, he said, had skied there often, and with the town's chief of police, no less. After a few flurried phone calls, Elena reported that Maynard's ancestors weren't from Susa at all, but nearby Venaus, and he and Lei Li were expected at the Venaus archives the next day.

And on the morning of his 48th birthday, Maynard tucked a bottle of wine under his arm and stepped from the narrow street and into the *municipio*, bustling that morning with Venausians filing papers and investigating titles and resolving their municipal matters. "I figured we were in the right place," Maynard would recall. "The nameplate on the counter said 'Ariana Marzo.'"

Ariana waved them toward an adjoining room, where Maynard saw not the bulging file cabinets and musty ledgers he'd expected but a trio of national and local reporters, the mayor, and a cluster of townsfolk who greeted him with a hearty "Hello! Welcome home!"

On the table was stacked all the information Maynard could have hoped for: maps and addresses and copies of birth certificates and death certificates and marriage licenses of Boniface Spirito Giacinto Marzo and Maria Clementina Durbiano, and of their daughter Maria Luigia Ernestina Marzo, his grandmother.

A visit from an American rock star was the most exciting thing to happen in the little town in quite some time, particularly a rock star with local roots. The next day, the newspapers would include spreads detailing Maynard's visit and his family tree, a tree that branched to include most of the people in Venaus. Even Mayor Nilo Durbiano was family, they discovered, a cousin on Clementina's side, and they toasted in Nagual del Marzo their unexpected reunion.

It wasn't surprising that so many shared common ancestors. Surviving the harsh alpine winters had never been easy, and people of the region had decades before relied on the bounty of neighboring villages to get them by until springtime. While blizzards raged over the mountains, the Marzos and the Durbianos had donned heavy coats and boots and mittens and scarves, tied bundles to their sleds, journeyed down the snowy peaks, and met their neighbors in the valley, where they exchanged food and supplies.

"When it came time to get married," Maynard would explain, "they picked a partner who could handle that trek." And Spirito, like so many others, chose as his wife a strong, capable woman he'd met on the wintry path. He chose Clementina Durbiano, a woman of the journey.

THROUGH THE NARROW STREETS THEY RODE, to the edge of town and up a steep incline that brought them face-to-face with the house. Its stonework had crumbled, its windows were long shattered, the roof was black with decay. But this was the house all the same, the house where Maynard's great-great-grandfather, great-grandfather, and grandmother had been born, where Marzos and Durbianos had celebrated Christmases and opened their windows to the first springtime day, where they'd told stories and sung songs and shared a glass or two of Spirito's wine.

Before the door rose precarious stone steps, steps Spirito and Clementina and baby Louisa had climbed, and Maynard and Lei Li rested there. In the distance were sun-washed green hills, and farther, snowcapped mountains, and across the narrow street, a weathered wooden fence laced with grapevines.

> It all unfolded because of that one connection I made in Denver five years be-
> fore. It happened because I kept in touch and opened my mouth at the right
> time. I had put my faith in just going. And then people put the pieces together
> that led me right where I was supposed to go. And my family was waiting for
> me.

Maynard stood in the wings of the Greek Theatre. He watched them arrive, singers and musicians, comics, family and friends, and a capacity audience. They'd come to L.A. for Cinquanta, a celebration of his 50th birthday.

The evening was a wave of contagious energy that spanned decades and generations, a seamless segue from Failure to A Perfect Circle to Puscifer. Boundaries blurred as the players changed partners in the spiraling dance. Carina stepped to the mic on APC's "The Package," Failure's Kellii Scott and APC's Jeff Friedl collaborated in a drum duo, Maynard lifted his voice in the second verse of Failure's "The Nurse Who Loved Me," and Billy Howerdel joined him on Puscifer's "Monsoons." And when Justin Chancellor opened the Tool favorite, "Sober," or Matt McJunkins kicked off APC's "Orestes," the crowd took its part and sang every word. And the evening was Devo, his dark, wavy hair framing his solemn face, in his debut solo before so large an audience, his cello shimmering in the splash of white light.

Green Jellö burst on the stage in all its masked chaos, Manspeaker a looming Big Bad Wolf and his son Damien a player in oversized puppet head. "I was so nervous," Manspeaker would recall. "There's all these serious songs about changing your life in positive ways, and I've got a song about pigs."

But the act was integral to the show's circling to a long-ago evening at Hollywood High. Manspeaker howled "Little pig, little pig, let me come in!" and Maynard delivered his falsetto response—his gold record response—"Not by the hair of my chinny-chin-chin!"

The moshing pigs exited the stage, and Laura Milligan stepped out as Hildy. She summoned Billy D from the Airstream, and Maynard in leisure suit and wig joined her in the old Libertyville campfire song, "Country Boner," while Danny kept the beat. "We've been able to stay together as long as we have because of the trust in each other," he would explain. "The end product will always be something more than the sum of the parts."

Cinquanta was just that, a collective of sound more complex and nuanced for the selfless collaboration.

> A show like that is not possible if people are unable to set aside their egos. It works when they look at a bigger common goal. Each band played pieces from their own heart and soul and then transitioned to the next set of people who shared each other's work. It made me want to do it all over again so even more people could feel this. That kind of magic can happen if you pay attention to where you are and where you're going—and where you've been.

They stood together—Maynard and Devo, Carina and Mat Mitchell, Jeff and Matt McJunkins and Billy, Danny and Juliette Commagere and Justin and Laura, Todd and Lei Li and Manspeaker and his family in the wings. They formed an arc across the stage, and the audience completed the circle's circumference. Their harmonies filled the night, and the gibbous moon rose higher in the sky.

A Perfect Union of Contrary Things

Nature, nurture, heaven and home
Sum of all, and by them, driven
To conquer every mountain shown
But I've never crossed the river

Braved the forests, braved the stone
Braved the icy winds and fire
Braved and beat them on my own
Yet I'm helpless by the river

Angel, angel, what have I done?
I've faced the quakes, the wind, the fire
I've conquered country, crown, and throne
Why can't I cross this river?

Pay no mind to the battles you've won
It'll take a lot more than rage and muscle
Open your heart and hands, my son
Or you'll never make it over the river

It'll take a lot more than words and guns
A whole lot more than riches and muscle
The hands of the many must join as one
And together we'll cross the river

Epilogue

===

L ei Li Agostina Maria is just tall enough to see over the bottom rail of the porch. Jerome is an idyllic place to be a little girl named in part for the grape her father brought back from the Tamale Ladies. Some call the Luglienga strain Agostenga, but it doesn't much matter: *Luglienga* and *Agostenga*, from the Italian words for *July* and *August*, the first months of the harvest.

The child stands on tiptoe and strains for a glimpse of her father's car. Across the road are apricot and almond and plum trees, an orchard just as magical as the ones her mother reads her stories about. Beyond are wisteria and star jasmine and the vineyard, where vines and leaves twist and turn in the most curious patterns. And in the yard hops Chet, the toad who faithfully returns every summer—tame as a house cat and all hers.

THE FIRST WAVE OF THE TOUR IS OVER. Maynard will be off again all too soon, but he'll have plenty to do in the meantime. He must check on his submerged cap fermentations and ask his bandmates about their progress on the next Tool album. There are jiu-jitsu sessions to schedule and a photo shoot to prepare for, and he still hasn't reserved the back table at the Neighborhood or reminded Kjiirt to meet him there before the upcoming Boston performance.

All that can wait. First, he'll join his family around the dinner table for homemade gnocchi and hear about their adventures while he's been away. After the baby has been put to bed, he'll decant a bottle of Kitsuné and talk with Lei Li, and they'll look into each other's eyes and whisper their joy.

On Saturday, he'll kneel beside his daughter in the garden and teach her to plant basil and transplant tomato seedlings from starter pots. He'll point out to her the black hawk soaring to its aerie on Mingus Mountain, teach her to identify the sound of cicadas chirring in the tree in the yard. He'll tell her tales of trout-splashed rivers and of the woods and the deer and rabbits that live there.

And in the morning, as the sun rises from behind the mountains, they'll watch for the day's first hummingbird—a small speck at first, then growing larger and larger as it flies straight and sure to the feeder at the edge of the porch.

Acknowledgments

The new era of art is an egoless collaboration. We're a huge patch of algae, single cells in a larger organism in sync. One person might coordinate it all, but they can't make it happen unless all the other elements are working together.　　　　—MAYNARD JAMES KEENAN

The authors are indebted to all who made this book possible, most especially Ann Collette, agent extraordinaire of the Rees Literary Agency; John Cerullo and the Backbeat team; and Alison Case for her dedication in reading and emending the sometimes indecipherable work in progress. And for graciously providing information, assistance, and support:

Steve Aldrich, Tim Alexander, Jim Allen, Debra Alton, Jen Ardis, Robert Arthur, Niels Bach, Nikki Bagley, Lisa McMaster Baldwin, Milan Basnet, Jon Basquez, Steve Begnoche, Nadia Bendenov, Nancy Berry, Steve Bishop, Boston Biographers Group, Mary Braman, Mike Burd, Tim Cadiente, Danny Carey, Todd Caris, Judy Carter, Stuart Cody, Fran Schulte Coffin, Carlos Coutinho, David Cross, John Crowley, Alex Cwiakala, Matthew Davis, Raffael DeGruttola, Richard Dickinson, Albert Drake, Michelle Duder.

Kathleen Cardwell Elkington, Sheila Falcey, Sheila Borges Foley, Murray Forbes, Rebecca Fox, Todd Fox, Peter Gago, Deborah Galle, Chad Galts, Leona Garrison and the Geary County Historical Society, Tim Genson, Colleen Shaw Gleason, Lori Green, Brian Greminger, Alex Grey, James Griffith, Paul Grout, Wayne Hansen, Thom Hawley, Limão Herédia, Billy Howerdel, Daniel Hungerford, Dakota Jensen, Kjiirt Jensen, Sue Ellen Jensen, Ann Johnson,

Acknowledgments

Axel Johnson III, Devo H Keenan, Jan Keenan, Lei Li Keenan, Mike Keenan, Susan Newkirk Kelly, Jeff Kiessel, Patti Klevorn, Michael Koran.

Marc LaBlanc, Linda Lawson, Sarah Llaguno, Terry Lowry and the West Virginia Archives and History Library, the *Ludington Daily News*, Ludington Visiting Writers, Lou Maglia, David Mallett, Bill Manspeaker, Matt Marshall, Sean F. S. McCormick, Anne Meeks, Pavle Milic, Jennifer Miller, Laura Milligan, Mat Mitchell, Tom Montag, Tom Morello, Steve Morse, Brian Mulherin, David Murphy, Jim Newkirk, Steele Newman, Lois Novotny, Jack Olsen, Anne-Marie Oomen, Mary O'Brien Overturf.

Nate Patrick, Bonnie Pfefferle, Rick Plummer, Tom Reinberg, Jack Ridl, Deb Rockman, Ramiro Rodriguez, Robby Romero, Liz Rotter, Laurie Rousseau, Julie Rowland, Richard Rowland, Jason Rubin, Ed Sanders, Monica Seide, Rebecca Solnit, Chris Stengel, Cheryl Strayed, Edgar Struble, Mark Tarbell, Chuck Tracy, Alan Trautmann, Karen Vallee, Pam Walling, Dan Whitelock, Connie Pehrson Wiles, Ted Winkel, Cindy Newkirk Yenkel, Moon Zappa, and Julia Paige Zeidler.